THE QUEST FOR JESUS
AND THE CHRISTIAN FAITH

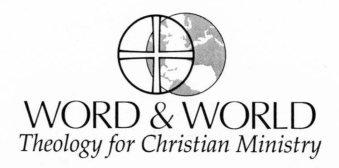

WORD & WORLD
Theology for Christian Ministry

EDITORIAL STAFF: Frederick J. Gaiser, Editor; Sarah Henrich, Associate Editor; Mark Throntveit, Book Editor; Sylvia C. Ruud, Managing Editor.

EDITORIAL BOARD: Charles Amjad-Ali, Paul S. Berge, Sarah Henrich, Kirsten Mebust, Elaine J. Ramshaw, Gary M. Simpson, Paul R. Sponheim, Walter Sundberg, Paul Westermeyer, and Frederick J. Gaiser, *ex officio*.

Supplement Series, 3

September 1997

Frederick J. Gaiser, Series Editor

Sylvia C. Ruud, Series Managing Editor

Word & World: Theology for Christian Ministry is published quarterly at Luther Seminary, 2481 Como Avenue, St. Paul, Minnesota 55108, U.S.A. Telephone (612) 641-3482.

ISSN 0275-5270
ISBN 0-9632389-2-2

THE QUEST FOR JESUS
AND THE CHRISTIAN FAITH

edited by
Frederick J. Gaiser

WORD & WORLD
Luther Seminary
St. Paul, Minnesota

Library of Congress Catalog Card Number 97-061607
ISBN 0-9632389-2-2

Printed in the United States of America

CONTENTS

ACKNOWLEDGMENTS

THE PAPERS INCLUDED IN THE VOLUME WERE FIRST PRESENTED AT A CONFERENCE ON "The Quest for Jesus and the Christian Faith" at Luther Seminary, St. Paul, Minnesota, June 3-5, 1997. The conference was a part of the seminary's Kairos program of continuing education.

Special thanks are in order to Peter Sethre, director of continuing education, and to the continuing education secretary, Annette Nickelson, for their work in planning and presenting this program. Thanks also to Lutheran Brotherhood for its financial support of Kairos participants through GEM scholarships. The planning committee for this particular Kairos session included Mary Knutsen, Craig Koester, Arland Hultgren, and Peter Sethre. We are grateful to Luther Seminary, its Board of Directors, administration, and staff, for their sponsorship and support of programs like this one.

We acknowledge also the Editorial Board of *Word & World* for agreeing to publish these essays as the third in the journal's series of supplemental volumes. The journal and the Kairos program provided financial support for this effort. Much of the work in putting the ideas into print and making them available to a wider audience comes from the creative efforts of Sylvia Ruud, managing editor of *Word & World*, and the office support of Katherine Jacobson, Circulation, and Alice Loddigs, Luther Seminary faculty secretary.

Finally, we thank the presenters themselves for agreeing to speak and publish in this important area of theological and ecclesiastical scholarship and to the participants in the conference for their stimulating attention and interaction.

F.J.G.

ABBREVIATIONS

ANCIENT SOURCES

Gos. Thom.	*The Gospel of Thomas*
Hippolytus, *Ref.*	*Refutation of All Heresies*
Irenaeus, *Adv. Haer.*	*Against Heresies*
Josephus, *Ant.*	*Jewish Antiquities*
Josephus, *War*	*The Jewish War*
Josephus, *Life*	*The Life*
LXX	The Septuagint
POxy	Oxyrhynchus Papyri

LUTHER'S WORKS

LW	*Luther's Works*, ed. Jaroslav Pelikan, Hilton C. Oswald, Helmut T. Lehmann, vols. 1-30 (St. Louis: Concordia, 1955-); vols. 31-55 (Philadelphia: Fortress, 1957-86)
WA	*D. Martin Luthers Werke: Kritische Gesamtausgabe*, 60 vols. to date (Weimar: Hermann Böhlaus Nachfolger, 1883-)

JOURNALS, REFERENCE WORKS, AND SERIALS

AB	Anchor Bible
ABD	*The Anchor Bible Dictionary*, ed. David N. Freedman, 6 vols. (New York: Doubleday, 1992)
ACNT	Augsburg Commentary on the New Testament
ANF	*The Ante-Nicene Fathers*, ed. Alexander Roberts and James Donaldson, 10 vols. (Buffalo: The Christian Literature Company, 1885-97; reprint, Peabody, MA: Hendrickson, 1994)
BA	*Biblical Archaeologist*
BARev	*Biblical Archaeology Review*
BASOR	*Bulletin of the American Schools of Oriental Research*
BIAC	*Bulletin of the Institute for Antiquity and Christianity*
BibRev	*Bible Review*
BTB	*Biblical Theology Bulletin*
CBQ	*Catholic Biblical Quarterly*
BZNW	Beihefte zur *Zeitschrift für die neutestamentliche Wissenschaft*
ExpTim	*Expository Times*
FFF	*Foundations and Facets Forum*
FOTL	The Forms of the Old Testament Literature
FRLANT	Forschungen zur Religion und Literatur des Alten und Neuen Testaments
HTR	*Harvard Theological Review*
HTS	Harvard Theological Studies
Int	*Interpretation*
JBL	*Journal of Biblical Literature*

JR	*Journal of Religion*
NHLE	*The Nag Hammadi Library in English*, ed. James M. Robinson, 3d ed. (San Francisco: Harper & Row, 1988)
NHS	Nag Hammadi Studies
NovT	*Novum Testamentum*
NovTSup	Novum Testamentum, Supplements
NTAbh	Neutestamentliche Abhandlungen
NTS	*New Testament Studies*
PSB	*The Princeton Seminary Bulletin*
SBLDS	Society of Biblical Literature Dissertation Series
SBLSBS	Society of Biblical Literature Sources for Biblical Study
SBLSP	*Society of Biblical Literature Seminar Papers*
SBT	Studies in Biblical Theology
SecCent	*The Second Century*
TSRev	*Trinity Seminary Review*
TToday	*Theology Today*
TU	Texte und Untersuchungen
USQR	*Union Seminary Quarterly Review*
VC	*Vigiliae Christianae*
WUNT	Wissenschaftliche Untersuchungen zum Neuen Testament
WW	*Word & World*
ZTK	*Zeitschrift für Theologie und Kirche*

Word & World
Supplement Series 3
1997

The Quest for Jesus and the Christian Faith: Introduction

Frederick J. Gaiser

Luther Seminary
St. Paul, Minnesota

Ask, and it will be given you; search, and you will find; knock, and the door will be opened for you. For everyone who asks receives, and everyone who searches finds, and for everyone who knocks, the door will be opened. (Matthew 7:7-8)

I. Who Are We?

ACCORDING TO JESUS HIMSELF, ASKING, SEEKING, AND KNOCKING—QUESTING— seems to be a good idea. So what is all the fuss about? What separates some questers from others? Are some quests valid and others not? If so, what are the criteria?

Those questions are not easily answered. To the degree that their quests are responsible, outward, and available to public scrutiny rather than inward, mystical, or gnostic, Christians (orthodox and not-so-orthodox) and non-Christians (kindly disposed to the Christian faith or not) use similar methods in their quests for the "historical Jesus." They are confined to the same data, they go to the same universities, they meet together in common conferences, they are often friends and colleagues. Perhaps the test will be found in another word of Jesus: "You will know them by their fruits" (Matt 7:16). This is not to suggest that there are no valid fruits of the investigations of the New Testament and the life of Jesus by those who are not orthodox Christians. On the contrary, some of their work has taught us much. Still, in his reference to the fruits test, Jesus is addressing the possibility of false prophets in the midst of the community. That remains possible. False prophets might be perfectly nice human beings. We might learn from them about the first-century world and the background of the gospels; but we might still judge their "prophecy" to be false, that is, their judgments about Jesus that go beyond historically observable phenomena. To try to discover what is historically knowable about Jesus' trial and death is useful work, even if the results are sometimes disconcerting. Christians dare not dismiss truth that will hold up to public canons of verifiability simply because it is inconvenient. On the other hand, to conclude work on Jesus' death by announcing that there was no resurrection moves out of the realm of research into the realm of "prophecy." Christian faith will label such prophecy "false"—at its best, not to shore up the institution and protect the privileges of power; not even, in fact, because it is out of step with millennia of faithful and meaningful Christian tradition (though that is no small matter); finally, Christians will label such prophecy false because it contradicts the presence of the living Christ experienced daily in word and sacrament, in prayer and meditation. Though not historically verifiable, the real presence of Christ is known to faith. It is announced to others in faithful "prophecy" not to enlarge the Christian power base but to set people free, to open to them the possibility of walking in a troubled world by faith in Jesus Christ given by the grace of God through the power of the Holy Spirit; it is a gift meant to turn them loose to serve God and neighbor in a world now given meaning and hope.

If that experience of liberation were not real, there would be no Christian faith, and the quest for Jesus would be merely an archival exercise—or, at best, a search for an historical role model for help in facing the challenges of the present, something like an attempt to know Socrates or Sojourner Truth, Martin Luther or Martin Luther King, Jr.—certainly not a bad thing, but a quest with no claim to transcendence and no prospect of grace.

The prospect of grace is precisely what marks the words of Jesus that introduce this section: "Ask, and it *will be* given you...knock, and the door *will be* opened for you." To be sure, human agency is not discounted—"search, and *you will find*"—but in Jesus' promise human agency works within a giving and an opening that comes from without. Indeed, in the small concentric structure formed by the three clauses of v. 7 (ABA), the active human agency of "finding" is surrounded by the grammatically passive experience of being "given" and having "opened": human agency works within and is surrounded by the grace of God.[1] Such agency, such questing, Jesus promises, will be successful. Quests with no such expectation will, by definition, not open themselves to Jesus' promise. Some time ago, Walter Brueggemann argued that "modernity cannot anticipate a breakthrough," that is, an intervention from outside the immediately visible world of cause and effect.[2]

---

[1]To be sure, the concentric structure does not carry over into verse 8 (where the seeker "receives," "finds," and the door "will be opened"—active/active/passive), though the mutuality between human seeking and divine opening remains.

[2]Walter Brueggemann, "The Formfulness of Grief," in *The Psalms and the Life of Faith*, ed. Patrick D. Miller (Minneapolis: Fortress, 1995) 94; the essay was originally published in *Int* 31/3 (1977) 263-275. In the original, Brueggemann used the German term for "breakthrough," i.e., *Durchbruch*. A line from Johann Ludwig Konrad Allendorf's 1736 hymn seems to respond directly: "Jesus ist kommen....Unser Durchbrecher ist nunmehr vorhanden" ("Jesus has come....Our breakthrough [lit. "he who breaks through"] is now upon us"). Allendorf's hymn proclaims the classic Christian faith.

While much of modernity may actually be more open now to surprise than it was when Brueggemann wrote (or at least more willing to admit it), his description still fits that form of enlightenment humanism that simply excludes the possibility of the providential and unexpected work of God in the physical world. Questing for Jesus with such a mentality is a legitimate and sometimes productive vocation; but it will discover neither the Christ of faith nor the Jesus known to faith because it has excluded that possibility from the outset. It has closed itself off from the promise of the grace inherent in Jesus' promise—or tried to, at least. Grace may have other ideas, and non-expectant questers may in the end find themselves, too, "surprised by joy."[3] In questing for Jesus, they take that risk.

There was no litmus test applied in the selection of authors for this volume, nor (as the results may show) did anyone know or determine from the start what each participant would do. We do know one another, however, so we know (to the degree that it is possible to know) that, despite all the differences among us in scholarly methodology, political orientation, and practical piety, each of us searches with the expectation of being found. It is within that perspective of Christian faith that we have embarked on this quest for Jesus.

II. WHAT HAVE WE SAID?

Though they all focus on Jesus and grow out of consideration of the recent quest for the historical Jesus, the papers included in this volume are quite diverse.

Mary Knutsen leads us into the discussion with a remarkably helpful introduction to the various modern quests for Jesus, a listing of the sources, methods, assumptions, and the several positions taken by leading figures in the third quest, an evaluation of that work, and an annotated bibliography of the major publications produced by these scholars.

Arland Hultgren carefully outlines and evaluates the sources used by the fellows of the Jesus Seminar and like-minded scholars. By focusing on Q and the *Gospel of Thomas* (indeed, particular readings of each), these scholars inevitably produce a picture of Jesus as sage and spirit-person. They then read (and emend) the canonical gospels through this filter. A different selection of sources would, of course, produce a different picture.

Walter Taylor, Jr. sketches the newer methods and discoveries used in the current quest for Jesus: archaeology, sociology, and cultural anthropology. These differ from older literary, form-critical, and redaction-critical methods in that they draw material from outside the texts to interpret the texts. Without doubt, they have contributed greatly to our understanding of Jesus, but they too can give a skewed picture if not used in relation to other methods—including fundamentally a simple reading of the texts themselves, as they stand.

Diane Jacobson, the only Old Testament scholar among the presenters, examines Jesus in relation to the wisdom traditions of the Old Testament and the

---

[3]See C. S. Lewis, *Surprised by Joy: The Shape of My Early Life* (1956; reprint, San Diego: Harcourt Brace Jovanovich, 1984).

intertestamental period. Without succumbing to the temptation to reduce Jesus to a mere wandering sage or to idolize him as a new god/dess, she makes a strong case that the New Testament, especially Matthew and John, portray Jesus as incarnate wisdom.

Donald Juel, while not rejecting an interest in the wisdom tradition, presents a solid and straightforward historical argument that Jesus was, in fact, crucified as the "King of the Jews." Thus, the title "crucified Messiah" best describes Jesus not only theologically, but historically as well.

David Tiede argues that the historical Jesus was a prophet who did signs, wonders, and mighty acts to manifest the special way God was at work in him for the restoration of Israel. In Jesus—the Jesus of history and the Jesus of the gospels—we see the manifest power of God.

The next three papers go in a different direction. More textual and literary, perhaps, than historical, each does detailed work on a section of the New Testament to help us understand Jesus and the witness to Jesus of the early Christian community.

Sarah Henrich examines Luke-Acts to discover what that literary complex understands as the saving work of Jesus. The question is relevant, of course, to the issue of whether, say, the traditional creeds adequately understand Jesus in their focus on his birth, death, and resurrection, or whether more attention needs to be paid to his earthly ministry. Henrich argues that since, according to Luke, there is continuity between the historical and the eschatological saving work of Christ, attention needs continually to be paid to the healing and community building work of the earthly Jesus—which Luke includes within his vocabulary of "saving."

Paul Berge turns his attention to the Johannine literature. Without directly entering the ongoing discussion about the historical reliability of the Fourth Gospel, Berge presents a careful literary and structural parallelism between John and 1 John. That coherence and artistry is, for Berge, its own witness to truth. It derives from and bears witness to the Johannine community's historical experience of Jesus as the word incarnate.

David Fredrickson provides new insight into the way Paul tries to work out how the unique historical Jesus has ultimate significance for all people everywhere. Fredrickson argues that in 2 Corinthians 1-7 Paul uses the available philosophical language of friendship, adopting it and radicalizing it, to make this case.

Two concluding papers suggest in different ways the legitimacy (perhaps the inevitability) of reading the New Testament as a whole in traditional Christian perspective.

Craig Koester contends that the resurrection of Jesus is essential to the reading of the New Testament as it stands. It is not a later level of tradition that can be pared away to discover a more fully human and historical Jesus, for its removal leaves essentially nothing. There are no New Testament texts that are not colored by the resurrection faith of those who knew and wrote about their encounter with the historical Jesus and/or the living Christ.

James Boyce reminds us that all knowing is a matter of perspective, that there is no "objective" reading or writing of texts. The New Testament takes the risk of presenting its treasure, Jesus, in the earthen vessel of rhetoric—language that always seeks to interpret and persuade, language that will always finally defy objectification. No other language is available to the writers of the New Testament. No other language is available to the Christian confession.

In the concluding *panel discussion*, some of the participants in the conference attempt to focus more sharply the question: "What difference does the quest for Jesus make for the Christian faith?" They believe it does make a difference, that Christians must enter this discussion and can learn from it. They do not believe the third quest for Jesus has at last identified the "real" Jesus, hidden so long beneath ecclesiastical tradition. The real Jesus for people of faith is not the Jesus of historical or dogmatic reconstruction (either of which might be done poorly or well and thus be more or less valuable) but the living Jesus of faithful proclamation. In that Jesus is life.

III. WHAT HAVE WE LEARNED?

Despite the diversity of these chapters, they seem to me to share many things in common—some of which we realized going in, some that emerged or were reinforced in this work together.[4]

1. We have met the Jesus Seminar and they are us

In part, this paraphrase of Pogo Possum refers simply to the observation above that the fellows of the Jesus Seminar and others writing now about Jesus are our colleagues and often our friends. We share academic backgrounds, scholarly methodologies, and, to a large degree, modernist worldviews. Like them, we are children of the enlightenment. We probably subscribe to most of the same magazines, and you couldn't distinguish us in a crowd.

There is perhaps a more significant similarity, however. Many of the present Jesus questers speak of their early (and sometimes present) alienation from the church and the tradition. Marcus Borg's experience of the dogmatic and moralistic interpretation of Jesus in his home Lutheran congregation in North Dakota was more or less common to many of us. All of us at one time or another have no doubt shared John Dominic Crossan's suspicion of the church's use of power to maintain its own privilege. Many of us have been struck by the slings and arrows of "good" church people who have not liked what we have said or written. Depending perhaps on our age, many of us would agree that the early teaching we received was often docetic in its denial or lack of interest in Jesus' true humanity. Many of us, like some in the third quest for Jesus, have worried that the church's Jesus has been much too interested in the comfort of the insiders and much too unlikely to consort with sinners and outcasts. In many and various ways, we share the experience of our colleagues who now seek a different Jesus from the one from which they find themselves alienated. We have met the Jesus Seminar and they are us.

---

[4]Though I speak in this section of "we" and "us," the formulations are my own. My colleagues are not responsible for them.

The difference between us seems to be not our experience of alienation but our experience of reconnection. For whatever reason, the biblical witness to a Jesus who is truly human and truly divine, to a Jesus who was the Son of God and crucified Messiah, to a Jesus whom God raised from the dead and who will come again to judge the living and the dead has struck a chord with us. We believe it. It sets us free. We find no conflict between this confession and our academic study. Problems continue, of course; alienations recur, and the church is imperfect. But Christian teaching does not lead us to expect otherwise. We find the source of renewal not outside the faith, but within it.

2. *The quest for the historical Jesus is a legitimate, even necessary, task for Christian believers*

Believers have nothing to fear from a rigorous examination of historical questions. Chaim Potok gets it right in his novel *In the Beginning*. When Lurie, the hero, takes leave of his beloved rabbinic teacher to go off to the dreaded University of Chicago to study the Bible, he confesses, "It is secular scholarship, Rebbe; it is not the scholarship of tradition. In secular scholarship there are no boundaries and no permanently fixed views." To which the teacher responds, "Lurie, if the Torah cannot go out into your world of scholarship and return stronger, then we are all fools and charlatans. I have faith in the Torah. I am not afraid of truth."[5]

Meier Sternberg argues that the Hebrew Bible is an open book, available to all, with no need of secret keys to unlock its mysteries.[6] Contrary to his assertion, so is the New Testament. To be sure, both testaments sometimes delve into mystery and sometimes make use of symbolic speech, but both are public and open. Both can be—and want to be—read by anyone. Both proclaim a God who is Lord of both history and nature, available in time, available to the senses, and eager to be found. Apart from such things as parabolic imagery and apocalyptic symbolism (which can also be learned), the language of scripture is transparent. It is not afraid of questions. Indeed, many of us, plagued by something like Marcus Borg's alienation from the dogmatic rigidity of our childhood, found the permission to raise historical and literary questions about Jesus and the Bible—and the insights that emerged from that study—magnificently liberating. It would not be putting it too strongly to say that such honesty permitted me to remain a Christian. But I never felt the need to leave the classic Christian faith in order to pursue honesty. On the contrary, once I got things figured out, the faith provided a firm place to stand while asking any and every question—especially questions about the faith itself. They are invited: "Great are the works of the Lord, studied by all who delight in them" (Ps 111:2).

More can be said. It is not just that the Bible is willing to be tested in the public arena—so is the God it proclaims. Because both Old and New Testaments view God as one who is always and forever inclined toward incarnation, that is, a

[5]Chaim Potok, *In the Beginning* (Greenwich, CT: Fawcett Crest, 1975) 415.
[6]Meier Sternberg, *The Poetics of Biblical Narrative: Ideological Literature and the Drama of Reading* (1985; Bloomington: Indiana University, 1987) 48-49.

God who is profoundly interested in and committed to history, so those who share biblical faith will also be interested in and committed to history. Asking historical questions is always asking theological questions—unless one brackets God out of history, which the Bible is never willing to do. As Hans Walter Wolff has said, it is the incarnational God who took the risk of making himself an object of historical study.[7] Had God not wanted people to engage in quests for the historical Yahweh (or the historical Jesus), God should have remained safely in heaven where gods belong. But God did not, and so we cannot—we cannot eschew the history that God embraced. Historical investigation is part and parcel of biblical faith.

3. Even after two millennia of Jesus scholarship, there is more to learn

One could be merely cynical about a third quest for the historical Jesus. A new generation of scholars, with dissertations to write and books to sell, needs a new gimmick. Scripture itself knows such suspicion. The Preacher, having declared that "all is vanity," goes on to say, "Of making many books there is no end, and much study is a weariness of the flesh" (Eccl 12:12).

But those of us who don't believe that Cynicism adequately defines Jesus need not be cynical about the present quest for Jesus. It is pursued by people of integrity whose scholarship is largely defensible and whose methods are often productive. All of us have learned from the study of the social world of the first century. Cultural anthropology provides genuine new insights into the values and worldview of a culture that is not ours. Archaeologists dig up artifacts and insights that were unavailable yesterday. Wisdom studies provide a whole new way of interpreting Jesus, historically and theologically. We may challenge all kinds of things, including what appears to be the touching faith of some in their ability to recover history "as it really was" (or at least what Jesus "really" said), but our own faith will not prevent us from learning some things from people with whom we disagree profoundly in other things. We may well differ with folks about their interpretation of data, but the data themselves are intriguing and enlightening. They invite and require us to rethink everything, which is exactly what every generation is called to do.

Biblical scholarship is no different from any other discipline. It sometimes discovers genuinely new insights, even as it sometimes goes down blind alleys and dead-end streets. It makes startling leaps forward; and sometimes it needs serious correction. One generation is often, if not regularly, amused by what was said by the previous generation and appalled by what is being said by the next. Yet all participate in a history of scholarship in which everyone's present work builds on what has been done before. And in the process real learning happens, insights appear that were not previously available in the same way.

Perhaps both advocates and critics take biblical scholarship too seriously. Those who assert that the Bible is inspired generally make no such assertion about biblical scholarship. Biblical scholarship makes no claim to be productive of faith,

---

[7]Hans Walter Wolff, "The Understanding of History in the Old Testament Prophets," in *Essays on Old Testament Hermeneutics*, ed. Claus Westermann (Atlanta: John Knox, 1979) 352.

though by providing knowledge it may nourish faith. By itself, it cannot destroy faith, though by raising questions it may, for a time, stir doubt. Faith is given by the Spirit—and was long before there was historical criticism—and faith is lost when, among other things, it no longer provides an adequate foundation for the believer's present world—and this, too, has happened in every generation. But though it does not claim to produce faith, biblical scholarship is productive—or can be. There is more to learn, and responsible Christians are happy to learn it.

4. Although historical work is essential work, it is not, for most of us, our primary work

The "us" here refers to the authors of these essays. Although each of us cares deeply about history, it seems fair to say that none of us is a student of the Bible because we were first interested in ancient texts.[8] We became interested in ancient texts because we were captured by the gospel—and the gospel comes in ancient texts. That is why, I think, most of us would not call ourselves, first and foremost, historians, not even biblical historians, but rather theologians—though, to be sure, biblical theologians.[9]

The point is not to drive a wedge between history and theology—precisely impossible in an incarnational faith—but merely to argue for the validity of the theological vocation. When I was a parish pastor in South Dakota in the late '60s and early '70s, colleagues were demitting the ministry right and left because they found it unable to deliver what they discerned that people needed: sociological, economic, and political liberation. They left the ministry and went to find "real work." It was a crisis of faith; they were unable to believe that the gospel of the forgiveness of sins had anything to do with people's "real" lives. They refused to be the in-house institutional chaplains they understood themselves to be called to be.

In some ways, the present quest for Jesus operates from the same perspective: a claim to free Jesus from the constraints of church and tradition and bring him into the "real" world—for some, as a liberator and social critic, ushering us into a new age of egalitarian commensality; for others, as a spiritual guide, a real *Mensch*, an honest-to-God human being and spirit-person in whom people of this generation can recognize and understand themselves. To both groups, traditional theology and traditional theologians remain suspect.

But what if Martin Luther were correct, that a true doctor of theology is not a defender of ecclesiastical tradition and order but one who properly distinguishes law from gospel?[10] Making such a distinction for Luther is not a matter of neat theoretical theologizing; it is a matter of liberating people from bondage to sin and to the institutional church. To turn gospel into law is, in John Dominic Crossan's language, to "broker the kingdom." To proclaim divine forgiveness and accep-

[8]Sarah Henrich and James Boyce were and are, to be sure, classicists. Still, they would not want to claim a dispassionate interest in the scriptures only because the scriptures are classical texts.

[9]True, Mary Knutsen is a systematic theologian, but she clearly understands herself to be a *biblical* systematic theologian.

[10]See, for example, Martin Luther, *Psalms 1 and 2* (1519-1521), *LW* 14:283-284; *Sermons on the Gospel of St. John* (1537), *LW* 24:293; *To the Christian Nobility* (1520), *LW* 44:205.

tance, while recognizing the reality of sin in the lives of people and the place of the cross in the life of God (i.e., without succumbing to cheap grace), is to set people free—not just in or for the church, but in and for their families and their world. Forgiven, they are free to act boldly despite the ambiguities and contingencies of life as we know it. Forgiven, they are free to risk themselves for others in family and society. Forgiven, they are free to work, furthering God's own creative development of the world.

From this perspective, one might suggest that some of the third-questers, in their enthusiasm to remove any ultimately transcendent dimension from Jesus of Nazareth, thereby eliminate the possibility of understanding the work of Jesus "for us," instead turning Jesus into a human role model par excellence. Christianity, if it survives at all, becomes then only a kind of *imitatio Christi*. Theologically, one must point out that this changes gospel into law. Jesus is not one who opens the kingdom of heaven "for us," but is a teacher we seek to emulate and a model to which we aspire. The work is ours. Again, it is not surprising that this is attractive on the contemporary American scene. Everything is about law in our world of jogging, self-help, and alternative healing. Everything is up to us. Do it yourself! And the "historical Jesus" becomes the great model of how to pull it off, or, at best, our helper in our own pulling it off. For the moment, the adrenalin flows. In the long term, we have created a new legalism.

Understanding the theologian as the one who announces God's freedom in Christ, Gerhard von Rad proclaimed himself to be much more interested in the "theological maximum" than in the "historical minimum"[11]—a statement that was widely misunderstood to mean that "nothing ever happened, but here is what it means." That something happened, that God entered and worked in history, was essential to von Rad. But he knew the futility of attempting to separate what happened from the interpretation of what happened. And an interpretation of events that is faithful to the biblical God who liberates from bondage and brings life out of death is where liberation and life are to be found in the present, not in a presentation of the minimally assured data of history.

And that is why we are theologians. We are dependent upon the work of historians. We are called to be conversant with it, to enter into it as it impinges on our work of theology, to argue intelligently and apologetically; but we are called to be theologians. And we find it a noble work.

5. The "historical Jesus" is as fully an ideological construct as is the Jesus of the classical creeds

If, over against the polytheistic assumptions of the entire ancient world, Old Testament and Jewish faith insisted that there is "one power in heaven," some participants in the present quest for Jesus lean toward the assumption that there is none. A "God" there may be, but not one that upsets the ways of the world or that is fully present in the life of a Palestinian carpenter. All three worldviews, polytheism, monotheism, and practical atheism, are theological or ideological constructs.

---

[11]Gerhard von Rad, *Old Testament Theology*, vol. 1 (New York: Harper & Row, 1962) 108, 118-119.

Western secular humanism gives pride of place to atheism—and many of us academic types have to fight against concurring. Truth to tell, many, if not most, moderns—no matter what their confession—function day by day with a kind of practical atheism; they (we) really do put our ultimate trust in human agency. No wonder a human (but spiritual and challenging) Jesus is more attractive than one with embarrassing claims to divinity. Such a Jesus fits just fine in a modern and sophisticated western culture.

But there are other ways to construe reality. That was clear to me beneath American fluorescent lights listening to these lectures; it is clearer still beneath an African sunset writing this introduction. If among American sophisticates the notion of God is quaint, here among African villagers the notion of atheism is unthinkable. Both the Bible's voice from the past and the contemporary voices of tribal people proclaim that the world cannot be understood apart from God (or the gods). And, of course, many modern westerners agree—and always have. It is quite fitting, of course, to have it out—to debate which view is more consistent with reality as we know it—and Christian theologians must be prepared for that difficult conversation; but the debate will not proceed without assumptions, and often the assumptions will determine the outcome. If people don't rise from the dead, Jesus didn't rise from the dead. If people didn't walk on water, Jesus didn't walk on water. But the Bible knows as well as the modern skeptic that people don't rise from the dead and don't walk on water—*unless they do!*—and it is that surprise that the Bible proclaims as the work of God in the life of Jesus. The biblical authors are open to a challenge of their own worldview, just as the Bible is willing to challenge the worldview of others.

To say it again: bracketing God out of the equation of history is as much an ideological construction as putting God in. The decision has little or nothing to do with historical verifiability. It has to do simply with where we choose to plight our troth—and, again, the test will be in the fruit. Many in the present quest for Jesus have been understandably alienated by a top-down imposition of orthodoxy, crushing the Jesus of history and the human quest of contemporary people. They would argue rightly that such an imposition has failed the fruits test. Now, therefore, they seek something else: a human Jesus who welcomes equally the spiritual seeker and the social outcast, challenging from beneath the Jesus controlled by the ecclesiastical hierarchy and the theological elite. Thus far they are in good company. Luther, at least, finds something right in that; although he stresses the insufficiency of preaching the historical Jesus,[12] he is quite clear that one gets to the Christ of faith from beneath, through the Jesus of history, not from above, through philosophy and dogma:

> We can, therefore, establish no firmer foundation for the divinity of Christ than that we wrap and seal our hearts in the promises of scripture. Scripture lifts us up with supreme gentleness and leads us to Christ—first, to Christ as a human being; thereafter, to Christ as the lord of all creation, and, finally, to Christ as

[12]See the quotation from *The Freedom of a Christian*, cited by David Fredrickson on p. 174 of this volume.

God. In that way I am brought carefully along and learn to recognize God [in Christ]. But the philosophers and those who are worldly wise want to begin at the top—which is where they become fools. We must begin from the bottom and only then move upward [in our knowledge], that Solomon's proverb not be fulfilled in us: "It is not good to eat much honey, or to seek honor on top of honor" (Prov 25:27).[13]

Perhaps the problem for some in and around the Jesus Seminar is that they have, indeed, started from beneath in their quest for the human and historical Jesus, but, at the same time, they have started from the top, replacing the dogmatism of the early and medieval church with the dogmatism of the present. They "know" in advance that the promises (which alone provide the firm basis for recognizing God in Christ) are not true or do not apply. The promises cannot be true because they sin against the regnant philosophy of this age, that God cannot or does not really do anything in the world. Thus, these scholars cut themselves off from the possibility of being gently lifted up and led to Christ—nor, if their Jesus is the true Jesus, can they allow it of others. And, in this at least, they, too, fail the fruits test.

6. *There is no single solution to the Jesus question*

Who is Jesus? The eschatological prophet? The divine logos? The Son of God? The suffering servant? The crucified Messiah? Or, moving to more recent designations, is he a peasant sage? A spirit-person? Wisdom incarnate? If the third quest has proved anything it is that the historical Jesus remains remarkably elusive. Most of the recent designations work, to some degree or another. The scholars have done their homework and know how to read texts. As long as we expect them to speak only of the Jesus of history, their results are more or less convincing—all of them. Just as the testimonies of scripture itself are convincing—all of them. So, too, properly understood, are many of the formulations of ecclesiastical tradition. Certainly some formulations are better than others. All probably can be pushed too far and used coercively. But all make a point. And in doing so, they remind us that Jesus transcends our labels—all of them. Intriguingly, the many-faceted Jesus of the third quest tends to suggest a transcendence that many participants in that quest want to deny. And it is precisely that transcendent Jesus that the biblical and ecclesiastical designations have sought to describe. Paul finally says it best: "For all the promises of God find their Yes in him" (2 Cor 1:20 RSV). No trajectory, no tradition, no title, no description will capture Jesus—the "historical" one or the biblical one. All the promises and all the titles that go with them will be just enough.

7. *Finally, it's not a Jesus question, it's a God question*

Most of what has been said so far leads inevitably to this conclusion. The Jesus portrayed in the Bible requires the assumption that God really was in Christ

---

[13]*Sermon on John 3:1-15 (Gospel for Trinity Sunday), WA* 10/1/2:297 (my translation; words in brackets added). I am indebted to Peter Petzling for bringing this passage to my attention. For an older English translation of the entire sermon, see *Sermons of Martin Luther: The Church Postils*, vol. 3, ed. John Nicholas Lenker (1907; reprint, Grand Rapids: Baker, 1995) 405-420.

(indeed, in the death and resurrection of Jesus) reconciling the world to himself (2 Cor 5:19)—and that there is a God who can and would do such a thing. The Jesus of the third quest—or at least some parts thereof—derives from the assumption that God does not enter history in ways that upset the observable laws of cause and effect. Yet, in the work of John Polkinghorne and others, we have very sophisticated models of how we might understand a "God who acts" in a post-Newtonian world. Mary Knutsen has addressed this issue in her essay, so it need not be elaborated here, but the point is important: how we portray Jesus has everything to do with what we think of God, and vice versa.

This does not imply that there is no Jesus question. Both historians and theologians want and need to understand Jesus in his own right. And there is legitimate disagreement or discussion about what categories and titles work best to describe Jesus. There is a legitimate debate about whether the church has paid too little attention to the life and sayings of Jesus because of its abiding interest in his death and resurrection. But all of these questions, too, are significantly impacted by what we make of Jesus' relation to God. Why, for example, the interest in Jesus' sayings and serving? Is it simply to establish that Jesus is humbler and wiser than most, perhaps than any? The latter case would, of course, be impossible to make historically. So what is at stake here? Jesus as better-than-average role model? Jesus as supporter of my favorite cause? That hardly seems enough. But what if Paul is correct in speaking of the divine kenosis or emptying: "[Jesus] emptied himself, taking the form of a slave, being born in human likeness. And being found in human form, he humbled himself and became obedient to the point of death—even death on a cross" (Phil 2:7-8)? Intriguingly, though Paul is clearly interested in establishing the ultimate humiliation of Jesus in his death and his glorious exaltation by God in resurrection and ascension, he (Paul) chooses a hymn that includes also Jesus' birth and human life, his humility and obedience, his service of others. These now become profoundly interesting, not necessarily because Jesus did them better than anyone else, but because the Jesus who did them was "in the form of God." In Jesus, God becomes the humble servant of humankind. Our interest in Jesus would have waned long ago were he nothing more than a first-century sage. But if, in Jesus of Nazareth, we see the incarnation of God, then interest in Jesus will never cease. As, indeed, it has not. Witness this book. ⊕

Word & World
Supplement Series 3
1997

The Third Quest for the Historical Jesus: Introduction and Bibliography

MARY M. KNUTSEN

Luther Seminary
St. Paul, Minnesota

THE FLOOD OF NEW BOOKS ON JESUS, SOME OF WHICH ARE SIX OR SEVEN hundred pages in length, can quickly exceed even the most avid reader's attempts to keep up. The purpose of this paper is to provide a context for what is being called the "third quest" for the historical Jesus, to highlight the major points of contention among contemporary Jesus scholars, and to survey some of the major books in the third quest.

I. BASIC TERMS AND SOURCES

A. Terms

It will be helpful at the outset to clarify terms. First, we must distinguish between the earthly life of Jesus in its full human actuality (the "earthly Jesus") and the earthly life of Jesus as it is historiographically reconstructed, in a variety of ways, by contemporary historians (the "historical Jesus"). As any lover of biographies knows, the same person's life can be historically reconstructed in different ways by different biographers, depending on differing foci (e.g., politics or personal life), sources, and interpretive frameworks (think of the still proliferating number of biographies of Abraham Lincoln). Yet no single biography, nor even all of them together, can exhaust the richness of a person's life and identity. Moreover, insofar as they are engaged in a strictly historiographical study, historians of the life of Jesus are bound by the same rules of evidence that would apply to their work with any historical human figure. There is no reason, in principle, for Christians to object to this. After all, Christians also confess that Jesus of Nazareth was "truly human," even if we recognize much more in him as well.

Second, Christians also claim that this Jesus of Nazareth is alive, resurrected from the dead as the first fruits of a resurrection that will finally open all the graves of history to new life; Jesus is alive in our midst, giving us the promise and foretaste of his future for us (the "risen Jesus"). From the outset, Christians found that the reality of the risen Jesus required them to reinterpret their understanding of Jesus as they had known him in his earthly ministry. So there was a double interaction: the reality of the risen one deepened and transformed their understanding of the earthly one, and the realities of the earthly ministry and death of Jesus shaped their understanding of the risen one. The result is the New Testament, which Christians claim is the truest paradigm (norming norm) for our understanding, experience, and proclamation of Jesus Christ as savior of the world the ("kerygmatic Jesus"). This does not mean that strictly historical reconstructions of the earthly life of Jesus are illegitimate, since Jesus was indeed "truly human." Such historical studies can challenge and enrich faith's image of Jesus. But Christians hold that they do not exhaust the fullness of who Jesus was and is as the earthly and risen Lord.

B. Sources

There is a range of resources for the historical reconstruction of the earthly life of Jesus. These include resources both within the canon of the New Testament (the letters of Paul, the synoptic gospels, and John) and outside the canon. Sources particularly important to the contemporary debates include:

Q: The majority of biblical scholars hold that the Gospel of Mark was a source for both Matthew and Luke. In addition, however, Matthew and Luke also contain in common a number of sayings of Jesus as well as a temptation narrative that are not found in Mark. Hence, scholars have postulated that Matthew and Luke had a second source, in addition to Mark, composed largely of sayings of Jesus; this source they refer to as Q (for *Quelle*, the German word for "source").

Gospel of Thomas: The Nag Hammadi library discovered in 1945 included a variety of "gospels" buried by Egyptian monks in the late fourth century which scholars have found to bear "gnostic" characteristics. The *Gospel of Thomas* is one of these, written in Coptic (although a third-century fragment of *Thomas* in Greek also exists); it is composed of 114 sayings of Jesus, several clearly paralleling sayings found in the synoptics (e.g., parables of the mustard seed and sower).[1]

Dead Sea Scrolls: The Dead Sea Scrolls, discovered in 1947 near the Dead Sea, do not speak directly of Jesus or the Jesus movement. Rather they have greatly expanded our understanding of the varieties of Judaism in the first-century, including the existence of fervent apocalyptic eschatology in the highly sectarian Essene community at Qumran.[2]

---

[1]A good source for the *Gospel of Thomas* is James Robinson, ed., *The Nag Hammadi Library in English*, 4th rev. ed. (New York: E. J. Brill, 1996).

[2]A good source for the Dead Sea Scrolls is Geza Vermes, ed., *The Dead Sea Scrolls in English*, 4th ed. (New York: Penguin, 1996).

Non-Christian writers: There are brief references to "Christ" and/or his followers in Josephus, Suetonius, Pliny the Younger, and Tacitus.[3]

Archaeology: Archaeological work in Galilee has also contributed to important changes in our understanding of the world in which Jesus ministered. Galilee was not simply the bucolic backwater some of us may have previously imagined, but contained bustling centers of hellenistic language, culture, and commerce in Roman cities like Sepphoris (just four miles from Nazareth). Many Galileans, especially those engaged in a trade (like Jesus), probably knew at least some Greek and had some familiarity with Greco-Roman culture.[4]

C. Criteria of Authenticity

What are the criteria by which historians can determine whether a saying or action can plausibly be included in an historical reconstruction of the earthly life of Jesus? Although these criteria, and their specific meaning and appropriate use, are passionately debated, some of those most frequently invoked include: (1) attestation in more than one stream of early Christian tradition; (2) the criterion of embarrassment—for material unlikely to have been retained by the church unless it had historical grounding; (3) the criterion of dissimilarity—for material unlikely to have been simply derived from other first-century sources, either Judaism or the early church (an especially tricky criterion, since it can artificially isolate Jesus from his culture); (4) the criterion of coherence with what has been established about Jesus by using the other criteria; (5) the criterion of crucifiability—for material that adequately explains why Jesus was rejected and crucified.

"Authenticity" can be misleading here, because it can suggest that anything not deemed by historians to be plausibly included in a historical reconstruction is thereby "inauthentic," i.e., a sheer invention or falsehood. Christians hold that the sayings of the risen Jesus (e.g., the great commission in Matthew 28) are "authentic"—i.e., come from Jesus—even though we acknowledge that such sayings cannot be included in a historian's reconstruction of Jesus' earthly life. It is important to keep in mind the specific use of the term in relation to the task of historical reconstruction.

II. Previous Quests for the Historical Jesus

Many are naming current work as part of a third quest for the historical Jesus. It is helpful to get a brief understanding of the previous quests and what is distinctive about this third quest.

A. *The first quest*, in the nineteenth century, was inaugurated by the nineteenth-century "discovery of time" in geology, biology, politics, historiography, biblical studies, and theology: everything and everyone, including God, has a

---

[3]For an accessible, brief review of these resources, see Luke Timothy Johnson, *The Real Jesus: The Misguided Quest for the Historical Jesus and the Truth of the Traditional Gospels* (San Francisco: HarperSanFrancisco, 1996) 112-117.

[4]A good source for this is John J. Rousseau and Rami Arav, *Jesus and His World: An Archaeological and Cultural Dictionary* (Minneapolis: Fortress, 1995).

history. Many of the studies of the "historical Jesus" which emerged at this time were shaped by the values of the enlightenment and were undertaken specifically to oppose Christian doctrines. Many also reflect the impact of Newton and a scientific worldview rooted in a mechanistic causality. These studies of Jesus tended to be

- rationalistic: explaining away the miracles of Jesus
- moralistic: Jesus as a teacher of universal moral truths
- optimistic: viewing humankind as moving at last toward true enlightenment and a fully rational society in which all would realize the "brotherhood of man" and the "fatherhood of God"

In reaction to the rationalistic and mechanistic worldview of the enlightenment, the nineteenth century also saw the emergence of romanticism with its view of the universe as a developing organism and its focus on human feelings. Romantic portraits of Jesus tended to focus on his subjective experience and, above all, his consciousness of God's presence in everything.

B. No quest: The first quest effectively ended with Albert Schweitzer's *The Quest of the Historical Jesus* (1906) and his argument that (a) nineteenth-century lives of Jesus really resembled their authors and (b) Jesus is a very strange figure to us indeed—a wildly apocalyptic prophet who sped his own death in hopes that it would hasten the coming of the kingdom.

After Schweitzer there came a period of no quest, dominated above all by the work of Rudolf Bultmann and his conviction that a reconstruction of the historical Jesus is historically impossible, existentially unnecessary, and theologically undesirable. What is needed instead is a philosophical reconstruction of the existential "understanding of existence"—the universal human situation—embedded in New Testament texts (which are to be stripped of their apocalyptic framework) and an encounter with the kerygmatic Christ who calls us to authentic existence in the risk of existential trust.

C. The new quest (second quest) for the historical Jesus emerged in the post-World War II era, which brought with it a sense that historical events really do change the world. An apocalyptic end and new beginning to the world was no longer so unimaginable. The new quest, inaugurated by Bultmann's student Ernst Käsemann in 1953, sought not to attack faith but to bolster it by investigating the continuities between the kerygmatic Christ proclaimed by the church and the historical Jesus who proclaimed the kingdom. Central to this work is a focus on Jesus' identity as eschatological prophet, understood to be the point of continuity between the ministry of Jesus and the church's kerygma. Jesus' proclamation of the kingdom of God already carries an implicit christology—that Jesus himself is the event of God's coming to us.

III. THE THIRD QUEST FOR THE HISTORICAL JESUS[5]

A. Context and Character of the "Third Quest"

While the first two quests were largely European (and particularly German) movements, the third quest is predominantly the work of English-speaking scholars, both British and North American, especially the latter. Although the third quest has been particularly marked by the public visibility of the Jesus Seminar and its members (especially Marcus Borg and John Dominic Crossan), other scholars are also writing books on Jesus that strenuously differ from the Jesus Seminar, Borg, and Crossan. The third quest includes many different viewpoints. The larger context of this third quest in North America includes:

- post-Constantinian culture, in which being a church-going Christian is no longer part and parcel of American citizenship, and in which there is also a widespread suspicion of institutions per se, especially among baby boomers.[6] Some of the members of the Jesus Seminar have made clear their deep dissatisfaction with their own earlier experiences of the church's authoritarianism, its fundamentalistic (Funk) or dogmatic (Borg) presentations of Jesus' message and ministry, and/or its hierarchical claims to control access to Jesus and the vision and power of God at work in his life (Crossan)

- pluralistic values, including a tendency toward revulsion against any kind of exclusive claims for Jesus or for Christianity. Jesus is one among many who open our eyes to the spiritual dimensions of everyday life, one of many revealers of the holy. The theological distinction between revelation and salvation becomes important here: in Christian tradition there can be many teachers through whom we come to know and understand the world, but there is only one savior in whom the destiny of creation and humanity is actually changed, whose cross and resurrection mean that death will no longer have the final word. There is a tendency among some third-quest scholars—particularly some members of the Jesus Seminar—to reduce Jesus to a "revealer" only. This appears to have to do not only with an embrace of pluralistic values (there are many revealers), but also with a theology that cannot imagine that God actually does anything in Jesus or in the world. Robert Funk has been particularly clear about this. The modern universe is a self-enclosed causal web, he argues; any appeal to God's agency is simply mythological, including any appeal to God's bringing about a coming kingdom or raising Jesus from the dead

- a widespread yearning for experiential access to the presence of the holy, of the sacred ("new age" religions, charismatic movements, etc.). Churches need to understand and connect with this yearning, even though it tends to invoke

---

[5]The fullest survey to date of contemporary Jesus scholarship is that of Ben Witherington III, *The Jesus Quest: The Third Search for the Jew of Nazareth* (Downers Grove, IL: InterVarsity, 1995).

[6]For a fine study of baby-boomer values and religious yearnings, see Wade Clark Roof, *A Generation of Seekers* (San Francisco: HarperSanFrancisco, 1993).

an "inert God"—a spiritual presence available for my use, enhancement, health and well-being, but not a God who acts

- a consumerist culture that is increasingly enslaved to work, and yet also increasingly longing for a sense of abiding connections with others—friends and community. Borg's emphasis on Jesus' effecting a social (not political) transformation rooted in divine compassion, and Crossan's emphasis on Jesus' open meals and open healing (not necessarily cure but healing—restoring the victim to community) speak to this

B. Specific Context in Contemporary New Testament Scholarship

The scholarly context of the new quest includes:

- a new confidence in the possibility of the historical reconstruction of the life of Jesus and in the significance of this for contemporary religious life
- a setting in secular universities and departments of religious studies rather than seminaries and divinity schools
- a broad range of new sources available in the past 50 years, both archaeological and textual (e.g., Nag Hammadi, Dead Sea Scrolls)
- new methods: literary, cultural anthropological, and social world approaches to the New Testament and to the world of the first century:

   — literary: the parables of Jesus (e.g., good Samaritan, leaven, mustard seed) are not moralistic tales but stories in which the hearers' social world and values are challenged and opened up

   — cultural anthropology: Jesus is a charismatic holy man, a shaman and miracle worker who also transforms the boundary markers of the "social body" that demarcate clean/unclean, honor/shame, insider/outsider. One of the major differences between the cultural anthropological orientation of the third quest and the rationalistic first quest is the affirmation by virtually all third questers that Jesus did indeed do miracles, as did many others in the first century

   — social world: Jesus is one who subversively undoes a socio-political system based on patronage (akin to Chicago ward politics), who eats with outcasts and sinners and refuses to found an institution; he is the enactor of an open, egalitarian "brokerless" kingdom

C. Plurality of the Third Quest

The third quest is not only composed of the publications of the Jesus Seminar, Robert Funk, Marcus Borg, and John Dominic Crossan. Many other scholars have published major new works on the historical Jesus, several of them in direct opposition to Crossan and others. A spectrum of these new portraits of Jesus includes the following (see bibliography for more detail):

- Jesus as hellenistic Cynic sage: Burton Mack argues that Jesus was an individualistic sage akin to the hellenistic Cynics, who wandered homelessly mocking the pretensions of society with wit and sarcasm. Jesus had no eschatology and was not much interested in things Jewish

- Jesus as aniconic Jewish sage: Robert Funk and John Dominic Crossan have both written extensively on the parables of Jesus, as has Bernard Brandon Scott, another member of the Jesus Seminar. All stress the world-undoing character of the parables: the mustard seed grows not into a mighty cedar of Lebanon but into a bushy weed; the leaven dirties the whole lump. Unlike Burton Mack, however, Scott argues that Jesus' disconcerting wisdom is Jewish in form and content. In his brilliant and homiletically very helpful book *Hear Then the Parable*, Scott analyzes all the New Testament parables in terms of their ultimate originating performance in Jesus' distinctively world-undoing voice, disclosing the no-image God of Israel. In another article, Scott argues that this voice can also be heard in a *Gospel of Thomas* parable that likens the kingdom to a woman carrying a broken jar of meal that is wholly empty when she arrives home: "In the end the voice exposes a non-presence without image. The parable, the proverb, the beatitude imitate in language the no-image God of Israel. The expected divine presence becomes a divine absence"[7]

- Jesus as Jewish Cynic peasant: While Burton Mack has argued that Jesus is best to be understood as a hellenistic Cynic sage and Brandon Scott argues that Jesus is a Jewish Cynic sage—the form and content of his wisdom sayings are Jewish, not hellenistic—Crossan adds that Jesus is a peasant Jewish Cynic. Jesus enacted the shattering of fixed, hierarchical worlds and an opening to the unmediated presence of God in the peasant language of the body: in open meals with sinners and outcasts, in freely given healing and forgiveness, and in constant itinerancy. The "brokerless kingdom of God" Jesus thereby enacted was non-eschatological, always available to all who have the courage to adopt his lifestyle

- Jesus as spirit person: Marcus Borg argues that Jesus was above all a charismatic holy man—a kind of shaman—who was profoundly in touch with the spiritual powers permeating all things and able to open others to an experience of this encompassing power—a power whose ultimate character is compassion, not purity

- Jesus as egalitarian prophet of wisdom: Both Elisabeth Schüssler Fiorenza and Ben Witherington have focused on the presence of wisdom categories (cf. Proverbs 8) in the New Testament to interpret the ministry and identity of Jesus. Fiorenza presents Jesus as a prophetic sage who understood himself as the child and spokesperson of Divine Sophia and who founded a radically egalitarian community in which women were primary leaders. Witherington disparages feminist scholarship on Jesus and wisdom, but argues that Jesus understood himself to be the incarnation of God's wisdom. In contrast to other presentations of Jesus as sage, however, both Fiorenza and Witherington argue that Jesus' wisdom is also suffused with eschatological overtones from

---

[7]Bernard Brandon Scott, "Jesus as Sage: An Innovating Voice in Common Wisdom," in *The Sage in Israel and the Ancient Near East*, ed. John Gammie and Leo Purdue (Winona Lake, IN: Eisenbrauns, 1990) 415.

its Jewish apocalyptic context: wisdom is not opposed to apocalyptic but suffused with it

- Jesus as prophet of the present and coming kingdom: The first two volumes of John Meier's three-volume book, *A Marginal Jew*, present Jesus as the bearer of a coming eschatological kingdom of God, already proleptically present in his miracles and exorcisms. Jesus is an eschatological prophet and miracle worker greater than Elijah

- Jesus as prophet of imminent restoration eschatology: Eschewing a focus on sayings of Jesus, E. P. Sanders turns to eight relatively undisputed deeds of Jesus and focuses his book *Jesus and Judaism* particularly upon two events: Jesus' overturning of the tables in the temple and prophetic announcement of a coming new temple, and Jesus' appointment of twelve to serve as judges over the restored twelve tribes of Israel. Thus, Sanders pictures Jesus as a prophet of the eschatological restoration of Israel

- Jesus as eschatological prophet, Messiah, and suffering servant: N. T. Wright's massive new book, *Jesus and the Victory of God*, is rooted in Wright's conviction that Schweitzer got it basically right: the New Testament presents an historically reliable portrait of Jesus as one who went to his death in the hope of concentrating in himself the eschatological woes and so speeding the coming of the final kingdom. What Schweitzer failed to see, however, is that Jesus did not thereby envision the end of the space-time universe; rather, he employed apocalyptic imagery in prophetic proclamation of a very specific first-century event: the destruction of the temple by the Romans in 70 A.D. with the eschatologically renewed Israel and the nations as the new dwelling place of God. By going to the cross, Jesus prophetically enacted and took upon himself the reality of this coming judgment of God; he enacted his own self-understanding as Israel's representative king and suffering servant

IV. EVALUATING THE THIRD QUEST

A. What's Good in the Third Quest

Without doubt, the publications of the fellows of the Jesus Seminar and others have brought new excitement to conversations about Jesus. Though there may be reason for concern about some of the content of this conversation, the broad interest it has generated presents an opportunity for the Christian church.

The recovery of Jesus as a subversive sage (parable-teller), charismatic holy man, and socio-religious prophet is broadly true to the sources (including the New Testament) and can challenge and enrich faith's picture of Jesus and his kingdom. Although none of these characterizations (nor all three together) is sufficient, they provide us with genuinely new insight into the Jesus of history.

The response touched off by this work of the third quest demonstrates the need for the church's gospel proclamation and story more fully to connect with people's lives and yearnings. Several of these authors (particularly Marcus Borg's best-selling *Meeting Jesus Again*) are connecting deeply with people, perhaps especially with baby boomers; the church needs to attend to this, to respond to the yearnings in its own way, even if it doesn't adopt Borg's specific construal of Jesus.

Finally, the church needs to investigate the life of Jesus with rigor, to rethink the saving work of Jesus biblically and theologically, in order to shape a more biblically faithful and effective ministry.

B. What's Debatable in the Third Quest

1. Jesus and Eschatology: A major dividing line between the first four portraits of Jesus sketched above and the last four is the issue of the relation of Jesus to Jewish apocalyptic eschatology (and the various construals of this apocalyptic eschatology among those who do ascribe it to Jesus). Most of the members of the Jesus Seminar have argued strenuously for a non-eschatological, non-apocalyptic historical Jesus, despite their recognition that both Jesus' Jewish world and the early church were deeply apocalyptic. Hence Jesus' sayings about the coming kingdom of God and all forms of future eschatology tend to be deemed not "authentic," i.e., later accretions by the early church. In part, scholars base this argument on their dating and interpretation of sources, particularly Q and the *Gospel of Thomas*. Their work demonstrates, however, that other factors contribute to this judgment concerning a non-eschatological Jesus. Funk argues that any appeal to God's agency is mythological, Borg suggests that an eschatological orientation seems to make ultimate claims for Jesus and that it undermines social transformation and a present sense of the Spirit, Crossan argues that it brokers the kingdom by not making it immediately and wholly accessible to all. I believe the problem is theological: a distinctively modern problem of conceptualizing divine agency. Leander Keck puts it vividly: "The Borg-Crossan construal tacitly posits an inert deity....In this interpretation of the kingdom, Jesus may refer to God but not defer to God's action."[8] The issues here are theological as well as historical-critical.[9]

2. Identification and use of sources: The denial of any apocalyptic eschatology in Jesus' message and ministry is fundamentally intertwined with the question of the identification and interpretation of sources. Debate has particularly focused on Q and the *Gospel of Thomas*.

Q: Two issues have been especially debated concerning Q. First, several scholars have attempted to distinguish earlier and later elements in Q, but in quite different ways. John Kloppenborg argues that the earlier strata of these sayings—those most likely to derive from Jesus—are composed of non-apocalyptic wisdom sayings, while the themes of apocalyptic eschatology are later.[10] Other scholars

---

[8]Leander Keck, "The Second Coming of the Liberal Jesus?" *Christian Century* (August 24-31, 1994) 787.

[9]For a very helpful discussion of how divine agency is to be conceived, see *TToday* 54/1 (1997), especially the article by Terence E. Fretheim, "The God Who Acts: An Old Testament Perspective," 6-18.

[10]John Kloppenborg, *The Formation of Q: Trajectories in Ancient Wisdom Collections* (Philadelphia: Fortress, 1987).

have argued just the opposite: that early Q (and Jesus' own ministry) is perfused with apocalyptic Jewish eschatology, and it is only the later strata of Q that introduce hellenistic wisdom ideas.[11] Secondly, there has been a continuing debate about the characteristics of the Q community, including the question of the degree to which the cross and resurrection of Jesus shaped its life and ministry (since Q is comprised almost entirely simply of sayings). John Dominic Crossan has argued, for instance, that the Q community was a wisdom-based community that continued unchanged after Easter, while M. Eugene Boring argues that Q bears all the marks of early Christian prophecy, which is rooted in the conviction that Jesus is risen and speaks through his prophetic spokespersons.[12]

Gospel of Thomas: John Dominic Crossan and some other members of the Jesus Seminar argue that the *Gospel of Thomas* represents a source for the sayings of Jesus that is independent of the synoptics and whose roots lie in the period immediately after Jesus' death, i.e., approximately 30-60 A.D. Others claim that the *Gospel of Thomas* shows dependence on the final redactional form of the synoptics and so is a later derivative from them. Christopher Tuckett argues persuasively, however, that although the extant texts of *Thomas*—a fourth-century Coptic text and a third-century Greek one—show dependence on the synoptics, we cannot be sure whether or not this dependence represents a later addition. Hence we need to avoid making sweeping generalizations one way or the other about *Thomas*'s status as an early, independent source for the sayings of Jesus.[13]

3. Relation to Judaism and the law: A closely related issue has to do with scholarly reconstructions of the various forms of first-century Judaism and of Jesus' relationship to this richly diverse Jewish world. Those who stress Jesus' Jewishness also tend to present an apocalyptic Jesus, while those who do not attend focally to Jesus' Jewishness (e.g., Crossan) or who stress his difference from some first-century forms of Judaism (e.g., Borg on Jesus' opposition to purity laws) tend to present a non-apocalyptic Jesus. A more specific subset of this issue has to do specifically with Jesus' understanding of the law, about which scholarly views differ.

4. The historicity of Jesus' trial(s), passion, and burial: John Dominic Crossan argues that the synoptic accounts of the trials, passion, and burial of Jesus are "prophecy historicized": Old Testament texts used as sources to invent Jesus' history. Jesus, he argues, was not tried before Jewish authorities (a moral point for Crossan as well, post-holocaust) and was not buried, but was most likely consumed by dogs and vultures or thrown into an open grave. Douglas Moo and

[11]For a clear and judicious discussion, see Chris Tuckett's article on Q in *ABD* 5:567-572, and, more fully, his book *Q and the History of Early Christianity* (Edinburgh: T & T Clark, 1996).

[12]M. Eugene Boring, *The Continuing Voice of Jesus: Christian Prophecy and the Gospel Tradition* (Louisville: Westminster/John Knox, 1991). For a clear discussion of this issue, which argues that the cross and resurrection are important to Q, see the chapter on the Q community in Arland J. Hultgren, *The Rise of Normative Christianity* (Minneapolis: Fortress, 1992).

[13]Christopher Tuckett, "Thomas and the Synoptics," *NovT* 30/2 (1988) 132-157.

Donald Juel argue, however, that the changes made to these Old Testament texts are so crazy that they reflect the press of actual historical events.[14]

C. A Vital Issue: The Resurrection of Jesus of Nazareth

At several points (e.g., at the close of *Jesus: A Revolutionary Biography*) John Dominic Crossan simply denies that Jesus was resurrected from the dead; the resurrection was invented by Paul in order to bolster his claims to post-Jesus apostleship, and all the resurrection appearances in the New Testament have to do with claiming authority for a particular Christian leader—and so a re-brokering of the kingdom. Crossan is clearly and intentionally exceeding the role of historian in his denial of the resurrection. His claim is avowedly theological: that his own historical reconstruction of the life of the earthly Jesus is itself the unsurpassable bearer of divine revelation—the historian as broker. At other points, Crossan appears to make a more modest claim: while some Christian groups found the resurrection to be central, others, particularly the Q community, did not; they just went on as they had before Jesus' death in accordance with Jesus' peasant Jewish wisdom, discovering in their praxis a continuing presence of divine power. The latter is the only viable option today as well for those who find the resurrection of Jesus untenable.

Others argue that the resurrection of Jesus is fundamental to virtually all early Christian literature, including Q. It is presupposed both in Q and in the *Gospel of Thomas*, both of which include sayings of the risen Jesus.[15] The resurrection of Jesus, understood as an eschatological event—the beginning of the ultimate transformation of all created life—is also clearly a fundamental presupposition in the letters of Paul[16] and shapes the very form of Paul's rhetoric.[17]

The resurrection of Jesus also shapes the distinctive genre of "gospel." Eugene Boring argues, for instance, that the gospels are not simply species of ancient biography, because from the outset their narratives of the earthly ministry of Jesus are transformed by and intended to mediate an encounter with the risen one through the story of his earthly life and death.[18] From the outset of Mark's Gospel, for instance, the reader is brought into the presence of the risen Jesus, a risen Jesus whose deepest identity is that of being the crucified Messiah. Mark's Gospel even reverses the usual Christian chronology of Jesus' life in order to press this point. The usual chronology was: (1) Jesus' ministry, suffering, and crucifixion;

---

[14]Douglas Moo, *The Old Testament in the Gospel Passion Narratives* (Sheffield: Almond, 1983); Donald Juel, *Messianic Exegesis: Christological Interpretation of the Old Testament in Early Christianity* (Philadelphia: Fortress, 1988).

[15]See M. Eugene Boring, *Sayings of the Risen Jesus* (Cambridge: Cambridge University, 1986), and idem, *The Continuing Voice of Jesus*.

[16]Richard Hays, "'The Word is Near You': Hermeneutics in the Eschatological Community," chapter 5 of *Echoes of Scripture in the Letters of Paul* (New Haven: Yale University, 1989).

[17]See Jouette Bassler, "Paul's Theology: Whence and Whither?" in *Pauline Theology*, vol. 2, ed. David Hay (Minneapolis: Fortress, 1993) .

[18]M. Eugene Boring, *Truly Human/Truly Divine: Christological Language and the Gospel Form* (St. Louis: CBP, 1984).

then (2) resurrection/exaltation; then (3) coming again with power and authority. Mark tells the story as (1) coming with power and authority (Mark 1-8); then (2) exaltation (Mark 9); then (3) suffering and cross (Mark 8-16). This may be part of the reason that Mark's gospel includes no stories of Jesus' resurrection appearances, but ends so abruptly at Mark 16:8: Mark shapes his story of the earthly life of Jesus to be itself a kind of resurrection appearance—a medium of encounter, for readers in every age, with the crucified one, alive.

For Christians, the "real Jesus" is the earthly and risen one, and so the New Testament, with its distinctive genres of proclamation and gospel narrative, has become paradigmatic (*norma normans, non normata*) for ways in which the church tells the story of Jesus, a story that is not yet over. Indeed, we regularly celebrate in our midst the living presence of the risen Lord, mediated to us through the telling of his apostolically shaped story and promise: this is the heart of Christian worship. To be sure, historical scholarship can enrich our understanding and hearing of that apostolic witness and its capacity to bear to us the promise and presence of the crucified one who lives, but it cannot supplant it.

V. Concluding Reflections: Four Models

Avery Dulles, that master of models, has suggested four basic models to relate the Jesus of the historians to the Christ of faith. I will simply indicate them here as resources for reflection, and indicate my own conviction that the final one is correct:[19]

1. The historically reconstructed life of Jesus set in hostile antithesis to Christian faith. This is specifically characteristic of some in the first quest (e.g., Reimarus) as well as some in the third quest (Burton Mack is the clearest example).

2. Historical reconstruction and faith held separate, each within its legitimate sphere, neither able to confirm or contradict the other. This is more characteristic of the period of "no quest" and Bultmann. Its best representative in the third quest, Dulles suggests, is John Meier.

3. Historical reconstruction as the ground of faith. This is particularly exemplified among some representatives of the "new quest" (second quest), Dulles suggests, particularly J. Jeremias and G. Bornkamm as well as the theologian W. Pannenberg (at least, in my opinion, in his early work). It may be that John Dominic Crossan best fits here.

4. The canonically based apostolic gospel proclaimed in the church as the ground of faith, enriched but not supplanted by historical reconstruction of the life of Jesus.

---

[19]Avery Dulles, "Historians and the Reality of Christ," *First Things* 28 (December 1992) 20-25.

VI. ANNOTATED BIBLIOGRAPHY:
SELECTED WORKS IN THE THIRD QUEST

1. The Jesus Seminar

Funk, Robert W., Roy W. Hoover, and the Jesus Seminar. *The Five Gospels: The Search for the Authentic Words of Jesus*. New York: Macmillan, 1993.

> This is the controversial result of the voting of the Jesus Seminar on the authenticity of the sayings of Jesus in the four canonical gospels and in the noncanonical *Gospel of Thomas*: red for yes, pink for maybe, gray for probably not, and black for not authentic. In Mark, there is only one saying in red: Mark 12:17 (pay to the emperor what belongs to the emperor and to God what belongs to God). Matthew has five red sayings: Matt 5:39-42a (cheeks, cloaks, extra mile, giving to beggars); 5:44 (love your enemies); 6:9 (only the "our Father" of the Lord's prayer); 13:33 (parable of the leaven); and 20:1-15 (the last hired receive the same wages). Luke has eight red sayings: Luke 6:20-21 (congratulations you poor, hungry, weeping); 6:29-30 (cheeks, cloaks, giving to beggars); 10:30-35 (good Samaritan); 11:2 (only the "Father" of the Lord's prayer); 13:20-21 (parable of the leaven); 16:1-8a (parable of the shrewd steward); 20:25 (pay to emperor/to God). John's Gospel has no red sayings at all, and indeed is entirely in black save for one pink line at 4:44 (a prophet gets no respect). The *Gospel of Thomas* has three red sayings: 20 (parable of the mustard seed); 54 (congratulations you poor); 100 (pay to emperor/to God).

Hays, Richard B. "The Corrected Jesus." *First Things* 43 (May 1994) 43-48.

> This article is often cited by other biblical scholars as summarizing many of their objections to the Jesus Seminar's methods. In this review of *The Five Gospels*, Hays characterizes Robert Funk as a contemporary P. T. Barnum and the Jesus Seminar as unrepresentative of contemporary biblical scholarship. He then identifies four specific methodological problems in the book: (1) Selection and dating of sources: the book discounts Mark as a source for knowledge of Jesus (Mark is too apocalyptic) and relies instead on the postulation of an early, pre-Marcan sayings source (early Q) and an early, pre-Marcan version of the gnostic *Gospel of Thomas*, all without supporting argument. (2) Criterion of dissimilarity: the book deems a saying authentic only when it is dissimilar both to antecedent Jewish tradition and to subsequent Christian tradition. The "Jesus" who emerges from this is a free-floating iconoclast, artificially isolated from his people and their scripture, and from the movement he founded. (3) A third methodological problem is the book's insistence on a "non-eschatological Jesus"—and use of this as a criterion for excluding many sayings; e.g., Luke 18:2-5 is deemed possibly authentic, but Luke 18:6-8 is not. Present is opposed to future, failing to recognize the possibility of a proleptic eschatology: the conviction that God's coming kingdom has already begun to impinge upon the present in such a way that God's final justice is prefigured—albeit not fully realized—now. (4) This method also isolates Jesus' sayings from a more comprehensive reconstruction of his life,

ministry, and death. Jesus becomes a "talking head" whose zen-like sayings are difficult to link to any possible reason for his execution as a political and religious threat. The method at work here, Hays concludes, is really an extension of the Bultmann-inspired existentialist theology briefly popular in the 1960s: the focus is on Jesus' existentialist "understanding of existence" detached from the reality of his particular setting, life, actions, and death. "The depiction of Jesus as a Cynic philosopher with no concern about Israel's destiny, no connection with the concerns and hopes that animated his Jewish contemporaries, no interest in the interpretation of scripture, and no message of God's coming eschatological judgment is—quite simply—an ahistorical fiction, achieved by the surgical removal of Jesus from his Jewish context" (46).

2. *Jesus as Cynic Sage*

Mack, Burton L. *A Myth of Innocence: Mark and Christian Origins*. Minneapolis: Fortress, 1988.

The book argues that the author of the Gospel of Mark invented the Jesus of Christianity, with disastrously anti-semitic results. Jesus was instead a wandering Cynic sage.

Mack, Burton L. *The Lost Gospel: The Book of Q and Christian Origins*. San Francisco: HarperSanFrancisco, 1993.

A reconstruction of a Cynic Jesus from an interpretation of Q.

Downing, F. Gerald. *Christ and the Cynics: Jesus and Other Radical Preachers in First-Century Tradition*. Sheffield: JSOT, 1988.

Eddy, Paul Rhodes. "Jesus as Diogenes? Reflections on the Cynic Jesus Thesis." *JBL* 115/3 (1996) 449-469.

A good synopsis of scholarly objections to the Cynic Jesus hypothesis.

3. *Jesus, Teller of Parables*

Crossan, John Dominic. "Divine Immediacy and Human Immediacy: Towards a New First Principle in Historical Jesus Research." *Semeia* 44 (1988) 121-140.

Crossan devoted a number of his early books to a study of Jesus' parables and proverbs, using structuralist analyses of the sayings of Jesus to uncover a process by which a familiar world is constructed and then shattered. This article is, in a sense, the culmination of that work: Crossan here postulates that the historical Jesus can be glimpsed as the originating voice behind all the versions of Jesus' parables and proverbs, an aphoristic voice through which Jesus discloses the unmediated presence of God. In Jesus' sayings, Crossan concludes, "one is stripped of all the perfectly normal and necessary, wise and prudent, helpful and human layers of protection and entitlement through which we face one another....Naked before the naked God, we are also naked to one another. And that...is what the historical Jesus considered the Kingdom was all about" (140).

Scott, Bernard Brandon. *Hear Then the Parable: A Commentary on the Parables of Jesus*. Minneapolis: Fortress, 1989.

> A rich study of all of the parables of Jesus in the New Testament, in all their versions (including the *Gospel of Thomas*), with each of the discussions concluding in a reconstruction of the "originating structure" of the parable. A continual theme is the way in which this "originating structure" undoes its hearers' expectations about the way the world works—all the mediating structures and images are undone. A rich resource for preaching.

Scott, Bernard Brandon. "Jesus as Sage: An Innovating Voice in Common Wisdom." In *The Sage in Israel and the Ancient Near East*, edited by John G. Gammie and Leo G. Perdue, 399-415. Winona Lake, IN: Eisenbrauns, 1990.

Robert W. Funk. *Honest to Jesus: Jesus for a New Millennium*. San Francisco: HarperSanFrancisco, 1996.

> At the heart of much of the work of the Jesus Seminar is the picture of Jesus as a teller of koan-like parables that subvert all our expectations. Funk begins his book by clearing away the barriers to Jesus, including basic Christian beliefs about Jesus, and by outlining the new sources and methods in the third quest. He focuses on Jesus as a teller of parables, parables intended to subvert every "mythological" cosmology and temporal narrative. Much of the rest of Funk's book, on Jesus' ministry and death, follows Crossan: Jesus is the enactor of a brokerless kingdom.

4. Jesus, the Peasant Cynic

Crossan, John Dominic. *The Historical Jesus: The Life of a Mediterranean Jewish Peasant*. San Francisco: HarperSanFrancisco, 1991.

> In this long book, Crossan places the structure-shattering words and ministry of Jesus in the religio-political context of the Roman empire and Roman occupation. Against the enslaving system of patrons, brokers, and clients that was the web of the Roman empire, Crossan lifts up in Jesus' miracles, meals, and itineracy the power of divine immediacy, which shattered imperial hierarchy in favor of an open egalitarian commensality. For instance, peasant life, he argues, fell victim to a "perfect circle of victimization" (324): Very heavy taxation brought in its wake hunger, sickness, and desperation. These were in turn interpreted as the effects of sin, for which temple taxes needed to be paid so that forgiveness (and so release from hunger, sickness, desperation) could be obtained. But payment of such taxes led to even more impoverishment, hunger, and sickness, which was interpreted as further evidence of sin, requiring even higher taxes—and on and on. By contrast, Jesus freely heals and forgives (e.g., Mark 2:1-12) and so offers free access to the divine presence and power which others would broker.

Crossan, John Dominic. *Jesus: A Revolutionary Biography*. San Francisco: HarperSanFrancisco, 1994.

> A much shorter, more popular version of the longer book. Crossan again presents Jesus as a peasant Jewish Cynic enacting in magic, meals, and

itineracy a "brokerless kingdom"—unmediated access to the presence and power of God, equally available to all. Unfortunately, some returned to such brokering, beginning with Paul, who invented the resurrection of Jesus in order to bolster his own status as an apostle. This subversion reached its climax with Constantine and the "church of the empire." Crossan closes this book with the argument that the body of Jesus was not buried; it was torn apart and eaten by dogs and vultures. Finally, in the last section of the book, he reiterates his theology: neither cross nor resurrection are important, because Jesus' significance is that his historically reconstructed words and deeds are a "revelation" of God's aniconicity.

Crossan, John Dominic. *Who Killed Jesus? Exposing the Roots of Anti-Semitism in the Gospel Story of the Death of Jesus*. San Francisco: HarperSanFrancisco, 1995.

Crossan here argues passionately against the historicity of the passion narratives, and particularly the trial of Jesus. These are "prophecy historicized" not "history remembered." It is crucial to establish this because some parts of the passion narratives have been employed in centuries of Christian anti-semitism. Crossan particularly attacks here the work of Raymond E. Brown (*The Death of the Messiah*, 2 vols. [New York: Doubleday, 1994]). Brown makes it clear that he is doing a redactional study of the gospels' theology and meaning, not a historical reconstruction, though he does occasionally comment on historical questions, including suggesting that Jesus' trial before the Sanhedrin may not have been impossible. Crossan erupts: after the holocaust, he argues, one can no longer be casual about such historical matters, even in a redactional study.

Carlson, Jeffrey, and Robert A. Ludwig, eds. *Jesus and Faith: A Conversation on the Work of John Dominic Crossan*. Maryknoll, NY: Orbis, 1994.

A collection of articles on Crossan's book. An especially insightful article on all of Crossan's work is Bernard Brandon Scott, "to impose is not/To Discover: Methodology in John Dominic Crossan's *The Historical Jesus*" (22-30).

5. Jesus, Spirit-Filled Holy Man

Vermes, Geza. *Jesus the Jew: A Historian's Reading of the Gospel*. 2nd ed. New York: Macmillan, 1993.

A Jewish scholar, Vermes explores Jesus' historical identity in two parts. Part I, "The Setting," has three chapters: (1) Chapter one, "Jesus the Jew," points out that rabbis were regularly called carpenters—those who build a dwelling place for us out of the Torah—and that Jesus also worked as an exorcist, teacher, and healer. (2) Chapter two places Jesus in Galilee, long the home of rebels: Ezekias the patriarch was executed in 47 B.C. by the young Herod. His son Judas the Galilean, in 4 B.C., robs the king's arsenal in Sepphoris; in 6 A.D. he leads a revolt against the census and its tax, and with Zadok cofounds the Zealots. Judas's sons, Jacob and Simon, are crucified for rebellion in 46-48 A.D.; his last son, Menahem, captures Masada in 66 A.D. at the start of the Jewish-Roman war, entering the temple in royal attire as its royal (messianic) claimant. Eleazar, his nephew, leads the resistance at Masada in 70-74. The bloodiest leaders of the 66-70 war are a Galilean contingent. Jesus is in many respects a Galilean: he loves the countryside, holds a chauvinistic antipathy toward gentiles, and one of his followers is Simon the Zealot—an ominous surname. Jesus also enters Jerusalem as a royal, Davidic messiah. Jesus and his followers could be recognized by their accents—as Peter was in the courtyard—and were looked down upon by the Pharisees as uncultured brutes. To be "Galilean" is itself to be politically and religiously suspect—and recognizable. (3) Chapter three, "Jesus and Charismatic Judaism," brings Jesus into the company of two other first-century Jewish charismatic miracle-workers: Honi the Circle Drawer and Hanina ben Dosa. All heal by divine power (link of sickness and sin), conduct exorcisms, are associated with miracle-working holy men like Elijah and Elisha, and address God intimately as Abba. Jesus, too, is a charismatic holy man and miracle worker. All tended to be disliked by religious officialdom. Part II, "The Titles of Jesus," explores Jesus' identification: (4) as eschatological prophet—an eschatological Elijah or Moses; (5) as Lord; (6) as Messiah; (7) as Son of Man; and (8) as Son of God. In his postscript, Vermes concludes: Jesus was "one of the holy miracle-workers of Galilee" (223).

Borg, Marcus J. *Jesus, A New Vision: Spirit, Culture, and the Life of Discipleship*. San Francisco: HarperSanFrancisco, 1987.

Part I, "Jesus and the Spirit," follows Vermes in depicting Jesus as profoundly in touch with a more encompassing spiritual world in which all life dwells and as drawing on that life-giving spirit as a miracle-worker; Jesus is a spirit-filled miracle-worker. Part II, "Jesus and Culture," explores the identity of Jesus as subversive sage, as founder of a revitalization movement, and as social prophet. In the conclusion, Borg argues that the significance of Jesus for our time is that Jesus' experience of a world of spirit challenges the modern worldview and opens us to richer religious imaginations and experience. It is in that sense, he argues, that Jesus "reveals" God—as the sustaining, lively, compassionate ground of all life—although he is not the only such "revealer." So, too, Jesus is a model for discipleship: for life lived in the Spirit and in the compassion which is the fruit of the Spirit.

Borg, Marcus J. *Meeting Jesus Again For the First Time: The Historical Jesus and the Heart of Contemporary Faith*. San Francisco: HarperSanFrancisco, 1994.

This book has become a popular bestseller. Borg begins with his own religious autobiography: growing up as a Lutheran in North Dakota, he was presented only with the dogmatic Jesus, whose entire mission is to pronounce doctrines about himself and demand belief in them as a condition for entry into heaven, and/or the moralistic Jesus, who adds some moral rules to the conditions for entry. All was cold, rationalistic, and very remote from the real concerns of human life. Then Borg had an experience of what he calls "nature mysticism" (14). He began to see Jesus as one whose experiential awareness of the Spirit was foundational for his life. So Christian faith is not a matter of believing doctrines or of obeying rules but of experiential relationship to the Spirit of God, the encompassing matrix of all life. Borg argues that Jesus initially was a disciple of the decidedly apocalyptic John the Baptist, but then Jesus had "a kind of conversion" toward a totally non-futurist and non-eschatological outlook. (Mark invented the eschatological kingdom of God sayings.) Jesus was above all a spirit-person or shaman like Honi and Hanina. He was not God, but experienced and was a means for others to experience the spirit of God, as do many mediators of religious experience. Borg concludes: Jesus' "own self understanding did not include thinking and speaking of himself as the Son of God whose historical intention or purpose was to die for the sins of the world, and his message was not about believing in him. Rather, he was a spirit person, subversive sage, social prophet, and movement founder who invited his followers and hearers into a transforming relationship with the same Spirit that he himself knew, and into a community whose social vision was shaped by the core value of compassion. Naturally, this image of Jesus leads to a quite different image of the Christian life" (119). To expand this image, Borg pleads for the recovery of a richer range of the biblical images of salvation and wholeness, beyond simply viewing Jesus as making a payment or serving as substitute victim for our sins. These images include the exodus story, with its picture of wandering in the wilderness with God towards a fuller life in God, and the story of exile and homecoming. The story of Jesus as sacrificial victim does let us announce that sinners are accepted, but it also has grave shortcomings: (1) a static understanding of Christian life—an endless cycle of sin, guilt, and forgiveness; (2) religious and political passivity; (3) primary orientation to afterlife; (4) portrayal of God as judge; (5) relative incredibility; and (6) irrelevance to real life.

Borg, Marcus J. *Jesus in Contemporary Scholarship*. Valley Forge, PA: Trinity International, 1994.

This title can be misleading. This book is a collection of Borg's articles from the past ten years or so, including his article, "A Temperate Case for a Non-eschatological Jesus," not a survey of contemporary scholarship on Jesus.

Borg, Marcus J. *The God We Never Knew: Beyond Dogmatic Religion to a More Authentic Contemporary Faith*. San Francisco: HarperSanFrancisco, 1997.

In this popularly addressed book, Borg charts his own journey from a view of God as a being "out there" over against us to a more fully panentheistic conception of God—of creation as dwelling within God.

6. Jesus as Wisdom

Johnson, Elizabeth A. "Wisdom Was Made Flesh and Pitched Her Tent Among Us." In *Reconstructing the Christ Symbol*, edited by Maryanne Stevens. New York: Paulist, 1993.

A clear, brief explication of some of the many ways the New Testament itself portrays Jesus in terms of the Old Testament figure of wisdom, through whom God makes all things and in whom people delight in creation's order, abundance, and extravagance.

Schüssler Fiorenza, Elisabeth. *Jesus: Miriam's Child, Sophia's Prophet.* New York: Continuum, 1994.

Fiorenza presents Jesus as a prophetic sage who understood himself as the child and spokesperson of Divine Sophia and who founded a radically egalitarian community in which women were primary leaders.

Witherington, Ben, III. *Jesus the Sage: The Pilgrimage of Wisdom.* Minneapolis: Fortress, 1994.

Probably the fullest exploration of the figure of wisdom in the Old Testament and its various New Testament applications to the figure of Jesus. Witherington is also convinced that Jesus understood himself as the embodiment of divine wisdom.

Witherington, Ben, III. *The Jesus Quest: The Third Search for the Jew of Nazareth.* Downer's Grove, IL: InterVarsity, 1995.

The fullest treatment to date of all the major new books in the third quest. Witherington includes his own position in his chapter on "Jesus the Sage: The Wisdom of God."

7. Jesus, Miracle-Worker and Eschatological Prophet

Meier, John P. *A Marginal Jew: Rethinking the Historical Jesus,* vol. 1, *The Roots of the Problem and the Person.* New York: Doubleday, 1991.

Meier is an extremely careful Roman Catholic biblical scholar. The major portion of this first volume is a discussion of methodology in the historical reconstruction of the life of the earthly Jesus, in which Meier argues that the canonical sources are the most reliable. The second part of the volume is on Jesus' birth and naming, his family, and his childhood.

Meier, John P. *A Marginal Jew: Rethinking the Historical Jesus,* vol. 2, *Mentor, Message, and Miracles.* New York: Doubleday, 1994.

Meier's careful work here extends into (1) Jesus' relationship to John the Baptist; (2) his preaching of the kingdom of God; and (3) his miracles. Jesus is the eschatological bearer of God's present and coming kingdom, made proleptically present in his miracles and exorcisms. For cautious, careful— but sometimes tedious—historical scholarship, Meier is the best of the books on Jesus.

8. Jesus, Prophet of Jewish Restoration Eschatology

Sanders, E. P. *Jesus and Judaism.* Philadelphia: Fortress, 1985.

Sanders focuses his book upon two things: Jesus' overturning of the tables in the temple and prophetic announcement of a coming new temple, and Jesus' appointment of twelve to serve as judges over the restored twelve tribes of

Israel. Thus, Sanders pictures Jesus as a prophet of Jewish restoration eschatology.

Sanders, E. P. *The Historical Figure of Jesus*. London and New York: Penguin, 1993.

This book covers the larger story of Jesus' ministry, message, self-understanding, and passion in a readable and reliable way.

9. Jesus, Eschatological Prophet, Messiah, and Suffering Servant

Wright, N. T. *Christian Origins and the Question of God*, vol. 2, *Jesus and the Victory of God*. Minneapolis: Fortress, 1996.

Wright's eagerly awaited magnum opus on Jesus begins by contrasting an approach like that of Wrede (contrasting the historical Jesus to the church's later story of Jesus) with one like that of Schweitzer; Wright clearly adopts the latter in two ways: the gospel narratives are read as providing broadly historically reliable information about Jesus' ministry and Jesus' self-understanding as eschatological Messiah and suffering servant, and that self-understanding is presented as including Jesus' belief that his own death was necessary to enact and focus God's curse on Israel (in the coming destruction of the temple), complete the eschatological tribulations, and so enable the ushering in of God's promise of renewal to Israel and, through Israel, to all the nations of the earth—a this-worldly apocalyptic renewal.

Wright, Tom. *Original Jesus*. Grand Rapids: Eerdmans, 1996.

A brief, winsomely confessional and beautifully illustrated little book on Jesus.

10. Jesus, The Risen One

Johnson, Luke Timothy. *The Real Jesus: The Misguided Quest for the Historical Jesus and the Truth of the Traditional Gospels*. San Francisco: HarperSanFrancisco, 1996.

Johnson argues passionately against the Jesus Seminar, Borg, and Crossan. He argues that some basic things can be known about the historical Jesus—plenty for Christian faith—and then argues against these "third questers" in three broad areas, the last by far the most important: (1) they choose bad sources and omit some good ones for information about Jesus—Paul's letters are an especially serious omission; (2) the narrative order of the gospels is needed to provide a meaningful context for the sayings and deeds; and, especially, (3) the "real Jesus" lived long ago but is also alive now, risen from the dead, and it is this living Jesus who is the real ground of Christian faith. He concludes: "Christians direct their faith not to the historical figure of Jesus but to the living Lord Jesus. Yes, they assert continuity between that Jesus and this. But their faith is confirmed, not by the establishment of facts about the past, but by the reality of Christ's power in the present" (143). ⊕

Word & World
Supplement Series 3
1997

The Use of Sources in the Quest for Jesus: What You Use Is What You Get

ARLAND J. HULTGREN

Luther Seminary
St. Paul, Minnesota

WHAT WE USE AND HOW WE USE IT IS CRUCIAL FOR OUR UNDERSTANDING OF JESUS of Nazareth. Already near the end of the second century, Irenaeus criticized the Ebionites for having a one-sided picture of Jesus based on their use of the Gospel of Matthew alone. He reproached Marcion for using an abbreviated Gospel of Luke. And he condemned the Valentinian Gnostics for their misuse of the Gospel of John and their use of the *Gospel of Truth*, which he called a "recent composition." According to him, the various heretics tried to establish their own preconceived teachings concerning Jesus by using the sources selectively. For Irenaeus himself, the only proper way to establish the truth concerning Jesus was to make use of the four gospels, no more and no less.[1]

In the present scene the portraits of Jesus provided in various books about Jesus are often based on those things Irenaeus complained about. On the one hand, there is a major undertaking these days to portray Jesus on the basis of a selective reading of the gospels. I refer here to the use of the hypothetical document Q as a prime source. On the other hand—in a move that would also anger Irenaeus—one finds interpreters going well beyond the four canonical gospels to reconstruct the teachings of Jesus, particularly by extensive use of the *Gospel of Thomas*, which has now been enhanced to the status of "the Fifth Gospel" by the fellows of the Jesus Seminar; it is not simply *a* fifth gospel but *the* Fifth Gospel.[2] It has thereby achieved

---

[1]Irenaeus, *Adv. Haer.* 3.11.7-9.

[2]Robert Funk et al., *The Five Gospels: The Search for the Authentic Words of Jesus* (New York: Macmillan, 1993).

a kind of canonical status for a number of scholars, if not for the church. Moreover, what is being promoted in some circles is the use of Q and the *Gospel of Thomas* as prime sources for our understanding of Jesus over against the narrative, canonical gospels.

This essay is an attempt to assess the use of sources in that project and to spell out some areas that, in my view, need further development.

I. AREAS IN NEED OF EXAMINATION

1. Going beyond the canonical gospels. The four canonical gospels have been, and still are, the prime sources for the study of Jesus of Nazareth. But they are not the only, nor the earliest, writings that refer to Jesus. The earliest known documents are the writings of Paul from the middle of the first century. From Paul, however, there is relatively little about the earthly Jesus per se and nothing that we do not know otherwise from the gospels. Paul records that Jesus was crucified and subsequently raised (1 Cor 15:3-7) and, at best, provides three quotations attributed to Jesus (1 Cor 7:10; 9:14; 11:23-25), of which two have parallels in the synoptic gospels. The exception is 1 Cor 9:14 ("the Lord commanded that those who proclaim the gospel should get their living by the gospel"), which has a rough parallel at Luke 10:7.

In addition to the undisputed letters of Paul, there are two other places where sayings are recorded of the earthly Jesus.[3] One is in Acts 20:35 ("It is more blessed to give than to receive"), which has no parallel in the gospels, and the other is in 1 Tim 5:18, which does (cf. Luke 10:7).

Outside the New Testament there are additional references to Jesus from the first century and early into the second. But little is gained by looking at them. Josephus mentions Jesus but adds nothing to what is already known from the canonical gospels.[4] The early second-century Roman writers Tacitus, Suetonius, and Pliny the Younger mention Jesus and the early Christians,[5] but they provide no additional information either. Finally, the writings of the apostolic fathers from the first half of the second century contain some sayings of Jesus, as well as some reports about him, but by and large have not been a very important source for the study of the earthly Jesus.

When interpreters go beyond the canonical gospels today in studies of the earthly Jesus, they go primarily to the *Gospel of Thomas*.[6] The use of that document as a major source regarding Jesus must be assessed. That it contains some authentic teachings of Jesus not found in the canonical gospels is probable.[7] That is not in

---

[3]We leave aside here the many sayings attributed to the post-Easter Jesus. These are found at various places, including Acts 1:4-5, 7-8; 9:4-6, 10-12, 15-16; 18:9-10; 2 Cor 12:9; Rev 1:11, 17-20, etc.

[4]The texts are his *Ant.* 18.63-64 and 20.200.

[5]Tacitus, *Annals* 15.44; Suetonius, *Life of Claudius* 25.14-15; Pliny the Younger, *Letters to Trajan* 10.96.

[6]Besides this document, the many other Nag Hammadi texts associated with it are dealt with by Majella Franzmann, *Jesus in the Nag Hammadi Writings* (Edinburgh: T. & T. Clark, 1996).

[7]Logia 25 and 95, for example, have the ring of authenticity.

dispute. But some extravagant claims have been made about its worth in the study of Jesus. Two claims are especially notable. The first has to do with the age of the document in its final form. The second has to do with its pre-history. We shall take up these two points in that order.

First, how old is the *Gospel of Thomas*? The usual judgment has been that it was produced in the middle of the second century A.D. and probably at or near Edessa in eastern Syria.[8] But recently some interpreters have claimed that it was produced in the first century or at least by the year A.D. 100.[9]

How can one assign a date to this document? In regard to external evidence, the *Gospel of Thomas* is first attested in the writings of Hippolytus (d. ca. A.D. 235) during the first quarter of the third century,[10] and then by Origen about A.D. 233.[11] In addition, three Greek fragments of this gospel—known as Oxyrhynchus Papyri 1, 654, and 655—come from about the same time. On paleographical grounds they have been assigned to the years A.D. 200-250.[12] Prior to these items, there is no external or textual evidence for the existence of the *Gospel of Thomas*. On external grounds, therefore, there is good evidence for placing the *Gospel of Thomas* in its

[8]Among others, the following can be mentioned: A. Guillaumont et al., *The Gospel According to Thomas* (New York: Harper & Brothers, 1959) vi; Henri-Charles Puech, "Gnostic Gospels and Related Documents," in *New Testament Apocrypha*, ed. Edgar Hennecke and Wilhelm Schneemelcher, 2 vols. (Philadelphia: Westminster, 1963-65) 1:305; Oscar Cullmann, "The Gospel of Thomas and the Problem of the Age of the Tradition Contained Therein," *Int* 16 (1962) 427; R. McL. Wilson, *Studies in the Gospel of Thomas* (London: A. R. Mowbray, 1960) 7-8; Bertil Gärtner, *The Theology of the Gospel according to Thomas* (New York: Harper & Brothers, 1961) 271; Gilles Quispel, "'The Gospel of Thomas' and the 'Gospel of the Hebrews,'" *NTS* 12 (1965-66) 378; Johannes Leipoldt, *Das Evangelium nach Thomas: Koptisch und Deutsch*, TU 101 (Berlin: Akademie, 1967) 17; Jacques-É. Ménard, *L'Évangile selon Thomas*, NHS 5 (Leiden: E. J. Brill, 1975) 3; Klyne R. Snodgrass, "The Gospel of Thomas: A Second Century Gospel," *SecCent* 7 (1989-90) 19-38; Michael Fieger, *Das Thomasevangelium: Einleitung, Kommentar, und Systematik*, NTAbh 22 (Münster: Aschendorff, 1991) 4, 7; and Beate Blatz, "The Coptic Gospel of Thomas," in *New Testament Apocrypha*, rev. ed., ed. Wilhelm Schneemelcher, 2 vols. (Louisville: Westminster/John Knox, 1991-92) 1:113.

[9]Helmut Koester, *Introduction to the New Testament*, 2 vols. (Philadelphia: Fortress, 1982) 2:152, has written: "It was probably written during I CE in Palestine or Syria"; cf. idem, *Ancient Christian Gospels: Their History and Development* (Philadelphia: Trinity International, 1990) 83-84. According to *The Five Gospels*, 474, "Thomas probably assumed its present form by 100 C.E." Ron Cameron, *The Other Gospels: Non-Canonical Gospel Texts* (Philadelphia: Westminster, 1982) 25, suggests "the second half of the first century" as the time of composition. Stevan Davies, *The Gospel of Thomas and Christian Wisdom* (New York: Seabury, 1983) 3, places the completed work as early as A.D. 50-70. According to Stephen J. Patterson, *The Gospel of Thomas and Jesus* (Sonoma: Polebridge, 1993) 120, the gospel was written "in the vicinity of 70-80 C.E." That the Gospel of John was written as a response to the *Gos. Thom.* (implying the existence of the *Gospel of Thomas* prior to the Fourth Gospel) is asserted by Gregory J. Riley, *Resurrection Reconsidered: Thomas and John in Controversy* (Minneapolis: Fortress, 1995). He thinks that John 2:19 is a Johannine revision of *Gos. Thom.* 71. That is hardly sufficient evidence for his thesis.

[10]Hippolytus, *Ref.* 5.2. The reference is according to that in the *ANF* 5.50. In other editions, it is found at *Ref.* 5,7.20. Hippolytus died ca. A.D. 235. Hippolytus not only refers to the *Gospel of Thomas* as a document but also cites a variant of logion 4 within it.

[11]Origen, *Homily on Luke* 1.

[12]Cf. *The Oxyrhynchus Papyri*, ed. Bernard P. Grenfell, Arthur S. Hunt et al., 31 vols. (London: Egypt Exploration Fund, 1898-1966) 4:1; and Harold W. Attridge, "The Gospel According to Thomas (Greek Fragments)," *Nag Hammadi Codex II, 2-7*, NHS 20, ed. Bentley Layton, 2 vols. (Leiden: E. J. Brill, 1989) 1:96-99. Attridge places POxy 1 "shortly after A.D. 200" (p. 97); POxy 654 "in the middle of the third century" (p. 97); and POxy 655 "between A.D. 200 and 250 (p. 98)."

final form somewhere in the second century. (The Coptic version from Nag Hammadi is usually dated as a fourth-century text.[13])

In regard to internal evidence, there are four items worth noting. First, the *Gospel of Thomas* contains within itself a veiled reference to the twenty-four books of the Old Testament (logion 52). That reference presupposes the canonization of the Old Testament following the Jewish numerical system.[14] And that, in turn, puts the gospel somewhere into the second century when the canon had been solidified in Jewish communities. Second, the fact that the book begins with the claim in its prescript that it is the work of Thomas, the twin brother of Jesus,[15] reflects a time when it was important to appeal to apostolic authorship to establish authority. The canonical gospels, by contrast, are anonymous and lack claims of apostolic authorship within them.[16] By attributing itself to apostolic authorship, the *Gospel of Thomas* must come from well into the second century when anonymity can no longer stand; an appeal to a specific apostle for the authority of a document is important.[17]

A third point is more complex. A good number of interpreters hold that the *Gospel of Thomas* shows no dependence upon, nor even influences from, the canonical gospels.[18] On the other hand, there have been, and still are, interpreters who have held the opposite view, saying that the *Gospel of Thomas* shows evidence of dependence in at least some cases where there are parallels.[19] Perhaps the issue cannot be resolved. But it is undeniable that some logia in the *Gospel of Thomas* having parallels to the canonical gospels bear the marks of specifically Matthean

[13]As attested in many studies; cf. Helmut Koester, "Introduction [to the Gospel of Thomas]," *Nag Hammadi Codex II, 2-7*, 1:38; Beate Blatz, "The Coptic Gospel of Thomas," 1.111; and Ron Cameron, "Thomas, Gospel of," *ABD* 6:535.

[14]According to *Gos. Thom.* 52, twenty-four prophets of Israel spoke of Jesus. The designation 24 "prophets" undoubtedly refers to the 24 books in the Jewish canon. Cf. B. Gärtner, *Theology*, 154.

[15]In the *Acts of Thomas* 39, Thomas is designated as "Twin of the Messiah." For text, cf. A. F. J. Klijn, *The Acts of Thomas: Introduction-Text-Commentary*, NovTSup 5 (Leiden: E. J. Brill, 1962) 85.

[16]Even John 21:24, which identifies the beloved disciple as the writer of the Fourth Gospel, does not claim apostolic authorship.

[17]J. Patterson, *The Gospel of Thomas and Jesus*, 116, argues that assigning apostolic authorship points to the time of the deutero-Pauline epistles (i.e., late first century). This is to overlook the fact that pseudonymous apostolic authorship continues unabated in succeeding centuries, e.g., in the case of pseudepigrapha attributed to Peter, Philip, James, Mary, and others, including Thomas (*The Acts of Thomas*).

[18]Gilles Quispel, "Some Remarks on the Gospel of Thomas," *NTS* 5 (1958-59) 277; H. Koester, *Introduction to the New Testament*, 2:153; R. Cameron, *Other Gospels*, 24; S. Davies, *Gospel of Thomas and Christian Wisdom*, 5; R. Funk et al., *Five Gospels*, 474; Bentley Layton, *The Gnostic Scriptures: A New Translation with Annotations and Introductions* (Garden City: Doubleday, 1987) 377; and B. Blatz, "Coptic Gospel of Thomas," 1:113.

[19]Harvey K. McArthur, "The Dependence of the Gospel of Thomas on the Synoptics," *ExpTim* 71 (1959-60) 286-87; Robert M. Grant and David N. Freedman, *The Secret Sayings of Jesus* (Garden City: Doubleday, 1960) 106-16; B. Gärtner, *Theology*, 35-68; O. Cullmann, "The Gospel of Thomas," 434; Wolfgang Schrage, *Das Verhältnis des Thomas-Evangelium zur synoptischen Tradition und zu den koptischen Evangelienübersetzungen: Zugleich ein Beitrag zur gnostischen Synoptikerdeutung*, BZNW 29 (Berlin: Alfred Töpelmann, 1964); J. Leipoldt, *Das Evangelium nach Thomas*, 16-18; Kurt Rudolf, *Gnosis: The Nature and History of Gnosticism* (San Francisco: Harper & Row, 1987) 263; Christopher Tuckett, "Thomas and the Synoptics," *NovT* 30 (1988) 132-57; K. R. Snodgrass, "The Gospel of Thomas," 19-38; M. Fieger, *Das Thomasevangelium*, 6-7; John P. Meier, *A Marginal Jew*, 3 vols. (New York: Doubleday, 1991—) 1:130-39; and N. T. Wright, *The New Testament and the People of God*, vol. 1 of *Christian Origins and the Question of God* (Minneapolis: Fortress, 1992) 442.

and Lukan redactional work,[20] which speaks against total independence in those specific cases. Most impressive are two logia of the *Gospel of Thomas*, which appear in Greek in the Oxyrhynchus Papyri and which therefore allow comparisons with their parallels in the canonical gospels of the Greek New Testament. The first of these is *Gos. Thom.* 5, a part of which exists in Greek within POxy 654 (lines 29-30). The portion of that logion that exists in Greek is worded exactly as it is in Luke's Gospel over against its wording in Mark (as well as in Matthew). The similarities are underscored below, supplemented by missing letters and words inserted by editors who have placed them in brackets. Here it is evident that the *Gospel of Thomas* in its Greek form was dependent on the Gospel of Luke, whose redaction is apparent at this point:[21]

> Mark 4:22: οὐ γάρ ἐστιν κρυπτὸν ἐὰν μὴ ἵνα φανερωθῇ.
>
> Matt 10:26: οὐδὲν γάρ ἐστιν κεκαλυμμένον ὅ οὐκ ἀποκαλυφθήσεται καὶ κρυπτὸν ὅ οὐ γνωσθήσεται.
>
> Luke 8:17: οὐ γάρ ἐστιν κρυπτὸν ὅ οὐ φανερὸν γενήσεται.
>
> POxy 654: [οὐ γάρ ἐσ]τιν κρυπτὸν ὅ οὐ φανε[ρὸν γενήσεται].
>
> Translation (POxy 654.29-30): "For there is nothing hidden that will not be made manifest."

The second instance is *Gos. Thom.* 26 where the corresponding Greek text appears in POxy 1 (lines 1-4). It corresponds to the saying of Jesus in Matt 7:5//Luke 6:42, and every word and form of expression can be found in those gospels. That is illustrated in the following quotations.[22] Where the texts of Matthew and POxy 1 agree against Luke's version, a single underscore is used; where the texts of Luke and POxy 1 agree against Matthew's version, double underscoring is used:

POxy 1.1-4	Matt 7:5	Luke 6:42
καὶ τότε διαβλέψεις	καὶ τότε διαβλέψεις	καὶ τότε διαβλέψεις
ἐκβαλεῖν τὸ κάρφος	ἐκβαλεῖν τὸ κάρφος	τὸ κάρφος
τὸ ἐν τῷ ὀφθαλμῷ	ἐκ τοῦ ὀφθαλμοῦ	τὸ ἐν τῷ ὀφθαλμῷ
τού ἀδελφοῦ σου	τού ἀδελφοῦ σου	τού ἀδελφοῦ σου ἐκβαλεῖν

Translation (POxy 1.1-4): "And then you will see clearly to cast out the speck which is in the eye of your brother."

In this instance the peculiarities of both Matthew and Luke show up in the fragment, and the conclusion to be drawn is that the writer of the papyrus had both texts before him when he wrote his own.

---

[20]These passages are surveyed by C. Tuckett, "Thomas and the Synoptics," 145-56. He examines *Gos. Thom.* 5, 9, 16, 20, and 55 in relationship to the synoptic gospels.

[21]The Greek text of POxy 654.29-30 is from the critical text edited by H. W. Attridge, "The Gospel According to Thomas (Greek Fragments)," *Nag Hammadi Codex II, 2-7,* 1:115.

[22]The Greek text of POxy 1.1-4 is from ibid., 1:118.

These instances, together with others that can be listed,[23] indicate that the Gospels of both Matthew and Luke were probably available to, and were used by, the author of the *Gospel of Thomas* in its earliest Greek version.

Finally, in *Gos. Thom.* 13 there is a scene reminiscent of the Caesarea Philippi event of the synoptic gospels in which Peter makes the true confession and which is elaborated fully in the Gospel of Matthew (16:13-20). In Matthew's account Peter is by all means chief of the apostles. Moreover, the apostle Matthew was obviously important to the community in which the gospel was produced and to whom it was attributed subsequently. What is striking in comparing the two accounts is that, in the scene within the *Gospel of Thomas*, Peter and Matthew are demoted in rank and Thomas is elevated as the greatest of apostles. Indeed, Thomas is considered *equal* to Jesus himself—which gnostic teachers held as a possibility for the true disciple[24]—for he has become fully intoxicated with the teachings of Jesus, and he is therefore no longer to speak of Jesus as his "Master":

> Jesus said to his disciples, "Compare me to someone and tell me whom I am like."
> Simon Peter said to him, "You are like a righteous angel."
> Matthew said to him, "You are like a wise philosopher."
> Thomas said to him, "Master, my mouth is wholly incapable of saying whom you are like."
> Jesus said, "I am not your [singular in Coptic] master. Because you [singular] have drunk, you [singular] have become intoxicated from the bubbling spring which I have measured out."
> And he took him and withdrew and told him three things. When Thomas returned to his companions, they asked him, "What did Jesus say to you?"
> Thomas said to them, "If I tell you one of the things which he told me, you will pick up stones and throw them at me; a fire will come out of the stones and burn you up."[25]

It is my judgment that in this passage the form of Christianity that the Gospel of Matthew represents—Matthean and Petrine in western Syria in or around Antioch—is being denigrated by that form of Christianity represented by the *Gospel of Thomas* at Edessa or its environs in eastern Syria.[26] Risking an anachronism, we may say that the Gospel of Matthew reflects catholic and orthodox Christianity. But it is being denigrated by that form of Christianity reflected in the *Gospel of Thomas*. The phenomenon of denigration is known elsewhere, particularly among the Va-

---

[23]The clearest of these are as follows: POxy 654.12 (=*Gos. Thom.* 3) and Matt 6:26; 654.15-16 (=*Gos. Thom.* 3) and Luke 17:21; 654.25-26 (=*Gos. Thom.* 4) and Mark 10:31//Matt 19:30; and POxy 655.39-46 (=*Gos. Thom.* 39) and Matt 23:13//Luke 11:52. On these and other texts, cf. Joseph A. Fitzmyer, "The Oxyrhynchus Logoi of Jesus and the Coptic Gospel According to Thomas," in *Essays on the Semitic Background of the New Testament*, SBLSBS 5 (Missoula: Scholars, 1974) 355-433.

[24]Cf. Irenaeus, *Adv. Haer.* 1.25.2, concerning the Carpocratian Gnostics. Also at *Gos. Thom.* 108, the gnostic is said to be equal to Jesus. According to Hippolytus, *Ref.* 7.22, a similar teaching was held by the Ebionites.

[25]Quoted from *The Nag Hammadi Library in English*, ed. James M. Robinson, 3d ed. (San Francisco: Harper & Row, 1988) 127-28.

[26]On the importance of Thomas and the insufficiency of the authority of Peter and Matthew in this gospel, cf. A. F. Walls, "The References to Apostles in the Gospel of Thomas," *NTS* 7 (1960-61) 268-69.

lentinian Gnostics, who considered catholic Christianity second-rate.[27] In light of this logion, there can be little doubt that the *Gospel of Thomas* in its present form comes from a time that is later than the composition of Matthew's Gospel.

Other interpreters have maintained that, in addition to the redactional elements from Matthew and Luke, the *Gospel of Thomas* contains some sayings with parallels that are specific to Mark, and still others with parallels only to John.[28] All this gives rise to the suspicion that the author had the fourfold collection of gospels available in his community. That would point to the second half of the second century, when such a collection is first attested in the writings of Irenaeus, Clement of Alexandria, and Tertullian. The view that the *Gospel of Thomas* was produced in the middle of the second century at the earliest remains compelling.[29]

But even if the *Gospel of Thomas* in its present form is from a time later than the canonical gospels, is it possible that an earlier edition existed? The claim keeps being made that indeed an early version—a written text—was composed in the middle of the first century. Such a claim has been made by a number of persons, such as Helmut Koester, Stephen Patterson, Stevan Davies, John Dominic Crossan, and the fellows of the Jesus Seminar.[30] But how does one establish such a claim? Too often the claim is simply asserted and repeated as though it were an "assured result" of gospel studies. When one looks for reasons for the claim, there seem to be three. The first has to do with its genre. The *Gospel of Thomas* is a sayings collection, and since the Q document—a sayings collection—is thought to come from the 50s of the first century, and the two documents have a lot of sayings in common, we can assume that an earlier version of the *Gospel of Thomas* did too.[31] The second claim is that some of the sayings having parallels in the canonical gospels seem to exhibit an arrested development, lacking the interpretive embellishments found in their canonical parallels; therefore they can be assigned to an earlier date of composition.[32] Finally, it is argued that the lack of christological titles speaks for the relative antiquity of the document.[33]

---

[27]Irenaeus, *Adv. Haer.* 1.7.5; Epiphanius, *Panarion* 31.7.6-7.11; and the (Valentinian) Nag Hammadi text, *The Tripartite Tractate* 118.14-34.

[28]Scholarly discussion is summarized by J. Meier, *A Marginal Jew*, 1:134-37.

[29]See note 8.

[30]According to Helmut Koester and Stephen J. Patterson, "The Gospel of Thomas: Does It Contain Authentic Sayings of Jesus?," *BibRev* 6/2 (1990) 37, much of the material in the *Gospel of Thomas* may have been written as early as the 30s or 40s of the first century. S. Davies, *The Gospel of Thomas and Christian Wisdom*, 3, says, "Thomas should be dated ca. A.D. 50-70." John Dominic Crossan, *The Historical Jesus: The Life of a Mediterranean Jewish Peasant* (San Francisco: HarperCollins, 1991) 428, claims that the first version of the *Gospel of Thomas* was composed by the 50s of the first century. According to the Jesus Seminar's *Five Gospels*, 474, "an earlier version [of the *Gospel of Thomas*] may have originated as early as 50-60 C.E."

[31]Helmut Koester, "Introduction [to the Gospel of Thomas]," *Nag Hammadi Codex II, 2-7*, 1:39; idem, "Introduction [to the Gospel of Thomas]," *The Nag Hammadi Library in English*, 125; R. Cameron, *The Other Gospels*, 24; S. Davies, *The Gospel of Thomas and Christian Wisdom*, 16-17; and J. Patterson, *The Gospel of Thomas and Jesus*, 117.

[32]Gilles Quispel, "The Gospel of Thomas and the New Testament," *VC* 11 (1957) 205; H. Koester, *Introduction to the New Testament*, 2:154; R. Cameron, *The Other Gospels*, 24; and S. Davies, *The Gospel of Thomas and Christian Wisdom*, 16.

[33]Helmut Koester, "Introduction [to the Gospel of Thomas]," *Nag Hammadi Codex II*, 1:40; idem, *Introduction*, 2:152; and S. Patterson, *The Gospel of Thomas and Jesus*, 118.

The first argument—the analogy to Q—is not convincing at all. It is certainly not necessary to posit the first edition of a sayings collection in the middle of the first century to account for the preservation of sayings of Jesus. Both Joachim Jeremias and Helmut Koester—scholars very unlike one another—have demonstrated that sayings of Jesus continued to exist in oral circulation well into the second century before they were written down. [34] Jeremias finds some that were written down for the first time by Tertullian and Clement of Alexandria near the end of the second century. Other analogous sayings collections, such as the discourses of the Fourth Gospel and the sayings of Jesus collected in the *Dialogue of the Savior* (conventionally dated from the second century), come from times much later than Q in their written form. The *Gospel of Thomas* could actually have been written for the first time in the middle of the second century, based on sayings preserved and collected over time.[35] In any case, the genre of a document has little to do with its date.

The second point—that some sayings in the *Gospel of Thomas* appear to be more primitive than their parallels in the canonical gospels—carries little weight either for at least two reasons.[36] First, it is commonly noticed, by analogy, that Matthew abbreviated materials taken over from Mark. The author of the *Gospel of Thomas* could likewise have abbreviated materials taken from the canonical gospels. Second, the controlling hermeneutic of the *Gospel of Thomas* is, as stated in its prescript, that the sayings are obscure, and their meaning must be acquired. Therefore it is actually fitting that the author of the *Gospel of Thomas* would have stripped any received sayings of their interpretations found in the canonical gospels.

Finally, the claim that the *Gospel of Thomas* lacks christological titles, and that that would be a reason to give it an early date, does not hold up. First of all, at least one christological title does appear: Jesus speaks of himself as the Son of Man in one saying (86) and of his lordship in another (90). But aside from that, the lack of titles cannot be considered a criterion, since the document consists of logia attributed to Jesus himself and thus lacks opportunities for christological titles to be used by his disciples. Moreover, one cannot use the amount or range of christological titles in a work as an index of its age (the fewer, the earlier; the more, the later). If that were decisive, one would have to date the Gospel of John earlier than the Gospel of Matthew, which is unlikely on other grounds. The upshot is that the claims being made for a mid-first-century edition of the *Gospel of Thomas* existing prior to the canonical gospels—claims which give a certain privilege to it—are by no means self-evident.

To be sure, there are some passages in the *Gospel of Thomas* that have parallels in the synoptic gospels and could be based on independent traditions, as some have suggested. The parables of the great banquet and the wicked tenants (logia

[34]Joachim Jeremias, *Unknown Sayings of Jesus*, 2nd ed. (London: SPCK, 1964); Helmut Koester, *Synoptische Überlieferung bei den apostolischen Vätern*, TU 65 (Berlin: Akademie, 1957).

[35]Cf. H.-C. Puech, "Gnostic Gospels," 1:305.

[36]The two points that follow are taken from J. Meier, *A Marginal Jew*, 1:132-33, who cites still other literature.

64-65) are two examples,[37] but it is difficult to know whether they are truly independent. They may well be, but even if they are, that does not mean a priori that they provide greater access to the voice of Jesus of Nazareth than their synoptic parallels do.

Finally, there are a few sayings in the *Gospel of Thomas* that have no parallels to those in the canonical gospels, and some of these could be authentic.[38] But when these sayings are factored into a composite picture of the teachings of the historical Jesus, they do not actually add much to our understanding.

In the current situation there are three major proposals to account for the composition of the *Gospel of Thomas*: (1) It was composed independently of the canonical gospels.[39] (2) A first edition of the gospel was composed independently of the canonical gospels at an early stage, but that was supplemented and edited at later stages in light of the canonical gospels.[40] (3) It was composed in the second century by an author who employed and edited sources and traditions distinctive to that gospel and materials from the canonical gospels.[41] (Allowances must also be made in this view for redactional work at both the Greek and Coptic stages of composition.)

In light of the foregoing discussion—and taking into consideration the textual, external, and internal evidence—either of the latter two views seem to provide a more satisfactory account for the composition of the gospel than the first. But either would also mean that the *Gospel of Thomas*, as attested in both its Greek and Coptic versions, was dependent upon the canonical gospels in various places. The view that the *Gospel of Thomas* was composed in stages remains speculative; there is no external evidence that would support such a view, nor can any internal evidence be brought forth for it. When all these factors are considered, there are good reasons to conclude that the third view stated above is the most satisfactory.

In the book of the Jesus Seminar called *The Five Gospels*, only three sayings in the *Gospel of Thomas* are printed in red, and each has a parallel in the synoptic gospels: logia 20 (the parable of the mustard seed), 54 (the beatitude concerning the poor), and 100 (the saying on paying taxes to Caesar).[42] Some 33 passages are printed in pink, but here again all but four have parallels in the synoptics.[43] So for all the emphasis on the *Gospel of Thomas* as a new and major source on Jesus, there is finally little there that is not already in the canonical gospels.

2. Going behind the canonical gospels. The hypothetical Q document—recon-

---

[37]Independence is claimed by, among others, J. Jeremias, *The Parables of Jesus*, 24; Helmut Koester, "Three Thomas Parables," in *The New Testament and Gnosis: Essays in Honour of Robert McL. Wilson*, ed. A. H. B. Logan and A. J. M. Wedderburn (Edinburgh: T. & T. Clark, 1983) 197-200; and Bernard B. Scott, *Hear Then the Parable: A Commentary on the Parables of Jesus* (Minneapolis: Fortress, 1989) 32-33.

[38]See note 7.

[39]See note 9.

[40]R. McL. Wilson, *Studies*, 51, 92, 148.

[41]See note 8.

[42]Cf. *The Five Gospels*, 485, 504, and 525.

[43]Logia printed in pink are: 2, 5-6, 9-10, 14, 31-33, 35-36, 39, 41, 45, 47, 62-65, 69, 76, 78, 86, 89, 92, 94-99, 109, and 113. Of these, 95, 97, 98, and 113 are truly distinctive.

structed from some 225 verses common to Matthew and Luke, not taken from Mark—has been called "the First Gospel" by one scholar and "the Lost Gospel" by others.[44] As in the case of the *Gospel of Thomas*, the use of Q in the study of Jesus needs a fresh assessment. The very existence of Q, of course, continues to be challenged by a number of scholars,[45] but studies of Q go on unabated nevertheless.[46] Since it is thought that the Q document originated in the middle of the first century in Palestine or Syria—in other words, close to the time and places of the ministry of Jesus of Nazareth—the sayings in Q are taken as prime materials for reconstructing the teachings of Jesus.

Major interpreters have suggested that the Q document was composed within a community for whom the preaching of the cross and resurrection was a presupposition for its existence.[47] But recently John Kloppenborg has proposed— and Burton Mack and others have followed him—that Q is a layered document, and that its earliest recension can be attributed to a band of followers of Jesus who treasured his wisdom sayings and placed no emphasis whatsoever on his crucifixion, death, and resurrection. Moreover, the apocalyptic material within Q as we now know it must be considered additional material imposed on the earlier nonapocalyptic layer. Finally, as one untimely born, the narrative of the temptation of Jesus was added at the third stage of development.[48]

But can one posit the existence of a Q community that treasured the wisdom sayings of Jesus apart from cross, resurrection, and apocalyptic? The only way to do so is to reconstruct an early version of Q that fits the proposal. Furthermore, one must assume that the Q community was a cell group, walled off from other Christian traditions and communities, and that the reconstructed document contained all that the Q people ever thought important about Jesus. But that is totally arbitrary. By analogy one could apply the same viewpoint to the Epistle of James. Since the Epistle of James mentions neither the cross nor the resurrection and contains a great deal of wisdom sayings, must we conclude that the author and his

---

[44]Arland D. Jacobson, *The First Gospel: An Introduction to Q* (Sonoma: Polebridge, 1992); Burton L. Mack, *The Lost Gospel: The Book of Q and Christian Origins* (San Francisco: HarperCollins, 1993); and *The Lost Gospel Q: The Original Sayings of Jesus*, ed. Mark Powelson and Ray Riegert (Berkeley: Ulysses, 1996).

[45]Cf. Michael D. Goulder, "Is Q a Juggernaut?" *JBL* 115 (1996) 667-81; and *Beyond the Q Impasse— Luke's Use of Matthew: A Demonstration by the Research Team of the International Institute for Gospel Studies*, ed. Allan J. McNicol with David L. Dungan and David B. Peabody (Valley Forge: Trinity International, 1996).

[46]A major volume in this area is *The Gospel behind the Gospels: Current Studies on Q*, ed. Ronald A. Piper, NovTSup 75 (Leiden: E. J. Brill, 1995), including the opening essay by R. A. Piper, "In Quest of Q: The Direction of Q Studies," 1-18.

[47]T. W. Manson, *The Sayings of Jesus* (London: SCM Press, 1949) 13-17; Heinz T. Tödt, *The Son of Man in the Synoptic Tradition* (Philadelphia: Westminster, 1965) 250; Werner G. Kümmel, *Introduction to the New Testament*, rev. ed. (Nashville: Abingdon, 1975) 74; Leonhard Goppelt, *Theology of the New Testament*, 2 vols. (Grand Rapids: Eerdmans, 1981-82) 1:5; and Marinus de Jonge, *Christology in Context: The Earliest Christian Response to Jesus* (Philadelphia: Westminster, 1988) 83-84.

[48]John Kloppenborg, *The Formation of Q: Trajectories in Ancient Wisdom Collections* (Philadelphia: Fortress, 1987); Burton L. Mack, *The Lost Gospel*, 35-39. For a critique of Kloppenborg's theory, cf. A. Jacobson, *The First Gospel*, 50-51.

community placed no positive evaluation whatsoever on the cross and resurrection of Jesus?

The view that Q reflects an early form of a Jesus movement that placed no emphasis at all on the cross and resurrection is mistaken. Within the Q document itself, if we do not posit the existence of hypothetical layers, there are allusions to Jesus' rejection, death, exaltation, and coming again as Son of Man to judge the world—the major points of the common Christian kerygma! These allusions can be mentioned briefly: his rejection is alluded to in the sayings that the Son of Man has no place to lay his head (Luke 9:58//Matt 8:20) and that prophets coming to Jerusalem are always killed (Luke 13:34//Matt 23:37). His vocation as one who eschews power and ease, and goes the way of obedient suffering, is alluded to in the story of his temptation in the wilderness (Luke 4:1-13//Matt 4:1-11). His entry into Jerusalem on Palm Sunday—the prelude to the passion narratives in the gospels—is alluded to in his lament over Jerusalem, concluding with the pronouncement, "I tell you, you will not see me until the time comes when you say, 'Blessed is the one who comes in the name of the Lord'" (Luke 13:34-35//Matt 23:37-39).[49] His death is alluded to most strikingly in the saying that a disciple must carry his *own* cross and follow after Jesus (Luke 14:27//Matt 10:38). His exaltation, reign, and parousia are alluded to allegorically in the parable of the pounds/talents, in which a man departs to receive a kingdom and then returns to exercise judgment (Luke 19:12-27//Matt 25:14-30), as well as in apocalyptic Son of Man sayings, which presuppose resurrection to receive transcendent status (e.g., Luke 12:40//Matt 24:44; Luke 17:26-30//Matt 24:37-39).

The view of Kloppenborg—with his multi-layered, stratified Q—allows him to claim that the earliest form of Q was "genre bound" so as to exclude all thought of the cross and resurrection.[50] And since the document would not have had such thought, neither did the community that produced it.[51] But how do we know that there was such an early edition? Because the earliest edition was a "wisdom-gospel," and a wisdom-gospel "must be understood without recourse to theological harmonization with...the passion kerygma";[52] moreover, "the notion of resurrection...is inappropriate to [its] genre and theology."[53] A good amount of circular reasoning is at work in all of this.

What is fascinating from all the work on Q are the results for understanding Jesus. Burton Mack claims that the members of the Q community were "Jesus people," not Christians,[54] and that their community existed alongside Christian

---

[49]In this passage Ps 118:26 (LXX Ps 117:26) is quoted. It is quoted elsewhere in all four gospels in connection with the entry into Jerusalem (Mark 11:9//Matt 21:9//Luke 19:38//John 12:13).

[50]J. Kloppenborg, *The Formation of Q*, 2, 25.

[51]John Kloppenborg, "'Easter Faith' and the Sayings Gospel Q," *Semeia* 49 (1990) 71, 76, 82, 90; cf. H. Koester, *Ancient Christian Gospels*, 160.

[52]J. Kloppenborg, *The Formation of Q*, 39.

[53]J. Kloppenborg, "'Easter Faith' and the Sayings Gospel Q," 90.

[54]B. Mack, *The Lost Gospel*, 4-5.

communities. He suggests too that they preserved memories of Jesus better than the Christians did.[55] At this point, the old view of the nineteenth century is being revived in new dress, namely, that the earliest source of all would give accurate access to the Jesus of history. In the nineteenth century H. J. Holtzmann, for one, thought that the earliest source, Mark, would provide such access.[56] But now Mack is saying, in effect, that the narrative gospels must be set aside—especially Mark, for Mark was the culprit who created the genre. The earliest source is Q, and it is the sayings in Q, not the narratives, that provide access to Jesus of Nazareth.

3. Categorizing Jesus. Studies in the *Gospel of Thomas* and Q have converged in recent years to provide a portrait of Jesus that has been taking center stage, that is, that Jesus can be understood primarily as a "sage."[57]

The understanding that Jesus was a sage is by no means new. Interpreters have highlighted the sheer amount of wisdom teaching that is transmitted in the gospels.[58] But what is new is the claim that the category of "sage" is the most fitting, the defining category, the one that is central to understanding who Jesus was. Along with that is the claim that the term "eschatological prophet," which has been in vogue for so much of the twentieth century, is no longer useful, and is in fact misleading when speaking of the earthly Jesus.[59] Marcus Borg is one of the major proponents of a non-eschatological Jesus.[60] Burton Mack has concluded that Jesus was understood first of all by his followers as a teacher of wisdom, not as a prophet, and certainly not as an eschatological prophet.[61] And the volume produced by the Jesus Seminar speaks of the rejection of an eschatological Jesus as one of the main pillars of Jesus research today; it goes on to claim that Jesus must be understood primarily as a "sage" or "traveling sage."[62]

In addition to the term sage, the closely allied term "Cynic" has been used as a designation for the identity of Jesus. For Mack, Jesus was remembered by his followers not simply as a sage, but as a "Cynic-like sage."[63] For John Dominic Crossan, the term "peasant Jewish Cynic" is the defining one. [64] But comparative

---

[55]Ibid., 10, 47, 245, 250.

[56]Heinrich J. Holtzmann, *Die synoptischen Evangelien: Ihr Ursprung und geschichtlicher Charakter* (Leipzig: Engelmann, 1863).

[57]An exception is the work of A. Jacobson, *The First Gospel*, who says that in Q Jesus "functions more as prophet than as wise person" (75).

[58]Charles E. Carlston, "Proverbs, Maxims, and the Historical Jesus," *JBL* 99 (1980) 91, estimates that there are about 102 wisdom sayings attributed to Jesus in the synoptic gospels.

[59]Cf. Marcus Borg, "Portraits of Jesus in Contemporary North American Scholarship," *HTR* 84 (1991) 14: the picture of Jesus as an eschatological prophet is "mistaken and misleading."

[60]Marcus Borg, *Jesus: A New Vision* (San Francisco: Harper & Row, 1987) 10-14; "A Temperate Case for a Non-Eschatological Jesus," *Foundations and Facets Forum* 2/3 (1986) 86, 95; and "Portraits of Jesus," 13.

[61]B. Mack, *The Lost Gospel*, 34-39.

[62]*The Five Gospels*, 1, 4, 7, 10, 27, 32-33.

[63]B. Mack, *The Lost Gospel*, 115 and passim.

[64]J. D. Crossan, *Historical Jesus*, 421-22.

study with the profile of the Cynic in antiquity has shown that that category is unsatisfactory for application to Jesus.[65] The archetypical Cynic Diogenes of Sinope went about attacking conventions that others held dear. In the case of Jesus, however, there is too much in the traditions that portray him as affirming the essential values of the Jewish tradition and teaching those core values with authority. His attacks were against human traditions which had eclipsed both the letter and spirit of the commandments, not the tradition at its best. Moreover, the Cynic movement hardly existed in the first century of the common era. It had flourished for three previous centuries and then practically died out, only to be revived sometime near the middle of the first century A.D. after the death of Jesus.[66]

Other interpreters have used alternative categories as central in defining Jesus. For Morton Smith, Jesus was essentially a magician.[67] For Graham Twelftree, Jesus was an exorcist, although he does not exclude other categories.[68] But other interpreters—to their credit—categorize Jesus more broadly. For Geza Vermes, Jesus was primarily a "charismatic holy man," "hasid," and "charismatic prophet."[69] For Marcus Borg, Jesus was a charismatic healer, a holy person, a subversive sage, a social prophet, a mystic, and the founder of a movement to revitalize Israel.[70]

No doubt all the categories listed by Vermes and Borg are fitting. But there is one more. There is plenty of evidence in all the major traditions coming into the synoptic gospels—Mark, Q, L, and M—that Jesus was also an eschatological prophet.[71] Borg, in my view, is incorrect in rejecting that category. According to Borg, Jesus was a proclaimer of the kingdom, but the term "kingdom of God" signifies the power of the Spirit, not an eschatological reality.[72] But that is to deny what is so obvious in the various strands of tradition that transmit the teachings of Jesus. It is still possible to join those interpreters—too many to name here, except to mention E. P. Sanders and John Meier—who speak of Jesus as an "eschatological

[65]Cf. Paul R. Eddy, "Jesus as Diogenes? Reflections on the Cynic Jesus Thesis," *JBL* 115 (1996) 449-69.

[66]According to Donald R. Dudley, *A History of Cynicism: From Diogenes to the 6th Century A.D.* (London: Methuen, 1937) 117-26, the first Cynic to attract attention in the first century was Demetrius (in Rome) during the reign of Caligula (A.D. 37-41). The title of the work of Harold W. Attridge, *First Century Cynicism in the Epistles of Heraclitus: Introduction, Greek Text and Translation*, HTS 29 (Missoula: Scholars, 1976), should not encourage a different view. Attridge places the writing of the epistles in the first century and a half of the empire, not necessarily in the first.

[67]Morton Smith, *Jesus the Magician* (San Francisco: Harper & Row, 1978).

[68]Graham H. Twelftree, *Jesus the Exorcist: A Contribution to the Study of the Historical Jesus*, WUNT 2/54 (Tübingen: J. C. B. Mohr [Paul Siebeck], 1993).

[69]Geza Vermes, *Jesus the Jew: A Historian's Reading of the Gospels* (Philadelphia: Fortress, 1981) 83, 224; and *Jesus and the World of Judaism* (Philadelphia: Fortress, 1984) 9, 11, 31-32.

[70]M. Borg, "Portraits of Jesus," 12, 14-15; *Conflict*, 230-47; *Jesus: A New Vision*, 97-171; and *Meeting Jesus Again for the First Time: The Historical Jesus and the Heart of Contemporary Faith* (San Francisco: Harper, 1994) 30.

[71]Mark 14:25; Luke 13:28-29//Matt 8:11-12 (Q); Matt 13:43; 16:19; 20:21; 25:34 (M traditions); Luke 14:15; 22:16, 30 (L traditions). Cf. also 1 Cor 15:24.

[72]M. Borg, *Jesus: A New Vision*, 198-99.

prophet,"[73] to which we should add a wide range of other categories, including sage, healer, exorcist, and charismatic leader.

II. AREAS IN NEED OF DEVELOPMENT

1. Accounting for the death of Jesus. The most notable and confirmable item in the career of Jesus of Nazareth is that he was "crucified under Pontius Pilate." His life ended in crucifixion, and the charge against him was that he claimed to be king of the Jews. He was, in the words made famous by Nils Dahl, "the crucified Messiah."[74]

Since that is the case, any portrait of Jesus must pass what I shall call here the "criterion of crucifiability." The criterion can be stated as follows: an adequate historical construction concerning Jesus must account for why the Roman authorities of the day, and perhaps others, concluded that he must be crucified on the basis of his words or behavior. Jesus as sage won't account for it.[75] Nor finally does the view that Jesus was a Cynic. This criterion demands the inclusion of sources that are being dispensed with by too many today—the narratives of the gospels.

2. Accounting for christological claims. The second area in need of development in the use of sources is accounting for the rise of christological claims concerning Jesus very soon after his death. On first thought, this seems out of order. As soon as we enter into this arena, we are in the realm of the post-Easter situation and faith claims made by certain followers.

Nevertheless, the historian should ask, "How is it that the earliest followers of Jesus came to believe in him as the Messiah—the one who had no credentials?" It seems that that is important as a historical question, especially if Jesus did not claim to be such.

It has been said that the teachings of Jesus can be understood without presupposing a messianic consciousness.[76] That may well be true, but it is being challenged forcefully in new ways by N. T. Wright.[77] In any case, one must look not simply at the words attributed to Jesus in the gospels but also to accounts of his behavior. There are elements that can be considered historical, and which give

---

[73]Among those that can be included are: Rudolf Bultmann, *Theology of the New Testament*, 2 vols. (New York: Charles Scribner's Sons, 1951-55) 1:4; Werner G. Kümmel, *Promise and Fulfilment: The Eschatological Message of Jesus*, SBT 23 (Naperville: Allenson, 1957) 141-55; Günther Bornkamm, *Jesus of Nazareth* (New York: Harper & Brothers, 1960) 54, 66; Hans Conzelmann, *Jesus* (Philadelphia: Fortress, 1973) 68-81; Richard H. Hiers, *The Historical Jesus and the Kingdom of God: Present and Future in the Message and Ministry of Jesus*, University of Florida Monograph Series 38 (Gainesville: University of Florida, 1973); A. E. Harvey, *Jesus and the Constraints of History* (Philadelphia: Westminster, 1982) 86-90; E. P. Sanders, *Jesus and Judaism* (Philadelphia: Fortress, 1985) 155-56, 170-73, 237-39, 319, 321, 326, 330, 335, 340; and J. Meier, *A Marginal Jew*, 2:1044-47.

[74]Nils A. Dahl, *The Crucified Messiah and Other Essays* (Minneapolis: Augsburg, 1974).

[75]That sages *could* be crucified is attested at Matt 23:34. But the ones spoken of are *Christian* sages (along with prophets and scribes), leaders of Christian communities who would suffer martyrdom because they were emissaries of Jesus.

[76]G. Bornkamm, *Jesus*, 169.

[77]N. T. Wright, *Jesus and the Victory of God*, vol. 2 of *Christian Origins and the Question of God* (Minneapolis: Fortress, 1996) 477-539.

pause. Among the data at least three can be mentioned here. First, his calling of the twelve;[78] what meaning can be attached to that except that Jesus was in some sense heading up a new or renewed Israel in a symbolic way and that he was to be the leading figure of the new people in a new age? Second, his entry into Jerusalem on a donkey in keeping with the description of the Messiah's entry portrayed in Zech 9:9 has symbolic significance. The incident is narrated in both the synoptic gospels (Mark 11:1-10//Matt 21:1-9//Luke 19:28-38) and in the Gospel of John (12:12-15); and it is alluded to in the Q material as well (Luke 13:34-35//Matt 23:37-39). Because of its multiple attestation in these three independent traditions, one cannot dismiss it as non-historical in spite of the legendary accretions added to it in the gospel accounts.[79] It is reasonable to conclude that Jesus, by these acts and others, was acting in parabolic ways, redefining the image of the Messiah. Finally, at his trial he was apparently accused of being "King of the Jews"; at least that was the basis for his crucifixion. The fact that he went to his death under that charge implies that, in the end, he accepted the title. There is no hint that he refuted the charge—or at least that anyone claimed that he did. As a matter of historical importance, it would have been very difficult, even impossible, for his disciples to claim that he was the Messiah within a matter of days if indeed he was known to have denied it.

III. CONCLUDING REMARKS

In one of his essays Jacob Neusner has said that works on the historical Jesus are "nothing other than constructive theology masquerading as history."[80] Perhaps he is correct. But we should at least hold out the hope that not all attempts are guilty of such a charge. Surely there are some things that can be known.

I refer to the remark of Neusner as heuristic. It seems to me that many of the attempts to portray Jesus primarily as a sage are laden with a theological agenda. That agenda is to reinvent Christianity. According to the argument, there are at least three things wrong with traditional Christianity: (1) Traditional Christianity—with its emphasis on the cross—is charged with portraying Jesus as one who suffered abuse, and therefore it commends the suffering of abuse to others. (2) Traditional Christianity portrays Jesus not only as risen from the dead but also as the Lord who reigns over the entire universe; and that encourages Christian triumphalism, the stamping out of other religious traditions. (3) Traditional Chris-

---

[78]Although some scholars—such as H. Conzelmann, *Jesus*, 34—have concluded that "the twelve" is a later, post-resurrection designation, that does not exclude their existence as a group during the ministry of Jesus. Cf. G. Bornkamm, *Jesus*, 150, and E. P. Sanders, *This Historical Figure of Jesus* (New York: Penguin, 1993) 120-22.

[79]According to Rudolf Bultmann, *The History of the Synoptic Tradition* (New York: Harper & Row, 1963) 261-62, the story contains legendary expansions, but has a basis in history. Cf. also Werner G. Kümmel, *Promise and Fulfilment*, 116-17; Vincent Taylor, *The Gospel According to St. Mark* (New York: St. Martin's, 1952) 452; and G. Bornkamm, *Jesus*, 158. For a concise review of criticism, cf. Joseph A. Fitzmyer, *The Gospel According to Luke*, 2 vols., AB 28-28A (Garden City: Doubleday, 1981-85) 2:1244-46.

[80]Jacob Neusner, "Who Needs 'the Historical Jesus'?" in *Rabbinic Literature and the New Testament: What We Cannot Show, We Do Not Know* (Valley Forge: Trinity International, 1994) 176.

tianity expects an end of this world and the reign of the saints in the world to come; and that encourages both an anti-environmental worldview, on the one hand, and bizarre apocalyptic movements on the other.

Therefore, the argument goes, it is better to interpret Jesus as a sage, one who fits into the broad spectrum of teachers of all ages and around the world. Then Christianity—if we would call it that—would fit better into the religions of the world as an equal partner at the table, rather than trying to be superior. It would be more in keeping with the religion of Jesus! It would dwell on his moral teachings, dispensing with cross, resurrection, and eschatology.

A quick response to such claims is to observe that, if Christianity is to be reinvented along those lines, Christianity will no longer exist, for all that is left is a religion of Jesus uncrucified and unresurrected. But the challenge of our times is to go beyond that type of quick response. For if we take that line alone, we can be accused of simply trying to defend traditional Christian interests.

To respond to the sage hypothesis, to claim that Jesus was much more than that, and to say that there are still good reasons to hold out that Jesus was a prophet of the kingdom is, in my view, the way to proceed. The older consensus concerning Jesus and Christian faith was, in shorthand, that the proclaimer (Jesus, prophet of the eschatological kingdom of God) became the proclaimed (the crucified and risen Christ proclaimed in the church). In that way of thinking, there is a continuity: (1) Jesus the proclaimer announced the coming saving work of God; and (2) the church proclaims that the saving work of God has been accomplished in Jesus' death and resurrection—with final wrap-up to come at his parousia. That older consensus needs constant testing. We must ask ourselves whether that way of thinking is merely "theology masquerading as history." I do not think that it is. I think it is based on a much more secure foundation in history than the portrait of Jesus as a non-eschatological sage—a portrait based on hypothetical multi-layered sources sponsored by hypothetical communities of hypothetical "Jesus people" who had more integrity than those Christians who are given voice in the canonical writings of the New Testament. ⊕

Word & World
Supplement Series 3
1997

Jesus within His Social World: Insights from Archaeology, Sociology, and Cultural Anthropology

WALTER F. TAYLOR, JR.

Trinity Lutheran Seminary
Columbus, Ohio

WHEN WE SEEK TO CHARACTERIZE THE CURRENT FLOOD OF INTEREST IN THE historical Jesus, we search unsuccessfully for a single essay or programmatic book that has popped the cork of the heady academic champagne being drunk so deeply these days. No one vineyard is responsible. No one vintner has been the catalyst. Rather, the contemporary quest for the historical Jesus results from the coalescence of textual discoveries, archaeological finds, and new and renewed methodologies. James Charlesworth labels today's round of study "Jesus research," which, he says, "may be defined simply as the attempt to understand the man of history in light of all the evidence that is now pouring our way."[1] Others name the present round of study "the third quest."[2] Whatever the label, no one center can be identified.

Perhaps what has been most consistent in our era's quest for Jesus has been the attempt to place him within his social world. Virtually no one today ap-

---

[1] James Charlesworth, "From Barren Mazes to Gentle Rappings: The Emergence of Jesus Research," *PSB* 7, N.S. (1986) 224. For an introduction to the current quest see Walter F. Taylor, Jr., "New Quests for the Historical Jesus," *TSRev* 15 (1993) 69-83.

[2] Colin Brown, "Historical Jesus, Quest of," in *Dictionary of Jesus and the Gospels*, ed. Joel B. Green, Scot McKnight, and I. Howard Marshall (Downers Grove, IL: InterVarsity, 1992) 326-41. N. T. Wright claims to have coined the term. He applies "third quest" only to "one particular type of contemporary Jesus-research, namely, that which regards Jesus as an eschatological prophet announcing the long-awaited kingdom, and which undertakes serious historiography around that point" (*Jesus and the Victory of God*, vol. 2 of *Christian Origins and the Question of God* [Minneapolis: Fortress, 1996] xiv). See also his article, "Jesus, Quest for the Historical," *ABD*, 3:796-802.

proaches Jesus as simply a purveyor of non-incarnate platitudes. He is to be situated firmly within the social world of which he was a part. Indeed, part of the fascination in observing and participating in the reaping of various insights is learning how the scholar will blend today's harvest with a given social context from antiquity. The results exhibit great differences, depending on the social world chosen and the evidence interpreted, but most "questers" would agree with Richard Horsley that "all particular terms and texts as well as artifacts and architecture [are]...embedded in a particular social world, such that ascribing meaning to them requires some sense of the historical social world...through which their meaning is mediated and in which it is discerned."[3]

The result for many scholars has been a certain rapprochement between the study of archaeology and the study of texts, especially in the quest for the historical Jesus.[4] Yet archaeology is not the only method being utilized. So too are sociology (both the reconstruction of social history and the application of sociological theories) and cultural anthropology. It is to these varying approaches that we turn to see what we might glean about Jesus within his social world.

I. ARCHAEOLOGY, SOCIAL DESCRIPTION, AND SOCIAL HISTORY: COSMOPOLITAN GALILEE

While most practicing archaeologists have not themselves published theories about the historical Jesus, historical Jesus scholars have in recent years regularly used archaeological finds, especially for two types of social criticism: social description, which seeks (in our case) to reconstruct the customs and everyday life of first-century Mediterranean people; and social history, which charts larger, more comprehensive changes, such as the economic developments of a given region.

In work related to the historical Jesus, the archaeological-social focus has been on Galilee and the status of its inhabitants during the first century. As Sean Freyne has written, the current quest for Jesus "is rapidly in danger of becoming the quest for the historical Galilee."[5] Capernaum, Bethsaida, Nazareth, Sepphoris, the "Jesus boat," coins, and texts have been studied and restudied, as scholars have tried to place these disparate pieces together to reconstitute the complicated puzzle of first-century Galilean life.

One of the most controversial and thus most debated theses is that first-century Galilee should be understood as urbanized and Greco-Roman: in short, as cosmopolitan. In this view, Galilee (especially lower Galilee) is seen as being just as cosmopolitan as any other portion of the Greco-Roman world, thus increasing the likelihood that Jesus was to some extent knowledgeable of and influenced by the

---

[3]Richard A. Horsley, "The Historical Jesus and Archaeology of the Galilee," *SBLSP* (1994), ed. Eugene H. Lovering, Jr. (Atlanta: Scholars, 1994) 91.

[4]Ibid., 92-93.

[5]Sean Freyne, "The Geography, Politics and Economics of Galilee," in *Studying the Historical Jesus: Evaluations of the State of Current Research*, ed. Bruce Chilton and Craig A. Evans (Leiden: Brill, 1994) 76. See Jonathan L. Reed, "Population Numbers, Urbanization, and Economics: Galilean Archaeology and the Historical Jesus," *SBLSP* (1994) 203, notes 1 and 2, for literature on key archaeological work and appropriation of it by New Testament scholars.

Greco-Roman world. In part the Greco-Roman influence is seen in the presence of Romans in towns such as Capernaum, where some scholars identify evidence for first-century Roman occupation.[6] In that interpretation, the centurion of Matt 8:5-13 //Luke 7:1-10 is Roman. Others are not so confident of a Roman presence in Capernaum in the first century.[7] Without doubt the Roman military presence grew after the reconquest of Galilee in 67 A.D. and especially after the Bar Kochba revolt in the next century, reaching 15,000 men. But such a force does not seem to have existed during the lifetime of Jesus.[8] Another sign of Roman presence in Capernaum is the second- or third-century Roman bathhouse discovered there. It may be that the first-century building that lies underneath the later Roman bathhouse will provide proof of earlier Roman presence and thus greater probability of occupation by Roman troops, but for the moment Horsley, for one, concludes that the only military presence at Capernaum early in the first century was the military that belonged to the Roman client rulers. On the other hand, the presence of a tax-office is quite likely and thus a tax-collector could be found in Capernaum (Mark 2:1, 13-14).[9]

Another argument for Greco-Roman urbanization that has now been modified involves population estimates. In 1981 Strange and Meyers pegged Capernaum at 12,000 to 15,000 people, a figure adopted by J. A. Overman.[10] Reed credits Howard Clark Kee with a figure as high as 25,000.[11] Reed argues that the best way to estimate a town's population is by utilizing two figures: the extent of the town's ruins and the population density of its living quarters. By multiplying the number of hectares by the number of people living per hectare, an approximate population can be determined. Strange and Meyers used such a formula to arrive at their figure, but they used an 1871 report to give them the size of the ancient town. They further figured on 400 to 500 people per hectare. Reed argues that the actual site of the first-century town was much smaller and that population figures for the city of Pompeii should be used as a guide to determine population density, since much of first-century Capernaum is unexcavated or has been destroyed. Pompeii is chosen because it has been fully excavated and its housing pattern is similar to Capernaum's. Reed concludes, on the basis of his calculations, that the largest Capernaum could have been in the first century was 2,250 people, but he thinks it likely that the population was nearer 1,700.[12]

[6]So J. C. H. Laughlin, "Capernaum: From Jesus Time and After," *BARev* 56 (1993) 55-61.

[7]David Kennedy implies that the centurion was both non-Jew and non-Roman ("Roman Army," *ABD*, 5:797).

[8]E. M. Meyers, "Aspects of Roman Sepphoris in the Light of Recent Archaeology," in *Early Christianity in Context: Monuments and Documents*, ed. F. Manns and E. Alliata, Studium Biblicum Franciscanum, Collectio Maior 38 (Jerusalem: Franciscan, 1993) 32.

[9]Horsley, "Historical Jesus," 103.

[10]J. Strange and E. Meyers, *Archaeology, the Rabbis, and Early Christianity* (Nashville: Abingdon, 1981) 58; J. A. Overman, "Who Were the First Urban Christians? Urbanization in Galilee in the First Century," *SBLSP* (1988), ed. David Lull (Atlanta: Scholars, 1988) 160-68.

[11]Jonathan L. Reed, *The Population of Capernaum*, Occasional Papers 2 (Claremont, CA: The Institute for Antiquity and Christianity, 1992) 3.

[12]Ibid., 9-15. See also his "Population Numbers," 204-12.

In many ways the key to the debate regarding the urbanization and Greco-Romanization of Galilee is the interpretation of the excavations at the city of Sepphoris. Sepphoris had been used by Herod the Great as the administrative center through which he ruled Galilee. After he died, the local revolt against his rule centered in Sepphoris but was suppressed by Roman troops in 4 B.C. When Rome assigned Galilee to Herod's son Antipas, Antipas began rebuilding the city as a specifically Roman city.[13] The result was a thriving metropolis called by Josephus the "ornament of all Galilee" and "the strongest city in Galilee." Jesus, of course, grew up in the village of Nazareth, according to the gospels, just four miles away. In part because of his upbringing in Nazareth and in part because of the rural nature of many of his sayings, Jesus has been viewed as a country boy, out of touch with Greco-Roman urban culture. No tradition ever places him in Sepphoris, although Josephus underscores the economic, political, and administrative importance of the city.[14]

Excavators at Sepphoris are in the process of discovering, according to Silberman, "a gleaming marble theater and surrounding public buildings that were not merely architectural innovations, but powerful, pervasive symbols of the new, Roman way of culture, economics, and life."[15] With the capital so close at hand, some ask, is it reasonable to think that Jesus never went to the city, only an hour away? And what would he find there? A typical Greco-Roman city, with its baths, theater, statues, and festivals. Richard Batey concludes,

> The stage on which he [Jesus] acted out his ministry was cosmopolitan and sophisticated, and his understanding of urban life was more relevant than previously imagined....The people to whom Jesus proclaimed his message of hope and salvation...were struggling with life's meaning in a culture where Jewish traditions and Greco-Roman urban values collided.[16]

Indeed, Meyers has suggested that Jesus and his father Joseph quite likely found construction work not only in Sepphoris, a city of about 24,000 people, but perhaps also at Caesarea Philippi, Tiberias, and/or Bethsaida-Julias.[17]

If Jesus were indeed in Sepphoris or other similar cities, the question still remains how much he might have been influenced by what he experienced there.

[13]Thomas R. W. Longstaff, "Nazareth and Sepphoris: Insights into Christian Origins," in *Christ and His Communities: Essays in Honor of Reginald H. Fuller*, ed. Arland J. Hultgren and Barbara Hall (Cincinnati: Forward Movement, 1990) 12; see also Richard A. Horsley, *Sociology and the Jesus Movement* (New York: Crossroad, 1989) 77.

[14]Josephus, *Ant.* 18.27; *War* 2.511; *Life* 232, 346.

[15]Neil Asher Silberman, "Searching for Jesus: The Politics of First-Century Judea," *Archaeology* 47 (1994) 37. For a brief history of the excavations, see Meyers, "Aspects," 29.

[16]Richard A. Batey, "Sepphoris—An Urban Portrait of Jesus," *BARev* 18 (1992) 62; see also his *Jesus & the Forgotten City: New Light on Sepphoris and the Urban World of Jesus* (Grand Rapids: Baker, 1991). The article is more focused.

[17]"Sepphoris," in John J. Rousseau and Rami Arav, *Jesus and His World: An Archaeological and Cultural Dictionary* (Minneapolis: Fortress, 1995) 251; see that page for extensive bibliography on Sepphoris. On the population estimate for Sepphoris, see Reed, "Population Numbers," 214. Horsley, "Historical Jesus," 101, points out that the application of the Pompeii numbers to Sepphoris would result in a population under 10,000. Even John P. Meier (*A Marginal Jew: Rethinking the Historical Jesus*, 3 vols.; two now published [New York: Doubleday, 1991—] 1:284) thinks it possible that Jesus worked in Sepphoris.

Jerome Murphy-O'Connor, who is not given to excesses, connects at least one saying of Jesus with Sepphoris:

> The most natural explanation of Jesus' use of *hypokrites* ("stage actor") in criticism of the religious leaders of his day (e.g., Mark 7:6) is that he went to this theatre [in Sepphoris], the nearest one to Nazareth. The word, which has no Semitic equivalent, would not have been part of the vocabulary of a village artisan.[18]

His evaluation, of course, depends on the assumption that this saying goes back to Jesus himself.

While the theater in Sepphoris is often being dated now up to a hundred years later than earlier estimates (and thus too late to have been seen by Jesus),[19] the thesis of a Greek-speaking Jesus has become ever more popular. Near Sepphoris, earlier archaeology had shown that 80 percent of the inscriptions in Jewish burial catacombs were in Greek. Already in 1974 Martin Hengel wondered if the disciples were not at least bilingual (Aramaic and Greek). Andrew and Philip had Greek names, and Simon-Cephas-Peter, Andrew's brother, later undertook extensive missionary journeys among the Greek-speaking Jewish diaspora.[20] Argyle points to widespread influence of Greek in Palestine, with the very name of the Jewish council, Sanhedrin, coming from the Greek συνέδριον. Moreover, he argues, any Jewish business person would learn enough Greek to carry on business with gentiles. He too thinks that the reference to "stage actor" presumes a Greek original, and he also maintains that the conversations between Jesus and Pontius Pilate, the centurion, and the Syro-Phoenician woman would have to have been carried out in Greek, since none of them except Jesus would have spoken Aramaic.[21] And what of Jesus' ministry in Bethsaida and the Decapolis? The discussion today is not *did* Jesus know Greek, but how much Greek did he know? As Howard Clark Kee has written, "I cannot imagine, on the basis of archaeological evidence, anyone surviving in Galilee who did not speak Greek."[22] On the other hand, Meier doubts that Jesus could teach and preach in Greek, although he probably could conduct business in the language.[23]

Douglas Oakman identifies indirect references to Sepphoris that also lead to the consideration of the influence of Sepphoris on surrounding villages. The first passage is Luke 9:57-58, which includes the saying, "Foxes have holes, and birds of the air have nests; but the Son of Man has nowhere to lay his head." The second

---

[18]Jerome Murphy-OConnor, *The Holy Land* (Oxford: Oxford University, 1992) 413. See also Richard A. Batey, "Jesus and the Theatre," *NTS* 30 (1984) 563-74. Meier, *Marginal Jew*, 1:314-15, n. 175, has an extensive argument against Jesus having used this word.

[19]Meyers, "Aspects," 29. But see James F. Strange, "Sepphoris," *ABD*, 5:1091, and Longstaff, "Nazareth and Sepphoris," 11 and n. 19.

[20]Martin Hengel, *Judaism and Hellenism*, 2 vols. (Philadelphia: Fortress, 1974) 1:105.

[21]A. W. Argyle, "Greek among the Jews of Palestine in New Testament Times," *NTS* 20 (1973/74) 87-89. So also Joseph A. Fitzmyer, "Did Jesus Speak Greek?" *BARev* 18 (September/October 1992) 58-63, and Rousseau and Arav, *Jesus*, 51.

[22]Howard Clark Kee, "Contexts #17: Archaeology in Galilee," *BIAC* 18 (1991) 14.

[23]Meier, *Marginal Jew*, 1:262-62.

passage is Luke 13:31-33, which embraces Jesus' reference to Herod as "that fox." Oakman seeks to understand the passages by using first-century Galilean social contexts. Sepphoris derives from the Hebrew word for bird. Who are the "birds of the air," then? They are the Sepphoreans, who control both the villages and the produce of the land. The result is:

> The large oil and wine presses, perhaps with their accompanying ritual baths, serve the elites. They are signs of the extraction of product, of its removal from profane or local use and of its transfer far away. The tentacles of commercial Tyre and the temple system reach across the land....The Herodian and Judean-oriented elite at Sepphoris have everything they need, but the ordinary person has nothing! The ordinary person meanwhile goes away hungry.[24]

The sayings, he believes, comprise a critique of that system.

Cities such as Sepphoris were in fact surrounded by smaller villages, and, while resentment did occur at the disparities between the economic level of some people in the cities and the economic level of most people in the villages, the larger cities "were important points of interchange for those who lived in the villages and, in all probability, essential for economic survival."[25] For Meyers the urban centers such as Sepphoris, which linked Galilee with the Greek west, were so dominant culturally that the villages associated with Jesus (Nazareth, Nain, Cana, Capernaum) could not have escaped that influence.[26] He wonders, therefore, whether "nothing good can come out of Nazareth" refers to the degree of hellenization that had occurred in the village rather than the usual understanding that the negative reference is to the village's rural location.[27]

For Strange, the public buildings of Sepphoris symbolize the laying of a cultural foundation different from that which preceded it. The Romans, via Herod Antipas, "imposed a distinctive *urban overlay* upon a base, namely the local, Jewish culture in first-century BCE Judea."[28] The local Jewish culture continued, but the overlay was successfully grafted onto the local culture because that culture was already urbanized and hellenized and thus ready to receive the overlay. The success of the grafting is seen in part by the pro-Roman stance taken by Sepphoris during the revolt of 66-67.[29]

If Sepphoris and the other major Greco-Roman city in Galilee, Tiberias, were

---

[24]Douglas E. Oakman, "The Archaeology of First-Century Galilee and the Social Interpretation of the Historical Jesus," *SBLSP* (1994) 236.

[25]Kee, "Contexts #17," 12.

[26]Eric M. Meyers, "Galilean Regionalism as a Factor in Historical Reconstruction," *BASOR* 221 (1976) 101. For a critique and further questions for assessing the degree of cultural influence from the cities, see Horsley, "Historical Jesus," 123-25.

[27]Meyers, "Galilean Regionalism," 97; see also his "The Cultural Setting of Galilee: The Case of Regionalism and Early Judaism," in *Aufstieg und Niedergang der Römischen Welt*, part 2, vol. 19/1, ed. W. Haase (Berlin: De Gruyter, 1979) 698-99. Charles R. Page II views Nazareth, on the other hand, as an "inwardly focused, fundamentalist village" (*Jesus & the Land* [Nashville: Abingdon, 1995] 63-64).

[28]James F. Strange, "Some Implications of Archaeology for New Testament Studies," in *What Has Archaeology to Do With Faith?* ed. James Charlesworth and Walter Weaver (Valley Forge, PA: Trinity International, 1992) 31.

[29]On the mixed population, see Longstaff, "Nazareth and Sepphoris," 12-13 and n. 23.

so important, why do we have no information that Jesus ever visited them? Jesus may have avoided Tiberias because it was built on top of a cemetery, but the larger framework, suggests Graham Stanton, is that "Jesus deliberately avoided both cities, for they were the power bases of the despised Herodian family and the ruling elite of the day. They posed a direct threat to Jesus and his followers."[30]

When we turn from the specifics of a given city, we find two basic positions being taken by those who identify strong Greco-Roman urbanization in first-century Galilee. The first position is taken by Strange, who identifies a healthy, vibrant syncretism in the interaction of the Jewish and Greco-Roman cultures. The second position is taken, albeit with distinctions, by scholars such as Horsley and Crossan. For Horsley there was a tense and frequently confrontative relationship between the Galilean peasants and the Roman officials (along with the urban aristocracy that supported them). The relationship grew ever tenser during the initial decades of the first century, since Antipas needed tax money to finance the major construction projects at Sepphoris and Tiberias.[31] Small farmers were in a "tightening noose of institutionalized injustices such as double taxation, heavy indebtedness, and loss of land."[32] The result, as recorded in Josephus and highlighted by Horsley, was rural unrest and banditry in Galilee that were symptomatic of broader economic unrest that affected Judea as well, with aristocrats and priests purchasing small family holdings, thus forcing the former owners to live as tenant farmers or hired laborers.

Crossan, too, envisions tensions between the Roman civilization and the native Jewish culture over which it hovers. He uses the archaeological work at Sepphoris to color his picture of the relationships between the two cultures in conflict. Crossan thinks that Jesus and his first followers were not backwoods people unconnected with the Greco-Roman cultural currents of their day. In fact,

> the main west-east road through Galilee ran from Ptolemaïs on the Mediterranean coast through Sepphoris to Tiberias on the Sea of Galilee....Sepphoris was also the terminus of the north-south mountain road from Jerusalem....The village or hamlet of Nazareth, while certainly off the beaten track, was not very far off a fairly well beaten track. To understand Nazareth, therefore, demands consideration not only of its rural aspects but also of its relationship to an urban provincial capital.[33]

Jesus and his followers had every opportunity to know the Greco-Roman currents

---

[30]Graham Stanton, *Gospel Truth? New Light on Jesus and the Gospels* (Valley Forge, PA: Trinity International) 114.

[31]See Richard A. Horsley, *Archaeology, History, and Society in Galilee* (Valley Forge, PA: Trinity International, 1996); idem, *Galilee: History, Politics, People* (Valley Forge, PA: Trinity International, 1995). The earlier work of Sean Freyne is also of interest: *Galilee from Alexander the Great to Hadrian, 323 B.C.E. to 145 C.E.* (Wilmington, DE: Glazier, 1980); and *Galilee, Jesus and the Gospels* (Philadelphia: Fortress, 1988). Meier, *Marginal Jew*, 1:283, denies that the tensions in Galilee were high.

[32]Richard Horsley, *Jesus and the Spiral of Violence* (San Francisco: Harper and Row, 1987) 237. See also Horsley, "Historical Jesus," 98-99.

[33]John Dominic Crossan, *The Historical Jesus: The Life of a Mediterranean Jewish Peasant* (San Francisco: HarperSanFrancisco, 1991) 18.

of the ruling nation, and they consciously rejected them—although part of Jesus' model of rejection was the Greco-Roman Cynic sage, according to Crossan.[34]

In sum, those who posit a cosmopolitan Galilee argue that that region, together with the entirety of Palestine, was increasingly being assimilated into the Greco-Roman cultural, political, and economic system. Thus a "Galilee of the nations" (Isa 9:1, quoted in Matt 4:15) was reality and not mere prediction. As Strange concludes, "It seems clear that the archaeological evidence...supports a picture of the Galilee that participates more or less completely in the Roman world of its day....They [Galilee's citizens] played by Rome's cultural rules. They were recognizably part of the Roman empire."[35]

II. Archaeology, Social Description, and Social History: Non-Cosmopolitan, Rural Galilee

Others have been less sanguine about a Greco-Roman Galilee. One of the chief defenders of a non-cosmopolitan, rural, and Jewish Galilee is E. P. Sanders. He begins his argument with Herod the Great, whom he styles as "in many ways" one who "was loyal to Jewish law and traditions."[36] Herod did utilize Roman troops to secure his kingdom, but he quickly got rid of them, in part by paying bribes. Sanders understands Herod as largely independent of Rome, as long as he paid tribute, kept the borders safe, quashed any rebellions, and contributed troops if Rome needed them.

Nor should Herod's building programs be understood as anti-Jewish. Sanders notes that the structures Herod built for Greco-Roman culture and entertainment were built "in new towns settled largely by gentiles (Caesarea, Sebaste), in areas that were already gentile (Paneion) or in places where there was only a small Jewish population (Jericho)."[37] Finally, he denies the conclusion often drawn from Josephus that Herod built a theater, amphitheater, and hippodrome in or near Jerusalem and that he held quadrennial Greco-Roman games in honor of Augustus and Rome. Only the theater, Sanders argues, was built in Jerusalem. Further, there is no evidence that Herod ever built a *gymnasion* anywhere in his kingdom, a salient fact since the *gymnasion* was the primary vehicle for spreading Greek culture.[38]

Almost without exception, says Sanders, Herod the Great's son Antipas, who inherited Galilee, adhered to the same standards set by his father. He, too, was able

[34]Oakman, "Archaeology," 233-34, raises this intriguing question: Does not the Cynic understanding of Jesus propounded by Crossan, Mack, and others *demand* a thoroughly hellenized Galilee, with a comparable minimization of Jesus' Jewish orientation? That is, without the thesis of such hellenization it becomes virtually impossible to understand how Jesus could have encountered enough Cynicism to be able to adopt it.

[35]James F. Strange, "First-Century Galilee from Archaeology and from the Texts," *SBLSP* (1994) 90.

[36]E. P. Sanders, "Jesus in Historical Context," *TToday* 50 (1993) 433.

[37]Ibid., 434.

[38]Ibid., 434-36. Rousseau and Arav, *Jesus*, 4, note that "despite the statements of 1 Maccabees, no remains of gymnasia have been found in Palestine, not even in Jerusalem, for the Late Hellenistic-Early Roman period. Nevertheless, this does not prove that they did not exist."

to keep Roman soldiers away from Galilee, and he also adhered to the Jewish law, at least in matters that affected the people as a whole or that were known to them. He built no *gymnasia*, although he may have built a theater in his two capital cities of Sepphoris and Tiberias. The one major area in which he failed to carry out the policies of his father was in his desire to divorce his first wife, who fled to her father King Aretas. For our purposes what is of significance is that, when Aretas attacked Antipas' army, he did not need to fear a Roman legion, since there were no Roman troops in Galilee. Eventually Roman troops were dispatched from Syria, but that is the point: they were not stationed on Galilean soil.[39] In addition, the number of soldiers relates to the number of gentiles present in Galilee at a given time. Armies bring with them not only their culture but also retainers, both official and unofficial. The larger the gentile population in a given city, such as Sepphoris, the stronger the case can be made that the city and region were being affected by the gentiles' Greco-Roman culture.

At the root of Sanders' objection is the observation that much of the reputed Greco-Roman context argument is anachronistic. Scholars have created whole new worlds, he thinks, by shifting later evidence to the time of Jesus.[40] Meyers, too, argues that there certainly were gentiles in Sepphoris in the first century, but that definite evidence for a gentile population of any size, including Roman soldiers, comes only from the end of the first or the beginning of the second century.[41]

Sean Freyne agrees that the concept of a cosmopolitan Galilee has been pushed too far. "The alleged urbanization of Galilee," he points out, "is often taken to mean that the region's inhabitants participated fully in every aspect of Greco-Roman culture, including its religious and philosophical assumptions about life."[42] Horsley expresses a similar concern: scholars can be too quick to see the whole Greco-Roman culture as present when the evidence points to only a part of it.[43] Another perspective needs also to be taken into account: the sheer presence of Greco-Roman culture and cultural symbols does not mean that Jews living in close proximity necessarily became any less Jewish, any less observant in their religious practices. In Sepphoris, for example, alongside the Roman baths and theater archaeologists have discovered almost thirty *mikvaoth* (ritual baths) used in Jewish rites of purification. At least some date from the time of Jesus. Burial also took place outside the city limits, in accord with Jewish practice. On the basis of such data Eric Meyers makes the following judgment from his work at Sepphoris:

> The archaeology and history of Sepphoris suggest that in the time of Jesus the city was overwhelmingly Jewish in population, traditional in orientation toward language and common [Jewish] religious practice, urban in character..., connected to the other towns and villages of Galilee by trade and the new require-

[39]Sanders, "Jesus," 438-40. He also argues for a smaller Roman role in the administration of Palestine in general and Jerusalem in particular (442-45).

[40]Ibid., 447; see also n. 61 on that page.

[41]Meyers, "Aspects," 34.

[42]Sean Freyne, "The Historical Jesus and Archaeology," *Explorations* 10/2 (1996) 6.

[43]Horsley, "Historical Jesus," 102.

ments of an expanding population base, somewhat aristocratic because of its priestly component, retainer class, and pro-Roman posture, and perhaps an uncongenial but not unfamiliar place for Jesus.[44]

Horsley, in turn, questions whether there is enough evidence to support Meyers' assertions regarding Jewish inhabitants and their religious practices. He wonders how much weight should be placed on the ritual baths and burial customs, which in and of themselves do not answer the question of how Jews related to the (supposed) gentile culture around them.[45]

Sanders, in conclusion, admits, as the evidence dictates, that the Judaism of Jesus' era was in a number of ways hellenized. But living in a culture that was in some ways affected by Greco-Roman culture (with less influence according to Sanders and more influence according to others we have surveyed) did not mean that Palestinian Jews were inevitably dominated by it—any more than all diaspora Jews inevitably became thoroughly hellenized.[46] Nor is it unavoidably the case that hellenism should be viewed only as an alternative to native cultures, in our case Jewish. Hellenism could also be viewed as "a framework that enabled local religions and cultures to flourish within a new setting without compromising its indigenous character and unique self-definition."[47] For that matter, Riches thinks that Galilean Jews would have been particularly interested in maintaining their distinctions from gentiles, since Sepphoris had in relatively recent memory been destroyed, the citizens sold into slavery, and the combatants crucified.[48]

On the other hand, we will not again be able to view Galilee as a backwater out of touch with the broader world.

III. ECONOMIC TENSIONS IN GALILEE

As we seek to understand Jesus within his social world we need to understand the economic changes that were occurring in first-century Galilee. As we have already seen, Horsley identifies economic tensions as a fact of life for Galilean peasants. The tensions were exacerbated by Antipas's building programs at Sepphoris and Tiberias. The tax burden exacted to finance those projects, when added to the tax burden Galileans already were shouldering, resulted in indebtedness, loss of land, and social unrest. Peasant farmers left, after paying taxes, with too little grain and oil to feed their families were forced to borrow, often at exorbitant rates. While borrowing provided temporary relief, "the continuing pressures of the system drove them increasingly into debt."[49] Debt, in turn, could easily result in loss of land and/or reduction to life as a tenant farmer or day laborer.

[44]E. M. Meyers, "Galilee in the Time of Jesus," *Archaeology* 47 (1994) 41.

[45]Horsley, "Historical Jesus," 118.

[46]Sanders, "Jesus," 448.

[47]Eric M. Meyers, "The Challenge of Hellenism for Early Judaism and Christianity," *BA* 55 (1992) 85.

[48]Josephus, *Ant.* 17.289; *War* 2.68. John K. Riches, "The Social World of Jesus," *Int* 50 (1996) 388.

[49]Horsley, *Sociology*, 89. Sanders, "Jesus," 445, does not think that Palestinian Jewish farmers were especially heavily taxed.

Horsley is not alone in his understanding of first-century economic realities. Riches points to the initial decades of the first century as "a time of growing tension between the peasant majority of the population and a ruling class that had found new prosperity and power through a developing market economy and through engagement in international politics."[50] Freyne, among others, has suggested that, under the rule of Herod Antipas, Galilee moved from the more traditional peasant economy, in which theoretically everyone shared the land's productivity, to a more market-driven economy, in which wealth and power were increasingly concentrated in the hands of a few landowners and the ruling class.[51] The lack of available productive land was, according to Applebaum, a significant cause of unrest.[52] The better land increasingly was owned by the wealthy elite.[53]

A shift in the concentration of economic power was thus occurring in first-century Galilee. Oakman adopts the model of Karl Polanyi to explain what was happening. In that model one form of the redistribution of wealth occurs when the rents, tithes, and taxes from rural producers are moved to urban areas with their temples and government offices and then redistributed *not* to meet the needs of the agricultural producers but to meet other needs determined by the urban elite. This process of distribution through a central institution (in the case of Palestine, the institutions of temple and government) resulted in other centralizations, especially the growth of the large landholdings we have already discussed.[54] Sepphoris and Tiberias would have functioned as just such instruments of economic transference from rural producers to urban elites.[55]

Freyne cites Thomas Carney's view that the kind of rapid movement toward a market economy seen in first-century Galilee necessarily brings with it changes in values that affect existing institutions and create new ones. In particular, the pivotal values of kinship/family and honor/shame are altered. When the extended family no longer is suited to the economic system, serious threats emerge to it and related entrenched values.[56] Thus we return to the perception of social unrest in first-century Galilee.

Jesus certainly was knowledgeable about economic and social conditions in Galilee. His work as a carpenter would have taken him not only to other villages but likely to large estates and urban centers. The results of broader economic

---

[50]Riches, "Social World," 390; see also Douglas E. Oakman, *Jesus and the Economic Questions of His Day*, Studies in the Bible and Early Christianity 8 (Lewiston, NY: Edwin Mellen, 1986) 77.

[51]Sean Freyne, "Jesus and the Urban Culture of Galilee," in *Texts and Their Contexts: Biblical Texts and Their Textual and Situational Contexts* (Oslo: Scandinavian University, 1995) 597-622.

[52]S. Applebaum, "The Struggle for the Soil and the Revolt of 66-73 C.E.," *Eretz Israel* 12 (1975) 125-28 [in Hebrew, with an English summary]. Sanders, "Jesus," 446, argues that the real cause of the lack of arable land was that families had too many sons.

[53]Sean Freyne, "Herodian Economics in Galilee: Searching for a Suitable Model," in *Modelling Early Christianity: Social-Scientific Studies of the New Testament in its Context*, ed. Philip F. Esler (London and New York: Routledge, 1995) 33.

[54]Oakman, *Economic Questions*, 78.

[55]See Josephus, *Life* 66, 376, for rural resentment against the cities.

[56]Freyne, "Herodian Economics," 41-44.

changes would have been evident to him, especially since the itinerant nature of his work would have put him into contact with people in varying economic and social conditions. His use of language from farming, construction, fishing, and boat-building and repair is a sign of his breadth of experience.[57] Freyne sees the Galilean economic and social situation reflected in many of Jesus' parables: "day laborers, debt, resentment of absentee landlords, wealthy estate owners with little concern for tenants' needs, exploitative stewards of estates, family feuds over inheritance, etc."[58]

Jesus does more, however, than merely reflect knowledge of the socio-economic conditions of his time. He also speaks against them. In addition to healings that cross social, economic, and gender lines, he advocates for the poor and powerless (e.g., Luke 6:20-21). Part of his advocacy is the parallel he draws between the forgiveness of sins and the forgiveness of debts (Matt 18:21-35; Luke 7:41-43), a parallel seen most pointedly in the forgiveness petition of the Lord's prayer (Matt 6:12//Luke 11:4).[59] Another part of his advocacy is directing people to practice generosity (Matt 7:1-5//Luke 6:37-42, especially v. 38; Matt 22:1-10//Luke 14:15-24; Mark 12:41-44 // Luke 21:1-4; Luke 10:29-37; 16:1-8). Further, in an economic situation in which the family is being marginalized, Jesus proposes a new kind of kinship based on one's relationship to God (Mark 3:31-35; 10:30). In these ways he proposed an alternative way of life that challenged the values of the growing market economy and of the centralization of economic life in cities, especially Jerusalem and the temple. Such an agenda naturally attracted the attention of those dedicated to maintaining the elite in their positions of privilege.

IV. Sociological Exegesis

The Jesus we have been studying is one who was profoundly interested in the social implications of one's relationship with God. A branch of the social sciences that has been especially concerned to study religion as a social entity is sociological exegesis.[60] Sociological exegesis is more than the study of social history, i.e., describing and analyzing the social matrix of ancient literature, history, and archae-

---

[57]Rousseau and Arav, *Jesus*, 12, 25, 29, 72. See also John J. Rousseau, "The Impact of the Bethsaida Finds," *SBLSP* (1995), ed. Eugene H. Lovering, Jr. (Atlanta: Scholars, 1995) 194: "In the Synoptics the references to boats, fishing, nets, and sailing amount to 92, those to agriculture and shepherding to 141 for a ratio of 9:14."

[58]Freyne, "Jesus and the Urban Culture," 609.

[59]Oakman, *Economic Questions*, 153-56. He writes, "Rather than release from infractions against God, Jesus primarily asked through this petition for release from the earthly shackles of indebtedness. The problem of debt, oppressing the people of Palestine and controlling their lives, is so vast that only God's power can effectively remove it" (155). Oakman also emphasizes the connection of the forgiveness petition with that for daily bread. Indebtedness threatens the ability of people, in fact, to have their daily bread.

[60]On religion as a social entity, see Walter F. Taylor, Jr., "Sociological Exegesis: Introduction to a New Way to Study the Bible. Part I," *TSRev* 11 (1989) 100. On first-century religion as embedded in society, see the articles by Bruce J. Malina, "Religion in the World of Paul: A Preliminary Sketch," *BTB* 16 (1986) 92-101; and "Religion in the Imagined New Testament World: More Social Science Lenses," *Scriptura* 51 (1994) 1-26. For a brief history of the sociological study of the New Testament, see Taylor, "Sociological Exegesis," 100-7.

ology. Rather, it refers to a more specific utilization of sociological theory. So, for example, what theories of leadership might help us to understand Jesus or his first disciples? What theories of conflict might help explain the disagreements between Jesus and the Pharisees?

One of the earliest and most significant applications of sociology to the New Testament was that of Gerd Theissen, who applied to Jesus and the so-called Jesus movement the sociological theory of structural functionalism.[61] For our purposes Theissen made three contributions that are still of interest when we ask about the historical Jesus.

First, Theissen proposed that the social historical view we have already outlined, namely, that strained economic conditions helped lead to the rise of various reform movements within Judaism (including that of Jesus) needs to be modified in an important way.

> One often comes across the rather naïve idea that economic pressure leads to changes of attitude and protest predominantly among the lowest classes. In reality, people are activated above all when their situation threatens to deteriorate or when improvements are in sight: only those who know or can expect better living standards react sensitively to poverty and wretchedness. Thus all trends towards improvements or declines in living standards instigate action, and they can emerge in all levels of society....Consequently we must pay less attention to the absolute extent of economic pressure than to its increase in the case of particular classes; less attention to established levels than to upward and downward trends; less attention to static structures than to change.[62]

The appeal of Jesus, while certainly inclusive of those at or near the bottom of the socio-economic structure, had a particular poignancy to those whose saw their positions in society deteriorating—people such as Galilean fishermen, farmers, and artisans. Thus much of the leadership of the Jesus movement came from people who were experiencing a downward movement in their position in the world.[63] At the same time these people had something to give up when following Jesus. They were not rootless people looking for the next meal but those who had something to lose—and had already been losing it.

Second, Theissen does not think that Jesus established communities of believers. Instead, he sent out groups of itinerant charismatic preachers. Socially, these preachers were outsiders who abandoned home, family, and jobs to proclaim the new era. Others attracted to Jesus stayed at home and formed a second component of Jesus followers, the resident sympathizers or settled hearers. For the study of the historical Jesus, however, what is more important is his somewhat casual observation that the itinerant preachers were similar in many ways to wandering Cynic philosophical preachers: "The wandering Cynic philosophers are in some way analogous to the earliest Christian wandering charismatics. They too seem to have

---

[61]Theissen defines the Jesus movement as "the renewal movement within Judaism brought into being through Jesus and existing in the area of Syria and Palestine between about AD 30 and AD 70" (Gerd Theissen, *Sociology of Early Palestinian Christianity* [Philadelphia: Fortress, 1978] 1).

[62]Ibid., 39-40.

[63]Ibid., 46.

led a vagabond existence and also to have renounced home, families, and posses-sions."[64] Theissen's comparison has been developed by others far beyond his original reference to draw a picture of Jesus himself as a Cynic. Much of the groundwork for that view was laid by F. Gerald Downing, but it is the work of Burton Mack and John Dominic Crossan that has especially brought the Cynic Jesus to the public eye. "The historical Jesus was, then," Crossan concludes, "a *peasant Jewish Cynic.*"[65]

Third, Theissen maintains that there is substantial continuity between Jesus himself and the movement he founded. He argues, in a way similar to, although independent of, Ben Meyer, that one can reason from the movement that resulted from the ministry of Jesus back to the historical Jesus himself.[66] While it is beyond the scope of this paper to develop that insight further, Theissen's thesis presents a challenge to the criterion of dissimilarity and may alter the set of texts from which people seek to determine the historical Jesus.

Horsley agrees with Theissen that the Jesus movement was in part a response to economic and political oppression, as we have seen. He sharply criticizes Theis-sen, however, both at the point of the sociological theory Theissen uses and in Theissen's application of it. Horsley identifies what to him are severe limitations of structural functionalism as a theoretical basis, rejecting it in favor of conflict theory as a more appropriate way to understand Jesus and the Jesus movement.[67] What the Theissen-Horsley debate illustrates is that the scholar seeking to utilize socio-logical theory (or cultural anthropological theory) needs to do more than simply apply a given theory. She or he must also be able to defend the appropriateness of a given theory or school of thought for the biblical question at hand. All sociologi-cal theories are not created equal. The historical Jesus quester thus needs to be as sophisticated in selecting and adopting a theoretical perspective as is the literary critic, narrative critic, or reader-response critic.

V. Cultural Anthropological Study

Scholars of the Bible who utilize cultural anthropology as a tool for their study operate with this thesis: modern readers come to the task of reading the Bible as strangers. How, then, are we able to visit the world of the New Testament? One

---

[64]Ibid., 14-15.

[65]Crossan, *Historical Jesus*, 421. The italics are his. Two studies by Downing enunciate his approach most clearly: *Christ and the Cynics: Jesus and Other Political Preachers in First-Century Tradition* (Sheffield: JSOT, 1988), and *Cynics and Christian Origins* (Edinburgh: T & T Clark, 1992). Burton Mack's chief work is *A Myth of Innocence: Mark and Christian Origins* (Philadelphia: Fortress, 1988). For Mack, what others have identified as earlier Jesus traditions (with emphasis on Jesus' Jewishness and his apocalyptic worldview) are later additions. For a withering critique of the Cynic comparison see Horsley, *Sociology*, 46-47. A more measured critique is provided by Hans Dieter Betz, "Jesus and the Cynics," *JR* 74 (1994) 453-75. See also Ben Witherington III, *The Jesus Quest* (Downers Grove, IL: InterVarsity, 1995) 58-92.

[66]Theissen, *Sociology*, 4. Theissen has reiterated his thesis in an essay printed with the latest edition of Rudolf Bultmann, *Die Geschichte der Synoptischen Tradition. Mit einem Nachwort von Gerd Theissen*, FRLANT 12, 10th ed. (Göttingen: Vandenhoeck & Ruprecht, 1995). See also Ben F. Meyer, *The Aims of Jesus* (London: SCM, 1979).

[67]Horsley, *Sociology*, 9-10, 27, 30-42.

way to visit is to make our journey as theological and literary "ugly Americans," who read first-century texts as though they had been written in the twentieth century. A different way to read the texts is to try to become culturally sensitive visitors who recognize our own culture and its presuppositions while trying sympathetically to enter other cultures. Cultural anthropology, its advocates say, provides us a method of study that enables us to be such culturally sensitive visitors when journeying to the ancient Mediterranean world.

Cultural anthropology is the social scientific study of human culture. Culture, in turn, is defined as "an organized system of symbols by which persons, things, and events are endowed with rather specific and socially shared meanings and values."[68] Cultural anthropological study of the New Testament operates with several presuppositions, two of which are of most immediate interest.[69] The first is that to read texts properly one must be able to interpret the social-cultural system of which they are a part. "To interpret any piece of language adequately," writes Malina, "is to interpret the social system that it expresses."[70] It is for exactly that reason that cultural anthropological models are used, since they are a tool to help us "hear the meaning of the texts in terms of the cultural contexts in which they were originally proclaimed."[71] Without attention to the original cultural contexts, interpreters supply their own contexts, which invariably reflect the contexts of the interpreters rather than those of antiquity.

The second presupposition is that models developed from studies of the Mediterranean region are especially appropriate for New Testament study. During the last two generations the anthropological study of the cultures of the contemporary Mediterranean basin has developed a sophisticated set of models and body of literature. Students of the Bible find the work of anthropologists such as David Gilmore, Jean Peristiany, and Julian Pitt-Rivers to be particularly relevant.[72] Bruce J. Malina and scholars associated with The Context Group, an international team of scholars first assembled in 1986, have made especially fruitful use of such research.

From the perspective of the proponents of cultural anthropology, then, one

---

[68]Bruce J. Malina, *The New Testament World: Insights from Cultural Anthropology,* rev. ed. (Louisville: Westminster/John Knox, 1993) 9.

[69]For a fuller statement of the presuppositions of the use of cultural anthropology in studying the New Testament, see Walter F. Taylor, Jr., "Cultural Anthropology as a Tool for Studying the New Testament—Part I," *TSRev* 18/1 (1996) 15-17.

[70]Bruce J. Malina, *Christian Origins and Cultural Anthropology* (Atlanta: John Knox, 1986) 2.

[71]Malina, *New Testament World,* xiii.

[72]David D. Gilmore, "Anthropology of the Mediterranean Area," *Annual Review of Anthropology* 11 (1982) 175-205; idem, ed., *Honor and Shame and the Unity of the Mediterranean* (Washington, DC: American Anthropological Association, 1987); Jean G. Peristiany, ed., *Contributions to Mediterranean Sociology* (Paris: Mouton, 1965); idem, ed., *Honour and Shame: The Values of Mediterranean Society* (Chicago: University of Chicago, 1966); idem, ed., *Kinship and Modernization in Mediterranean Society* (Rome: Center for Mediterranean Studies, 1976); idem, ed., *Mediterranean Family Structure* (Cambridge: Cambridge University, 1976); idem, ed., with Julian Pitt-Rivers, *Honor and Grace in Anthropology* (Cambridge: Cambridge University, 1992); Julian A. Pitt-Rivers, *The Fate of Shechem or the Politics of Sex: Essays in the Anthropology of the Mediterranean* (Cambridge: Cambridge University, 1977); idem, ed., *Mediterranean Countrymen: Essays on the Social Anthropology of the Mediterranean* (Paris: Mouton, 1963).

cannot hope to reach the historical Jesus or the Jesus of the canonical gospels without utilizing models and data from cultural anthropology, especially that of the Mediterranean region.

VI. HONOR AND SHAME

While we could at this point explore many topics, including the grid-group model, models of the pre-industrial city, patron-client relations, kinship patterns, and the evil eye,[73] we need to limit our examples to two: honor-shame and purity-impurity.

Honor and shame provide our first example of insights to be gained from cultural anthropology. Honor and shame are what anthropologists call values. "The word 'value' describes some general quality and direction of life that human beings are expected to embody in their behavior. A value is a general, normative orientation of action in a social system. It is an emotionally anchored commitment to pursue and support certain directions or types of actions."[74] In the Mediterranean cultures of antiquity honor and shame were, in addition, core values, i.e., values expected in all human interactions.[75]

"'Honor' is a claim to worth (on the part of an individual, family, or group) accompanied by the public acknowledgment of, and respect for, that worth."[76] Honor, therefore, has two parts, one internal and one external: "Honor is the value of a person in his or her own eyes (that is, one's claim to worth) plus that person's value in the eyes of his or her social group."[77] Honor is, moreover, a limited good. There is only so much of it available; no more honor is available in a given society than already exists. Thus a person must always be on guard to make sure that someone else is not taking his or her honor.

Honor is either ascribed or acquired. Ascribed honor comes about because one is honorable or as a grant from someone else who is honorable. Honor can also be acquired by the activities of the individual in the societal "game" called challenge and riposte (see below). Further, honor is gained through beneficence, through giving away rather than keeping one's wealth. Shame is the loss of honor, which occurs when public opinion evaluates the person's deeds as dishonorable or likewise negatively evaluates something that has been done to the person or to (or by) someone who is closely associated with the person (such as a family member).[78]

Social relations, as a result, involve constant challenges to and for one's honor rating. Indeed, "in the first-century Mediterranean world, every social interaction

[73]See Walter F. Taylor, Jr., "Cultural Anthropology as a Tool for Studying the New Testament—Part II," *TSRev* 18/2 (1997) 69-82.

[74]John J. Pilch and Bruce J. Malina, eds., *Biblical Social Values and Their Meaning: A Handbook* (Peabody, MA: Hendrickson, 1993) xiii.

[75]Ibid., xvii. See also the literature cited in n. 70 above.

[76]John H. Elliott, "Disgraced Yet Graced: The Gospel According to 1 Peter in the Key of Honor and Shame," *BTB* 25 (1995) 168.

[77]Bruce J. Malina, *New Testament World*, 31.

[78]On the dyadic (group-oriented) nature of the Mediterranean personality and on the gender aspects of honor and shame, see Taylor, "Cultural Anthropology—Part II," 70.

that takes place outside one's family or outside one's circle of friends is perceived as a challenge to honor."[79] "In these honor and shame cultures, social relations are viewed as essentially conflictual in nature, with life itself constituting one challenge or conflict after another." [80] Since honor is a finite or limited good, if one person gains honor someone else necessarily loses it. A standard way in which honor is gained is by challenging others, calling their honor into question in some way, and winning the challenge. By failing to defend him/herself, the challenged person is shamed. Since Mediterranean life is lived much more publicly than life in the United States, the society is aware of the challenge and response.

Jesus, as presented in the New Testament gospels, is constantly involved in challenge and riposte scenes. In the Gospel of Mark, e.g., five such scenes have been gathered together in the narrative (2:1-12; 2:15-17; 2:18-22; 2:23-28; 3:1-6), and other challenge-riposte scenes are scattered through the rest of the gospel (3:20-35; 7:1-8; 10:1-12; 11:27-33; 12:13-17; 12:18-27). Jesus shows great skill at the "game" and "thereby reveals himself to be an honorable man, capable of defending God's honor, his group's honor, and his own honor."[81] On the other hand, the passion cycle shows a Jesus who is shamed and who acts in dishonorable ways. At Gethsemane Jesus "falls apart" instead of facing his upcoming suffering stoically (14:33-36). His own in-group of followers desert him, with one being so eager to escape he flees naked (14:50-52). Jesus is mocked, i.e., his head and body are dishonored (15:16-20), and he is submitted to a slave's death, with further mocking (15:29-32). "Lastly, he is physically and publicly exposed on the cross, which is the extreme denial of honor, he is closely ranked with criminals, given vinegar to drink, and his clothing (which is an extension of personhood) is divided by lot among the soldiers."[82] The climax of his defeat and dishonor is the cry of dereliction in 15:34. The resurrection, in this model, is not only the vindication of Jesus by God but also ascribing to him the highest honor (Phil 2:5-11).

Mark 6:1-6 gives us an example of a peremptory strike by Jesus in a challenge and riposte setting. Jesus returns to his hometown, presumably Nazareth, where people "take offense at him" when they record his honor rating: a carpenter, who as a traveling artisan was unable to fulfill the proper role of protector of the females in his life; the son of Mary, an unusual designation that raises questions about the identity of his father, since the normative phrase would be "son of Joseph"; and the brother of men and women known to the Nazarenes. By what right did a person with such a modest honor rating teach in the synagogue? In the Markan story Jesus does not wait for the people to draw their final conclusions. He takes the offensive

[79]Malina, *New Testament World*, 37.

[80]Elliott, "Disgraced," 168. Another term for this phenomenon is "agonistic culture," ἀγών being the Greek word for struggle or fight.

[81]Pilch and Malina, *Biblical Social Values*, 100. For an outline of the four stages in a challenge-response scene, see Esler, *First Christians*, 28. For other examples of honor and shame in Mark, see Malina, *New Testament World*, 59-60.

[82]Pilch and Malina, *Biblical Social Values*, 45; see also 44 and 102-3. On the shame of nakedness, see 121. On the whole passion story, see Bruce J. Malina and Richard L. Rohrbaugh, *Social-Science Commentary on the Synoptic Gospels* (Minneapolis: Fortress, 1992) 267-76.

and quotes a proverb, "Prophets are not without honor, except in their hometown, and among their own kin, and in their own house" (6:4). As John Pilch phrases it, "With one fell swoop Jesus insults his neighbors, his relatives, and his family. He shames them before they can shame him." Indeed, says Pilch, Jesus was "a shrewd man of his culture. He could readily size up a situation and respond with a perfectly appropriate comment. In the vast majority of instances, the perfectly appropriate comment is an insult. Throughout the Gospels, Jesus demonstrates that he is a master of insult."[83]

VII. PURITY AND IMPURITY

Our second example deals with another pervasive reality of first-century Jewish culture: purity and impurity. The work of the anthropologist Mary Douglas has been eminently helpful in understanding what at first may seem to be a strange phenomenon.[84] Purity and impurity have to do with boundaries. Boundaries are drawn by all cultures and serve to define what is "clean," unpolluted, or pure and what is "unclean," polluted, or impure. "The process of ordering a sociocultural system was called 'purity,' in contrast to 'pollution,' which stands for the violation of the classification system, its lines and boundaries."[85] Purity, then, is the "system of space and time lines that human groups develop to have everything in its place and a place for everything."[86] In America, where people think they do not have purity rules, purity and impurity are expressed by terms such as deviant or normal, and legal or illegal.

Douglas illustrates the basic concept of purity-impurity by means of the term dirt. "Dirt" is matter that is out of place. Soil found in one's garden or on a farm is not dirt, for soil found in garden or farm is soil that is in place. If, however, the gardener or farmer comes into the house with muddy shoes and proceeds to deposit muddy soil on the kitchen floor and the living room carpet, what was outside the house labeled as good soil now becomes "dirt," since it is out of place.[87] What is "in place" and what is "out of place" can likewise refer to behavior. "Dirt" always implies a larger framework:

> It [dirt] implies two conditions: a set of ordered relations and a contravention of that order. Dirt, then, is never a unique isolated event. Where there is dirt there is a system. Dirt is the by-product of a systematic ordering and classification of matter, in so far as ordering involves rejecting inappropriate elements.[88]

[83]John J. Pilch, *The Cultural World of Jesus: Sunday by Sunday, Cycle B* (Collegeville, MN: The Liturgical Press, 1996) 107. For more on honor and shame, see Halvor Moxnes, "Honor and Shame," in *The Social Sciences and New Testament Interpretation*, ed. Richard Rohrbaugh (Peabody, MA: Hendrickson, 1996) 19-40.

[84]Mary Douglas, *Purity and Danger: An Analysis of the Concepts of Pollution and Taboo* (London: Routledge and Kegan Paul, 1966); idem, "Pollution," in *The International Encyclopedia of the Social Sciences*, ed. David Stills, 18 vols. (New York: Macmillan, 1968-79) 12:336-42; idem, *Natural Symbols: Explorations in Cosmology* (New York: Vintage Books, 1973).

[85]Jerome H. Neyrey, "The Idea of Purity in Mark's Gospel," *Semeia* 35 (1986) 91.

[86]Malina, *Origins*, 20.

[87]Mary Douglas, *Implicit Meanings* (London: Routledge and Kegan Paul, 1975) 51.

[88]Douglas, *Purity and Danger*, 35.

Nor is that system capricious in origin. The purity-impurity lines express the culture's abstract values. "Purity arrangements help people to make sense of the significant features of their experience by marking off a place for everything. Purity arrangements likewise structure values by defining what is valuable and important."[89] More specifically, a culture needs to express and, in a sense, embody its core values. The central value helps determine how events, people, and actions are classified. "The core value, moreover, is replicated throughout the system, giving it direction, clarity, and consistency. What accords with this value and its structural expression is 'pure'; what contravenes it in any way is 'polluted.'"[90]

The ordering of reality in any culture results in lists or "maps" that indicate the proper ordering of life in relation to that culture's core value. The core value for Judaism in antiquity was God's holiness. For first-century Jewish Palestine, the resulting maps are maps or lists of holiness: maps of places in terms of their degree of holiness, of people, of potential marriage partners, of times, of uncleanness, of things, of meals.[91] Since the individual human body replicates the culture's core value and its concern for maintaining that value, the body also becomes an object of potential holiness (purity) or potential unholiness (impurity). The boundaries of the body become, therefore, the objects of special attention.

For the purity system of first-century Judaism and for our purposes in studying the historical Jesus, the boundaries of the body are of particular consequence. Those boundaries include both bodily surfaces (skin and hair; by extension, clothing) as well as the body's orifices. The orifices

> are gateways to the body interior, just as walled cities have gates, and countries have ports of entry and customs checkpoints. These orifices are the object of great scrutiny; for, since they are the gates to the interior, they must screen out what does not belong and guard against a pollutant entering within. The guarded orifices tend to be the eyes, mouth, ears, genitals, and anus.[92]

In terms of Mark 7, the text to which we will turn shortly, the chief interest is in the mouth and the need to guard it against unclean foods that would pollute the body.

In Mark 7:1-23 we have typical challenge and riposte material in which the Pharisees and scribes challenge Jesus because of the behavior of his disciples, to which Jesus responds. The unholy behavior observed by the Pharisees and scribes is the failure of Jesus' disciples to conform to the traditional norms of the Pharisaic understanding of Judaism. The opponents challenge Jesus by means of their criticism of his disciples' actions (not ritually washing their hands). His response or riposte is an insult ("you hypocrites," v. 7) followed by a quotation from Isaiah 29. That in turn is followed by his own charge that his opponents seek to circumvent God's command by means of their traditions. The corban discussion (vv. 9-13) is his proof. Jesus then makes the conflict more public by calling in the crowd to witness his next put-down of the opponents (vv. 14-15). The section concludes

[89]Bruce J. Malina, "A Conflict Approach to Mark 7," *Forum* 4 (1988) 12.

[90]Jerome H. Neyrey, "A Symbolic Approach to Mark 7," *Forum* 4 (1988) 66.

[91]See ibid., 67-71, and Neyrey, "Purity," 94-99, for detailed lists.

[92]Neyrey, "Symbolic Approach," 72.

with a private explanation to his disciples (vv. 17-23).[93] As John Pilch summarizes the flow of the narrative:

> The Pharisees hoped to shame Jesus, but Jesus shames them instead by insulting them, quoting Scripture creatively, and hurling a counterchallenge: they value their human tradition much more than the Torah, the Law of Moses.
>
> Next Jesus changes the topic, a strategy he frequently uses in conflict situations. The Pharisees asked about "the way" the disciples ate (with ritually defiled hands). Jesus changes the topic to "what" disciples might eat, that is, defiling and nondefiling foods (v. 15).[94]

Why are the Pharisees so concerned about the purificatory practices of Jesus' disciples? Obviously any behavior that did not yield to the tradition of the Pharisees in some ways threatened that tradition. But in addition to that, purity practices help to define group boundaries. They tell the people in the defined group who they are by telling them who is in the group and who is outside the group. People who did not follow the proper procedures that defined them as Jews (from the Pharisaic perspective) immediately raised questions by their behavior about their loyalty to the people of Israel and to Israel's God. Were Jews no different from gentiles? Were the disciples of Jesus—and implicitly Jesus himself—removing one of the basic marks that distinguished Jew from non-Jew? The larger matrix for their concern is the struggle within Judaism from at least the time of Daniel (165 B.C.) to define what a Jew really is. Each of the many groups within the Judaism of the first century maintained that its way of interpreting Judaism was the correct way. A popular teacher with a growing following and a unique understanding was a threat to all other groups.

The Pharisees had strong purity concerns and therefore set strong boundaries. When the disciples of Jesus (and Jesus) refused to follow the Pharisaic purificatory rules, they were rejecting the entire system developed by the Pharisees to mediate the core value of holiness. The same rejection existed no matter what the rule was: sabbath observance, touching a leper or corpse or being touched by a woman with a flow of blood, fasting, associating with sinners and gentiles, washing hands.[95]

What is the area of the body about which Jesus is concerned, according to Mark? The heart (2:6, 8; 6:52; 8:17; 11:23; 12:30, 33). And so in Mark 7 Jesus criticizes the Pharisees because their heart is far from God (v. 6). Food does not make a person unclean, since food does not enter the heart (v. 19). What does make a person unclean is what comes "from within, from the human heart" (v. 21; see also

---

[93]The preceding is a summary of Malina, "Conflict Approach," 11. Also reflected in the conflicts between Jesus and his opponents is the negative attitude of the Jerusalem religious leadership toward the Galileans of the north.

[94]Pilch, *Cultural World*, 131.

[95]David Rhoads ("Social Criticism: Crossing Boundaries," in *Mark and Method: New Approaches in Biblical Studies*, ed. Janice Capel Anderson and Stephen D. Moore [Minneapolis: Fortress, 1992] 149) lists examples from Mark. See also Neyrey, "Purity," 105-11. As Neyrey writes, "The issue of clean hands, then, symbolizes the issue of purity systems. A lot rides on a little" ("Symbolic Approach," 84). For Paul, the symbol was circumcision.

v. 23). "Jesus' concern, therefore, lies not with bodily surfaces and orifices, but with bodily interior and heart. Hence, lips and mouth do not need to be guarded, but the heart should be constantly examined."[96]

In his focus on the heart, Jesus provides an alternative system of purity. That system is extended to impure (unclean) people, for in his contacts with them Jesus extends cleanness, healing, and/or wholeness (1:41; 2:5, 11, 17, 23-28; 3:1-6; 5:15, 28-29, 41-42; 7:35; 8:25).[97]

In addition to a plethora of intriguing insights, the application of cultural anthropology to the study of the historical Jesus does two things for us. First, such study is cross-cultural and therefore has the potential to enable the interpreter to look at Jesus with eyes other than those of a twentieth-century westerner. Second, such study helps us to identify more closely the issues Jesus confronted in his ministry and in his life. Cultural anthropology can help us understand how his words "cut," as we come perhaps several steps closer to grasping what Jesus meant. We meet in that process a Jesus who challenged in even stronger and more pointed ways than previously thought the dominant social and political structures of his day. Or, if the interpreter does not agree with the words "stronger" and "more pointed," at a minimum she or he might well agree that the use of cultural anthropology helps us to see that Jesus challenges his era's assumptions in ways different from what we previously thought.

VIII. CONCLUSION

We opened with a remark about the heady academic champagne being drunk these days regarding the search for the historical Jesus. We have sampled from several different vineyards the results of planning, planting, plucking, and processing. Some may wish to keep the resulting scholarly wines separate and pure. Others, including this author, anticipate that the greatest contribution will come in the blending of the different vintages.

Our study of Jesus within his social world has yielded the following general results, in addition to the specific insights already detailed:

- insights from the social world of the first century based on archaeology, sociology, and cultural anthropology do not provide a magic solution to reconstructing the historical Jesus, but they do provide crucial interpretative frameworks in general and often significant interpretative keys to specific texts. It is more problematic to use these approaches to identify a specific saying or event as going back to the earthly Jesus

[96]Neyrey, "Symbolic Approach," 86. Two good introductions to purity in the New Testament are Rhoads, "Social Criticism," 143-59; and Jerome H. Neyrey, "Clean/Unclean, Pure/Polluted, and Holy/Profane: The Idea and the System of Purity," in *The Social Sciences and New Testament Interpretation*, 80-104.

[97]The passages are gathered by Neyrey, "Purity," 112. He also provides a summary chart comparing the purity systems of the Pharisees and Jesus (116); see also Rhoads, "Social Criticism," 151-52. On other elements of Jesus "program," see Neyrey, "Purity," 119-23, and Rhoads, "Social Criticism," 154-58.

- Jesus can no longer be understood simply as a backwater rural figure who has no contact with the broader Greco-Roman world. The value of that observation is compromised by excessive claims at either end of the spectrum. Thus Sanders is much too dismissive of Greco-Romanization in first-century Galilee. Many members of the Jesus Seminar, on the other hand, seem to posit a Jesus so thoroughly hellenized that one wonders if they think he was a Jew at all. Thus Crossan's label of Jesus as a Jewish Cynic seems to be an oxymoron. The next step beyond the current work of the Jesus Seminar is to ask more profoundly this question: How do we understand Jesus as a Jew within the context of Greco-Romanization?

- archaeological and sociological study are of inestimable value in setting the broader political and social setting within which Jesus lived and ministered. The work of Horsley is a positive example of what we can learn from social history, and he generally operates with a level of care in applying insights that is more well-developed than sometimes one finds in members of the Jesus Seminar. The use of archaeology and sociology is a reminder that a historical Jesus reconstructed from acontextual, isolated sayings is at best a sketchy figure—or even a stick figure

- cultural anthropology provides a cross-cultural resource that better enables interpreters to understand the dynamics and meanings of Jesus' actions and words by placing him firmly within the culture of which he was a part. Cultural anthropology may thereby help to sharpen the criterion of dissimilarity by showing more exactly where Jesus is the same as *and* different from those around him. At the same time cultural anthropology helps to raise questions about over-reliance on dissimilarity, which focuses on the uniquenesses of Jesus and not the ways in which he reflected his culture's perspectives. Dissimilarity, in fact, is probably the quintessential *western* criterion for determining an authentic saying of Jesus, since it reflects the west's attention to individualism. The way scholars have traditionally gone about their historical Jesus task thus tends to produce a western rather than a near eastern Jesus. One could critique the Jesus Seminar from just that perspective

- the student of Jesus who uses the methods we have investigated needs to be ready to engage in theoretical discussion about the methodologies used. Crossan, for example, is among the most sophisticated questers in his use of the social sciences. But can the construction of a pan-Mediterranean culture based on field work among *modern* Mediterranean people be utilized without argument or qualification as a key to understanding the Jesus of the first century?

- finally, how might the methodologies discussed in this article be useful in ministry? Their basic value consists in the new and renewed questions they bring to the study of the text and ultimately to the study of the historical Jesus. The value of the questions brought by contemporary archaeology, sociology, and cultural anthropology is seen in the way our understandings of early

Christianity have changed as a result of using their questions and approaches. The three methodologies, in different ways, have more firmly anchored the study of the New Testament in the cultures and societies within which its documents were written and read—which is to say, these methodologies have further incarnated for us the first-century world. The many new insights we have encountered in this article point to even more new possibilities for application and proclamation

Given the fruitful contributions of these methodologies for understanding Jesus, it is hard to imagine their absence from future scholarly menus designed to investigate the historical Jesus. ⊕

Word & World
Supplement Series 3
1997

Jesus as Wisdom in the New Testament

DIANE JACOBSON

Luther Seminary
St. Paul, Minnesota

A S A PROFESSOR OF OLD TESTAMENT, MY INTEREST IN THIS PAPER IS THE wisdom literature of the Old Testament and the Apocrypha, primarily Proverbs, Job, Qoheleth, Sirach, Baruch, and Wisdom of Solomon. I am particularly interested in the literary figure of woman wisdom found in this literature. After fifteen years of teaching this material I am more and more drawn to echoes of wisdom found in the New Testament, particularly in the picture of Jesus. I didn't look for these echoes under the influence of the third wave of the quest for Jesus. I didn't come with an agenda to find a kinder, gentler Jesus or to undermine belief in his death and resurrection. In fact, I, like many of my generation of scholars, thought that most of the connections between Old Testament and New Testament came through some sort of *heilsgeschichtlich* or prophecy/fulfillment connection. I looked to the prophetic, psalmic, and apocalyptic literature for ties. Even in Old Testament studies, wisdom always played second fiddle to the "real" biblical books in Torah and prophets.[1] The notion that wisdom might be important, even crucial, for New Testament studies as well as Old, had not crossed my mind—with one significant exception. My teacher Raymond Brown, himself trained in ancient near eastern studies, argued early on that the Gospel of John reflected not so much pure hellenistic or gnostic influence as influence from the hellenized Old Testament figure of wisdom.[2] As it turns out, and as other scholars were just beginning

---

[1]See J. Crenshaw, "Prolegomenon," in *Studies in Ancient Israelite Wisdom*, ed. J. Crenshaw (New York: KTAV, 1976) 1ff., for some possible explanations for this neglect.

[2]See Raymond E. Brown, *The Gospel According to John: A New Translation with Introduction and Commentary*, 2 vols., AB 29-29A (Garden City, NY: Doubleday, 1966), especially LII-LXIV. If I had had ears to hear, I would also have heard early rumbling from Bultmann and others.

to intuit, the connection between Jesus and wisdom in John was just the tip of the iceberg.

The discovery of the influence of wisdom on the New Testament has now come into its own and with it an onslaught of theories, perspectives, and, not surprisingly, naysayers and critics. Some say that wisdom stands at the center of New Testament christology; some say it is incidental at best. I would like to do three things: first, indicate some aspects of wisdom thinking and some features of the figure of woman wisdom that are crucial to the discussion of Jesus as wisdom; then, look into connections between Jesus and wisdom in two gospels—John and Matthew; finally, introduce some of the critical questions involved in this study and indicate where this study intersects with the quest for the historical Jesus and Christian faith.

I. Wisdom in Jewish Tradition

We begin by looking at wisdom in Proverbs. Formally wisdom material is made up of teaching material: proverbs, instructions, disputations, aphorisms, psalms, etc.[3] Using these forms, the Old Testament sages passed on observations about how the world works. They gave advice through which they hoped to form character and shape society. Additionally, the sages engaged in a more philosophical or theological quest. They tried to discover how God is involved with the world. They asked questions of theodicy, about how God is related to and communicates with humanity, about the meaning of life. In and among all the proverbs and instructions, these sages made use of metaphors to plumb the depths of those big questions. The central metaphor in much of the material was the figure of woman wisdom. Texts about her are found principally in Proverbs 1-9, Job 28, and throughout Sirach, Baruch, and Wisdom of Solomon. I want to concentrate on two aspects of this figure: images used and ideas behind the images.

In Prov 1:20-33, wisdom is pictured as a prophet.[4] As prophet, wisdom stands at the city gates and calls out to the people to follow her by heeding her reproof and responding to her call, which they have previously refused. She issues warnings and reproaches. To those who ignore her, she proclaims:

> Then they will call upon me, but I will not answer; they will *seek* me diligently, but will not *find* me....Therefore they shall eat the fruit of their way and be sated with their own devices....But those who listen to me will be secure and will live at ease, without dread of disaster. (Prov 1:28-33)

That is, wisdom rejects those who reject her and abides with those who heed her call.

---

[3]For details about Old Testament wisdom forms, see R. E. Murphy, "Form Criticism and Wisdom Literature," *CBQ* 31 (1969) 475-485; idem, *Wisdom Literature*, FOTL 13 (Grand Rapids: Eerdmans, 1983); Carol Fontaine, *Traditional Sayings in the Old Testament: A Contextual Study* (Sheffield: Almond, 1982); James G. Williams, *Those Who Ponder Proverbs* (Sheffield: Almond, 1981).

[4]See Phyllis Trible, "Wisdom Builds a Poem," *JBL* 94 (1975) 509-518. For this image and those which follow, also see Claudia Camp, *Wisdom and the Feminine in the Book of Proverbs* (Decatur, GA: Almond, 1985).

In Proverbs 8, woman wisdom is portrayed first as a teacher and sage who also stands at the gate. She teaches only truth, the opposite of which is not falsehood, but wickedness. By means of wisdom rulers rule justly, and all who follow her walk along righteous paths. Then, wisdom's portrayal takes a new and startling turn: "The LORD created[5] me at the beginning of his work, the first of his acts of long ago" (v. 22).

In this verse, wisdom is portrayed as a child of God, God's daughter. She was the first of God's acts of long ago; she was with God before the beginning of the earth. In the verses which follow, she announces that she, wisdom, was there when, or perhaps *in*, God's specific acts of creating heaven, earth, and sea. She is minimally a witness, more probably an associate in God's initial creation. She is thus part architect and master planner, and part dancing child, an unlikely combination captured in a Hebrew pun: "Then I was beside him, like a master worker [little child]; and I was daily his delight, rejoicing before him always, rejoicing in his inhabited world and delighting in the human race" (vv. 30-31).[6]

Wisdom is portrayed here as a mediating figure between God and humanity. In the beginning and within creation she works and plays before God, and then she calls to humanity with these words: "And now, my children, listen to me: happy are those who keep my ways....For whoever finds me finds life and obtains favor from the LORD; but those who miss me injure themselves; all who hate me love death" (vv. 32, 36).

Note that Proverbs 8 continues the contrast between those who accept wisdom and those who reject her: one gets life, the other death.

The portrait of wisdom continues:

Wisdom has built her house, she has hewn her seven pillars.
She has slaughtered her animals, she has mixed her wine, she has also set her table.
She has sent out her servant girls, she calls from the highest places in the town,
"You that are simple, turn in here!" To those without sense she says,
"Come, eat of my bread and drink of the wine I have mixed.
Lay aside immaturity, and live, and walk in the way of insight."...
For by me your days will be multiplied, and years will be added to your life.
(Prov 9:1-6, 11)

Here wisdom calls to humanity like a lover, like a wife, and like a wise woman. She builds up the household; she sends out her maidens; she sets the table inviting the simple to eat of her bread and drink of her wine. Some see this last behavior as priestly, others see a superattenuated version of the woman of worth, described in the final chapter of Proverbs.[7]

---

[5]The Hebrew word is קנה, better translated here "procreated." For this meaning, see Bruce Vawter, "Proverbs 8:22: Wisdom and Creation," *JBL* 99 (1980) 205-16.

[6]The unpointed Hebrew is אמון. If pointed אָמוּן, it means "little child." If pointed אָמוֹן, it means "master-worker" or "architect." Notice that everything that comes before this word would suggest the metaphor "master-worker," while the remainder of verses 30-31 suggest "little child."

[7]See Camp, *Wisdom*, and Carole Fontaine, "Proverbs," in *The Women's Bible Commentary*, ed. Carol Newsom and Sharon Ringe (Louisville: Westminster, 1992).

Two more images of woman wisdom found in Proverbs are worthy of note. In Prov 3:18, wisdom is called a "tree of life to those who lay hold of her,"[8] and Prov 16:22 reads, "Wisdom is a fountain of life to one who has it."[9] These images are stunning because, along with the picture of wisdom as God's child, her association with kings and with creation, and her gifts of truth and life, these images point to an underlying association between the figure of woman wisdom and certain manifestations of Egyptian and Canaanite goddesses.[10] The sages made use of this goddess imagery while very carefully avoiding making wisdom into a goddess. They used the language for the purpose of marking wisdom's unmatched close association with God.

The portrait of woman wisdom in Proverbs is able to accomplish a number of purposes: (1) She undergirds the divine authority of the wisdom of the sages. Humans are called upon to follow her. They can do this, according to Proverbs, by following the advice of the sages. (2) Woman wisdom provides the key to understanding the world and how it works. If you are searching for the glue that holds the world together, that keeps the world an ordered place, look to wisdom who is manifest cosmically, socially, and personally. Here a caveat is called for. In Job 28, only God knows the way to wisdom, so while humans can have faith that God understands how the world works, they cannot discover wisdom on their own. (3) Woman wisdom becomes a mediator between God and humanity. Through wisdom, God communicates divine order, purpose, will, and justice. Here the power of the metaphor is most apparent. Cosmic order and divine intention are not conceived abstractly. On the contrary, only a metaphor that portrays a dynamic relationship, personal and living rather than static, can adequately represent this mediating reality. A pure abstraction will not suffice for the living God.

Now, one can argue that woman wisdom is a fairly minor character or metaphor in the Old Testament. She is confined to one, perhaps two books. This is true, but her portrayal broadens and takes on great variety in the intertestamental wisdom books. One can offer a number of reasons for the increased interest, but central among them are apologetic and didactic concerns. These writers were trying to keep their young men down on the Jewish farm after they had experienced the "Paree" of hellenism.

Sirach, written in Jerusalem about 180 B.C., expands upon many of the images of woman wisdom already found in Proverbs. We find wisdom offering bread to eat and water to drink (15:3; 24:19, 21). She is an ever flowing river (24:30-31) and a tree whose branches are long life (1:20). In chapter 24, the tree becomes a vine with branches whose fruit is abundant and glorious (24:16-17). In Sirach, unlike Proverbs, wisdom is very clearly a creation of God, made not begotten. She first dwells with God in heaven, but then she is given a command by God to tabernacle, to make her home, among the people of Israel. She thus descends from heaven to

[8]See also Prov 11:30; 13:12; 15:4; cf. 12:12.

[9]See also Prov 10:11; 13:14; 14:27; cf. 18:4; 25:26.

[10]See Camp, *Wisdom*, and Bernhard Lang, *Wisdom and the Book of Proverbs: An Israelite Goddess Redefined* (New York: Pilgrim, 1986).

earth and finds a specific home in Israel by becoming embodied in torah. Wisdom in Sirach is identified with and as torah.

Most scholars say that this identification of wisdom and torah is original with Sirach and very surprising. But I would contend that similar connections were already suggested in certain Old Testament torah psalms.[11] In these psalms, as in Sirach, the cosmic wisdom of the universe is equated with torah.[12] Thus, an Israelite wishing to be wise and to live according to divine wisdom need only love and obey that which is already revealed, God's holy torah. Israelites need not search elsewhere for wisdom, because she stands before them. This identification between wisdom and torah becomes solidified in Pharisaic and Rabbinic Judaism.[13]

Wisdom of Solomon, written between 50 B.C. and 30 A.D. in Alexandria, takes yet another path. Unlike Sirach, who generally resists the surrounding hellenistic culture,[14] Wisdom of Solomon is a thoroughly hellenised Jewish work, written to convince Jews in Alexandria that Judaism has more wisdom to offer than either Greek philosophy or the Isis cult.[15] In Wisdom of Solomon, the figure of woman wisdom, now sophia,[16] is transformed by hellenistic vocabulary and thought.

As in Proverbs and Sirach, wisdom brings life, but now that life is eternal life, immortality, which leads to a kingdom (6:17-20; cf. 8:13). She lives with God who loves her, and she is an associate in his works (8:3-4). Wisdom fashions what exists (8:6), has foreknowledge of signs and wonders (8:8), and is said to have acted very directly within Israel's history. That is, wisdom delivered Adam (10:1), recognized and preserved Noah (10:5), rescued Lot and Jacob and Joseph (10:6, 10-12, 13-14), and guided Israel through the wilderness (10:15-11:14) by, among other things, "entering the soul of Moses."

In Wisdom of Solomon, sophia is compared to light and found superior (7:29-30); she is identified as a spirit (1:6; 7:22; 9:17). She is said to be "a breath of the power of God," "a pure emanation of the glory of the Almighty," "a reflection of eternal light," and "a spotless mirror of the working of God" (7:25-26). Such claims move the personification of wisdom to a new level in her relationship with the divine. This description is then followed by a verse which becomes very important in certain speculative theories about the identification of Jesus: "Though she is but one, she can do all things, and while remaining in herself, she renews all things; in

---

[11]For the category "torah psalm," a designation which overlaps with but is not the equivalent of "wisdom psalm," see James L. Mays, "The Place of Torah Psalms in the Psalter," *JBL* 106 (1987) 3-12.

[12]In the beginning of Psalm 19, for example, the firmament declares God's handiwork without words, but later in the psalm, the particular words of torah are declared to be perfect, true, and enduring forever. Similarly , in the very middle of Psalm 119, the long love song to torah, the psalmist declares that the "word" of the Lord "is firmly fixed in the heavens" (v. 89).

[13]See, for example, *Midrash Rabbah* on Gen 1:1.

[14]Though resisted, a certain amount of hellenistic influence is certainly to be found in Sirach. See A. Di Lella, "Conservative and Progressive Theology: Sirach and Wisdom," in *Studies in Ancient Israelite Wisdom*, 401-416, and Jack T. Sanders, *Ben Sira and Demotic Wisdom* (Chico, CA: Scholars, 1983).

[15]See John S. Kloppenborg, "Isis and Sophia in the Book of Wisdom," *HTR* 75/1 (1982) 57-84.

[16]In fact, חָכְמָה, Hebrew for "wisdom" is already translated into Greek σοφία in the LXX and in the Greek version of Sirach.

every generation she passes into holy souls and makes them friends of God, and prophets" (7:27). This verse, together with the verse about Moses and an overall impression given in Wisdom of Solomon, becomes central to the theory that sophia, who herself resides in heaven, regularly sends envoys and prophets to deliver her message.

Woman wisdom has quite a different face in Wisdom of Solomon. She overlaps with wisdom as we have known her, but the shift in language has a profound effect. Sophia is more ephemeral, spiritual, and exalted than in Proverbs or Sirach. This book in particular invites us into the world of wisdom speculation about Jesus. For now we have a very extravagantly developed metaphorical figure which has the potential to help Christians of the first and second centuries to make sense of Jesus.

Now, to the question at hand: What does all of this have to do with Jesus either historically or in the portraits drawn of Jesus by the writers of the New Testament? My answer: more than many are willing to say, but less than others claim.

II. Jesus and Wisdom in John and Matthew

In my opinion, some influence of wisdom thinking is apparent in much of the literature of the New Testament: in all of the gospels, in Paul, in the pseudo-Pauline books, and in James. But two preliminary comments deserve emphasis: First, none of the writers in the New Testament describe Jesus exclusively in terms of wisdom. We are here talking about only one stream of characterization among many. Second, the various writers come to quite different conclusions about the nature of the relationship between Jesus and wisdom. James is a straightforward book of Christian wisdom instruction. Luke, I think, portrays Jesus more as a wisdom teacher or, possibly, as wisdom's envoy. Paul emphasizes Christ crucified as the wisdom of God. But the two books I will look at in more detail, John and Matthew, both identify Jesus directly as woman wisdom, that is, Jesus is incarnate wisdom. Somewhere in this mix is the historical Jesus. We will look at the work of these two gospels before we turn to the question of Jesus himself and the various critical issues which remain to be addressed.

A. Wisdom in John

Wisdom abounds in the book of John. Many of the connections were observed already by Ray Brown in his two-volume commentary. As I have read subsequent scholarly investigations on wisdom in John, there is little that Brown did not observe first.[17]

I will concentrate on three types of evidence pointing to the identification of woman wisdom and Jesus in John and add a nod towards a fourth: the λόγος hymn; the "I am" speeches; Jesus' relationship with his disciples; and the possible pattern of wisdom descending from heaven, being rejected, and returning to heaven. The links I propose are sketched out in the chart of parallel texts on pp. 78-81.

[17]Brown, *John*, CXXII-CXXV.

PARALLELS BETWEEN JESUS IN JOHN AND WOMAN WISDOM

John 1:1-3
In the beginning was the Word, and the Word was with God, and the Word was God. He was in the beginning with God; all things were made through him, and without him was not anything made that was made.

John 17:5 (last discourse)
So now, Father, glorify me in your own presence with the glory that I had in your presence before the world existed.

Proverbs 8:22-23
The Lord created me at the beginning of his work, the first of his acts of old. Ages ago I was set up, at the first, before the beginning of the earth.

Sirach 24:9
Before the ages, in the beginning, he created me, and for all the ages I shall not cease to be.

Wisdom of Solomon 9:1-2, 9
O God of my ancestors and Lord of mercy, who have made all things by your word, and by your wisdom have formed humankind....With you is wisdom, she who knows your works and was present when you made the world.

John 1:4-5
In him was life, and the life was the light of all people. The light shines in the darkness, and the darkness did not overcome it.

John 8:12
Again Jesus spoke to them, saying, "I am the light of the world. Whoever follows me will never walk in darkness but will have the light of life."

John 9:5
"As long as I am in the world, I am the light of the world."

Proverbs 8:35
For whoever finds me finds life and obtains favor from the Lord.

Wisdom of Solomon 8:13
Because of her I shall have immortality.

Wisdom of Solomon 7:26, 29
For she is a reflection of eternal light....She is more beautiful than the sun, and excels every constellation of the stars. Compared with the light she is found to be superior.

Baruch 4:2
Turn, O Jacob, and take her; walk toward the shining of her light.

Proverbs 8:31
...rejoicing in his inhabited world and delighting in the human race.

John 1:10
He was in the world, and the world came into being through him; yet the world did not know him.

Proverbs 1:30
[They] would have none of my counsel, and despised all my reproof.

John 1:12
But to all who received him, who believed in his name, he gave power to become children of God.

Wisdom of Solomon 7:27b
In every generation she passes into holy souls and makes them friends of God, and prophets.

PARALLELS BETWEEN JESUS IN JOHN AND WOMAN WISDOM

John 1:14
And the Word became flesh and dwelt among us, full of grace and truth.

John 6:38-40
For I have come down from heaven, not to do my own will, but the will of him who sent me. And this is the will of him who sent me, that I should lose nothing of all that he has given me, but raise it up on the last day. This is indeed the will of my Father, that all who see the Son and believe in him may have eternal life.

Proverbs 8:2-3a, 31
On the heights, beside the way, at the crossroads she takes her stand; beside the gates in front of the town....rejoicing in his inhabited world and delighting in the human race.

Baruch 3:37
Afterward she appeared on earth and lived with humankind.

Sirach 24:8
Then the Creator of all things gave me a command, and my Creator chose the place for my tent. He said, "Make your dwelling in Jacob, and in Israel receive your inheritance."

John 1:17
The law indeed was given through Moses; grace and truth came through Jesus Christ.

Sirach 24:23
All this is the book of the covenant of the Most High God, the law that Moses commanded us.

Baruch 4:1
She is the book of the commandments of God, and the law that endures forever. All who hold her fast will live, and those who forsake her will die.

John 6:35
Jesus said to them, "I am the bread of life. Whoever comes to me will never be hungry, and whoever believes in me will never be thirsty."

John 4:13-14
Jesus said to her, "Everyone who drinks of this water will be thirsty again, but those who drink of the water that I will give them will never be thirsty. The water that I will give will become in them a spring of water gushing up to eternal life."

John 7:37-38
While Jesus was standing there, he cried out: "Let anyone who is thirsty come to me, and let the one who believes in me drink. As the scripture has said, 'Out of the believer's heart shall flow rivers of living water.'"

Proverbs 9:5
"Come eat of my bread and drink of the wine I have mixed."

Sirach 15:3
She will feed him with the bread of learning, and give him the water of wisdom to drink.

Sirach 24:19, 21, 30-31
Come to me, you who desire me, and eat your fill of my fruits....
Those who eat of me will hunger for more, and those who drink of me will thirst for more....
As for me, I was like a canal from a river, like a water channel into a garden.
I said, "I will water my garden and drench my flower-beds." And lo, my canal became a river, and my river a sea.

PARALLELS BETWEEN JESUS IN JOHN AND WOMAN WISDOM

John 14:6
Jesus said to him, "I am the way, and the truth, and the life. No one comes to the Father except through me."

John 11:25
Jesus said to her, "I am the resurrection and the life. Those who believe in me, even though they die, will live."

Proverbs 8:7a, 20a, 35a
...for my mouth will utter truth....I walk in the way of righteousness....For whoever finds me finds life.

Baruch 4:1
All who hold her fast will live.

John 15:1, 5
"I am the true vine, and my Father is the vinegrower....I am the vine, you are the branches. Those who abide in me and I in them bear much fruit, because apart from me you can do nothing."

Proverbs 3:18
She is a tree of life to those who lay hold of her; those who hold her fast are called happy.

Sirach 1:20; 24:16-17
To fear the Lord is the root of wisdom; and her branches are long life.
...I spread out my branches, and my branches are glorious and graceful. Like the vine I bud forth delights, and my blossoms become glorious and abundant fruit.

John 1:36-38, 43
...and as [John] watched Jesus walk by, he exclaimed, "Look, here is the Lamb of God!" The two disciples heard him say this, and they followed Jesus. When Jesus turned and saw them following, he said to them, "What are you looking for?" They said to him, "Rabbi" (which translated means Teacher), "where are you staying?"...The next day Jesus decided to go to Galilee. He found Philip and said to him, "Follow me."

Proverbs 1:20-21; 8:1-4, 17b
Wisdom cries aloud in the street; in the markets she raises her voice; on the top of the walls...at the entrance of the city gates.... Does not wisdom call, does not understanding raise her voice? On the heights beside the way, in the paths she takes her stand....and those who seek me diligently find me.

Sirach 4:11
Wisdom teaches her children, and gives help to those who seek her.

Wisdom of Solomon 6:16
...because she goes about seeking those worthy of her, and she graciously appears to them in their paths.

John 7:34; 8:21
"You will search for me, but you will not find me; and where I am, you cannot come."
Again he said to them, "I am going away, and you will search for me, but you will die in your sin. Where I am going, you cannot come."

Proverbs 1:28; 8:17
Then they will call upon me, but I will not answer; they will seek me diligently, but will not find me.
I love those who love me, and those who seek me diligently find me.

Sirach 6:27
Search out and seek, and she will become known to you; and when you get hold of her, do not let her go.

Wisdom of Solomon 6:12
Wisdom...is found by those who seek her.

PARALLELS BETWEEN JESUS IN JOHN AND WOMAN WISDOM

John 3:13	*Baruch 3:29*
No one has ascended into heaven except the one who descended from heaven, the Son of Man.	Who has gone up into heaven and taken her, and brought her down from the clouds?
	Enoch 42:1-2
	Wisdom could not find a place in which she could dwell; but a place was found (for her) in the heavens. Then Wisdom went out to dwell with the children of the people, but she found no dwelling place. (So) Wisdom returned to her place and she settled permanently among the angels.

The λόγος hymn (John 1:1-18) has been long recognized for its links with wisdom. Sophia was already linked to λόγος in Wisdom of Solomon, a link that was also made by Philo.[18] This link between word and wisdom is also anticipated in the torah psalms and in Sirach. Woman wisdom's place at the beginning of creation, as one through whom all things were made, is also well established. What is startling in John is the masculine gender: *"He* was in the beginning with God." But what is dramatically important is the claim that the word was not only *with* God, but actually *was* God. Not even Wisdom of Solomon goes this far. Significantly John makes this new claim while also holding on to the earlier notion that wisdom was also *with* God. Thus he maintains both identity and difference. John goes on to identify this λόγος as one in whom there is life and light. The claim to give life is central to wisdom's identity. Though this gift becomes the gift of immortality only in Wisdom of Solomon, wisdom's gift of life always promised more than mere existence. Wisdom's gift was true life, and both Baruch and Wisdom of Solomon associated this gift with light.

Verses 10-12 of John's hymn introduce the notion that many in this world reject this λόγος, while those who believe receive power. This theme, to which I will return, of wisdom's rejection by some and acceptance by others, is already present in wisdom's prophetic speech in Proverbs 1.[19]

Verse 14 is considered by many to be the quintessential incarnational verse, marking Jesus as unique. But very clearly woman wisdom also appears on earth throughout the wisdom tradition. She stands in public places and wanders around calling to people. Very specifically, she is commanded by God in Sir 24:8 to make her dwelling, to tabernacle, in Israel. The Greek word for dwelling is σκηνήν, tent, just as in John the λόγος is said to ἐσκήνωσεν, to tent among us. The tie is apparent. Still the unique claim of the text is also there, primarily in the form of an argument that becomes more explicit in verse 17. John declares, "The law (νόμος)[20] indeed

---

[18]See Pheme Perkins, "Jesus, God's Wisdom," *WW* 7/3 (1987) 273.

[19]Note also that in Prov 8:32 those who respond to wisdom's appeal are addressed by her as children.

[20]תּוֹרָה is consistently translated νόμος in the LXX. Both terms are used much more broadly than the English word "law"; the lack of an appropriate English equivalency has caused no end of interpretative difficulties.

was given through Moses; grace and truth came through Jesus Christ." Sirach identifies tabernacled wisdom as torah. John says no; wisdom is incarnate not in law, but rather in Jesus Christ, finally named in v. 17, in contrast with Moses, the giver of torah. Jesus, not torah, is the one who bestows grace and truth.[21]

One of John's major means of identifying Jesus as wisdom is the various "I am" speeches. Traditionally, Jesus' use of "I am" in John has been associated with the divine name, thus undergirding Jesus' divine claims. I have little doubt that this conclusion is true. But throughout the wisdom material, woman wisdom also speaks in the first person. And when one looks at the specific predicates which complete the "I am" claims, the association with wisdom is undeniable. Note, for example, the claim that Jesus was "the light," made already in the λόγος hymn and repeated in 8:12 and 9:5, where Jesus says, "I am the light of the world." Images of walking on right paths and contrasts of wisdom's light with darkness are found throughout the texts about woman wisdom.

Jesus declares in John 6:35, "I am the bread of life; whoever believes in me shall not hunger, and whoever believes in me shall never thirst." Most remarkable here is the contrast with Sir 24:19, 21: "Come to me, you who desire me, and eat your fill of my produce....Those who eat me will hunger for more, and those who drink me will thirst for more." Once again the argument with Sirach is explicit. Torah is never finally fulfilling. True fulfillment, true release from hunger and thirst comes with Jesus. This contrast is all the more striking given the frequency in Judaism of associating torah and water.

Jesus' claim in 14:6 to be the way, the truth, and the life has so many ties to the claims of woman wisdom that gathering all the texts would fill up an entire page. These stand at the heart of wisdom's claims. Perhaps more interesting is Jesus' claim, "No one comes to the Father except through me." Jesus' address of God as "Father" may well have had wisdom roots.[22]

Finally, Jesus claims to be the "true vine" (John 15:1). Again the ties with wisdom are clear in Sirach. Of interest there is Sirach's move to identify wisdom as vine after describing wisdom as a tree. Thus wisdom's identity as "tree of life" is indirectly linked to Jesus' identity as true vine. The scriptural depth of both of these images stands behind this identification.[23]

---

[21]John uses the term λόγος, rather than σοφία. One might speculate about the reasons for this: sophia is feminine; sophia is too associated with a goddess; etc. But one might also look at this another way. John needs three crucial ingredients to make his point, and he gets all three by using the term logos: (1) association with woman wisdom—woman wisdom has been explicitly associated with "word" in Wisdom of Solomon and Philo; (2) association with creation—the notion of creation by word is central to Genesis 1; (3) association with torah—torah is identified as "word" any number of places, including Psalms 19 and 119. In addition, of course, John's argument establishes links with the enormous history of λόγος in the Greek world. The contrast with woman wisdom is certainly not the only agenda or message of John 1, but the contrast does constitute a major theme. Moreover, John's argument as well as his identification of Jesus and wisdom continue throughout the gospel.

[22]The address to God as Father is rare in the Old Testament but is found in the prayers of both Sirach and Wisdom of Solomon (Sir 23:1, 4; 51:10; Wis 14:3; note also Wis 11:10 and especially 2:16). This identification might come as a natural address of wisdom, God's daughter, to God. See also Ben Witherington III, *Jesus the Sage* (Minneapolis: Fortress, 1994) 339-340.

[23]Note especially Psalm 80; Isaiah 5; Jeremiah 2; 5; 6; 8; Ezekiel 17; 19; Hosea 10.

The identification of Jesus as wisdom is clear in these speeches, but the associations do not end even there. In each of the first seven chapters of John, Jesus is associated with water. Brown notes that water was a symbol of torah not only in Sirach but also in rabbinic literature and at Qumran.[24] This association lends depth to reading the story of the wedding at Cana as yet another allusion to Jesus as wisdom. The water at Cana is already associated with a Jewish rite. The step to associating the water with torah is not large, though certainly not as explicit. Jesus, true wisdom, turns the water of legal requirements into superior wine. Jesus, like wisdom in Proverbs 9, becomes the true host of the feast. The story thus provides an interesting alternative to the way that Matthew and particularly Luke deal with the motif of wisdom hosting the banquet.

The wedding at Cana is the first story in John after Jesus calls the disciples. The action of calling disciples also adds to the picture of Jesus as wisdom.[25] Like wisdom, Jesus has followers. Like wisdom's followers, they both *seek* to find him and are *sought out* by him. Like wisdom, Jesus cries aloud in public places. Like wisdom, Jesus addresses his followers as children. Like wisdom, Jesus makes disciples into friends. Like wisdom, Jesus enjoins his followers to love him and gives love in return. The mutual relationship of love is key for both the relationship between wisdom and her followers and for Jesus and his. Particularly instructive is the link between love and commandment: "They who have my commandments and keep them are those who love me; and those who love me will be loved by my Father, and I will love them and reveal myself to them" (John 14:21). By connecting love and commandment, John once again pits the identification of Jesus as wisdom over against her identification as torah.

Finally, as is true for wisdom, so also for Jesus in John, though some disciples heed the call, others turn away. They reject not only the message, but more significantly they reject the messenger. We caught a glimpse of this theme of rejection already in the λόγος hymn, but it extends far beyond that point. Catherine Cory incorporates this theme into the tabernacles discourse in John 7:1-8:59.[26] She suggests that this discourse can be read as a rescue of Jesus, the wisdom of God, from enemy hands, from those who reject him. In this she sees a foreshadowing of Jesus' being lifted up in death as a vindication of Jesus. In death, Jesus is lifted up as wisdom, able to judge those who have rejected him. She thus claims that Jesus' death and ascension are not outside of John's portrait of Jesus as wisdom.

With this claim, Cory joins others who see reflected in John's portrait of Jesus, as well as in Matthew and in the early christological hymns, a particular pattern of

---

[24]Brown, *John*, 328.

[25]For what follows, see the expansive list of parallels in Brown, *John*, CXXIII, and the comments of Witherington, *Jesus the Sage*, 378-379.

[26]Catherine Cory, "Wisdom's Rescue: A New Reading of the Tabernacles Discourse (John 7:1-8:59)," *JBL* 116/1 (1997) 95-116.

behavior based on the character of woman wisdom.[27] This pattern is most clearly articulated in Enoch 42 (the final text on the chart of parallels). This so-called V pattern or vindication pattern centers on the idea that wisdom, who resides in heaven, descends to earth, hoping to dwell there. On earth wisdom is met with rejection, so she ascends once again to heaven, where her vindication is marked by the judgment of those who rejected her. The pattern varies among those who suggest it, and certainly many reject it out of hand.[28] Ben Witherington claims that the basic pattern is discernible in all of the early christological hymns. He suggests that in the λόγος hymn, the only such hymn to begin a gospel, only the first two elements are present because the third element of return is delayed until the final portion of the gospel.[29]

Even without this final, somewhat questionable suggestion of a vindication pattern, one can see that John's claim that Jesus is wisdom is all pervasive. It fits well with John's replacement theology. Jesus replaces torah as wisdom just as surely as he replaces every other Jewish festival or tradition in John. But the extent of the referent and the magnitude of the claim is surprising.

So, John identifies Jesus as wisdom. This may have something to teach us about one gospel writer's profession of faith about Jesus, but what does it have to do with the historical Jesus? Were it only John claiming such identification, the answer might be nothing. John's portrait of Jesus is often seen as the least historical in ordinary terms. But the truth is, John is not alone. Perhaps what is reflected in John is not some late, pre-gnostic influence, but rather early speculation about Jesus. Perhaps this speculation came from Jesus' role as teacher, and possibly from hymnic reflection on his life story. To emphasize the point that John is not alone, I will move on to Matthew, with his dependence on Mark and Q.

B. Wisdom in Matthew

Matthew is an entirely different book from John, with a birth narrative instead of a λόγος hymn and teaching of a very different order. Jesus' teaching in Matthew is less grand and philosophical, more homey and down to earth—if one can speak of kingdom parables as down to earth! At one level, Matthew, like Luke and even Mark, presents Jesus as a wisdom teacher. Jesus is consistently addressed in Matthew as rabbi or teacher. While no one will dispute that Jesus was a teacher, some might question the designation *wisdom* teacher. The rationale for that desig-

---

[27]See, e.g., Witherington, *Jesus the Sage*; Fred W. Burnett, *The Testament of Jesus-Sophia: A Redaction-Critical Study of the Eschatological Discourse in Matthew* (Lanham, MD: University Press of America, 1981); Celia Deutsch, *Hidden Wisdom and the Easy Yoke* (Sheffield, England: Sheffield, 1987); M. Jack Suggs, *Wisdom, Christology and Law in Matthew's Gospel* (Cambridge: Harvard University, 1970); Elisabeth Schüssler Fiorenza, "Wisdom Mythology and the Christological Hymns of the New Testament," in *Aspects of Wisdom in Judaism and Early Christianity*, ed. Robert L. Wilken (Notre Dame, IN: University of Notre Dame, 1975) 17-42.

[28]See Marshall Johnson, "Reflections on a Wisdom Approach to Matthew's Christology," *CBQ* 36 (1974) 44-64, for an important critique. Burnett, *Testament*, 26, for example, continues the pattern by speaking of sophia's reappearance from heaven as, or associated with, the son of man.

[29]Notice the references to ascending in John 3:13; 6:62; 20:17.

nation lies in the formal characteristics of Jesus' teaching as well as in the manner of reasoning employed.

The forms of Jesus' teaching have been well categorized.[30] Leo Perdue surveyed the various forms found in the wisdom books of the Old Testament and the Apocrypha[31] and marked their presence in Matthew, Mark, and Luke. He found in these gospels a few folk proverbs and a few more literary proverbs—more often antithetical than synonymous. While he did not find a great number of comparative proverbs (such as Prov 25:14: "Like clouds and wind without rain is one who boasts of a gift never given"), Perdue noted that "this type of saying seems to provide the basis for many New Testament parables, e.g., those of the kingdom in Matthew 13:44-50" ("the kingdom of heaven is like treasure hidden in a field or a merchant in search of fine pearls").[32] A parable can be characterized as a proverb in narrative form. Perdue found a number of rhetorical questions, and, of course, a sizable number of beatitudes. He described the temptation narrative as a wisdom disputation (not so surprising for the opening and only story of the ever elusive Q). But among all the forms the most frequently used are admonitions and aphorisms; these are usually collected together in groupings very like wisdom instructions found in Proverbs and elsewhere.

Although formally identical, a proverb is spoken by a sage who is passing on a traditional saying or observation. An aphorism is a saying that comes from an individual wishing to pass on a personal insight. Often this insight is undermining, rather than supportive, of traditional authority. Perdue calls the aphorism "a subversive saying wearing the disguise of a proverb."[33] Aphorisms are used "to reorient hearers to a new and different meaning system."[34] In the case of Jesus, the new meaning system centers on the new reality of the kingdom of God, thus, I might add, combining wisdom and apocalyptic. Not surprisingly, Jesus makes use primarily of parables and aphorisms, though Perdue notes that in Matthew, as in Mark and Q, traditional wisdom is also present.

So formally, much of Jesus' teaching can be characterized as wisdom teaching, so long as we note that it is primarily wisdom of a counter order.[35] The manner of reasoning employed by Jesus in Matthew might also be designated as wisdom reasoning. Jesus doesn't speak like a traditional prophet. He doesn't use introductions like "Thus says the Lord." Rather he appeals to reason, to logic, to experience,

---

[30]Leo G. Perdue, "The Wisdom Sayings of Jesus," *FFF* 2/3 (1986) 3-35. See also Fontaine, "Proverbs," and Charles E. Carlston, "Proverbs, Maxims, and the Historical Jesus," *JBL* 99/1 (1980) 87-105.

[31]These include folk proverbs, literary proverbs (synonymous, antithetical, and synthetic), comparative proverbs (similitudes/parables, *a minore ad maius* and reverse, better sayings), numerical sayings, riddles, questions (rhetorical, impossible), beatitudes, admonitions, instructions, disputations, wisdom psalms, and wisdom poems.

[32]Perdue, "Wisdom Sayings," 11.

[33]Ibid., 28.

[34]Ibid., 29.

[35]This designation is used by Witherington, *Jesus the Sage*, 161. Note that Jesus also teaches about his impending death, so that at a very basic level his passion is not separated from his teaching.

and to nature. Jesus in Matthew uses irony and paradox, both parts of the heritage of wisdom. He does appeal to authority, but that authority is his own. To get a feel for how Matthew sees Jesus as a wisdom teacher, one need look no further than the sermon on the mount. Jesus begins: "When Jesus saw the crowds, he went up the mountain; and after he sat down, his disciples came to him. Then he began to speak, and taught them, saying:..." Then follows a series of beatitudes, a common wisdom form: "Blessed are the poor in spirit, for theirs is the kingdom of heaven..." (Matt 5:3). Just as interesting is the end of the sermon: "'Everyone then who hears these words of mine and acts on them will be like a wise man who built his house on rock....' Now when Jesus had finished saying these things, the crowds were astounded at his teaching, for he taught them as one having authority, and not as their scribes."

Jesus tells a parable of a wise man and a fool. He enjoins his hearers to be wise! And they are astonished because he doesn't cite earlier authorities but rather claims an authority of his own. Between this wisdom-marked beginning and ending, we find a number of different kinds of teaching, including some straight-forward proverbs that are then explained and given a twist: "You are the salt of the earth; but if salt has lost its taste, how can its saltiness be restored?...You are the light of the world. A city built on a hill cannot be hid" (Matt 5:13-14).

These proverbs are frequently given an eschatological or apocalyptic cast. And a good deal is said about the law and about teaching:

> Do not think that I have come to abolish the law or the prophets; I have come not to abolish but to fulfill. For truly I tell you, until heaven and earth pass away, not one letter, not one stroke of a letter, will pass from the law until all is accomplished. Therefore, whoever breaks one of the least of these command-ments, and teaches others to do the same, will be called least in the kingdom of heaven; but whoever does them and teaches them will be called great in the kingdom of heaven. (Matt 5:17-19)[36]

The commandments are taught, but, in good rabbinic tradition, they are given a twist: "You have heard that it was said to those of ancient times, 'You shall not murder'; and 'whoever murders shall be liable to judgment.' But I say to you....You have heard that it was said, 'You shall not commit adultery.' But I say to you..." (Matt 5:21-22; 27-28). Jesus teaches wisdom, and as wisdom, he teaches torah. Still, Jesus doesn't teach torah exactly like the rabbis. He doesn't explain it or interpret it from within and cite other authorities. Rather Jesus teaches even torah aphoristically, giving it a radical edge, a bite, a new direction that invites formation of a new community.

Like John, Matthew is very interested in the relationship between torah and Jesus. Unlike John, Matthew does not reject the identification of wisdom and torah, but neither does he stop there. I suggest that Matthew sees torah as a preliminary stage of wisdom's revelation. Wisdom is not fully revealed in torah because, for Matthew, the full embodiment of wisdom is not torah but Jesus.

---

[36]It is worth noting that teaching, not only baptism, is also part of the great commission (Matt 28:19-20).

Before we leave the sermon on the mount, we should take note of Jesus' saying:

> Ask, and it will be given you; seek, and you will find; knock, and the door will be opened for you. For everyone who asks receives, and everyone who seeks finds, and for everyone who knocks, the door will be opened....In everything do to others as you would have them do to you; for this is the law and the prophets. (Matt 7:7-8, 12)

Here Jesus paraphrases the golden rule from Lev 19:18, 34 through the notion of "seeking and finding" found in Proverbs, Sirach, and Wisdom of Solomon.

In considering the portrait of Jesus as wisdom teacher, a few brief comments are in order about Jesus as one who teaches in parables. The parable is a wisdom form, albeit not frequently used in Old Testament wisdom literature. B. B. Scott says that Jesus' use of the parable falls, like the aphorism, into the category of subversive literature.[37] In these parables, the poor, the outcast, and the unclean become the bearers of truth. As such they subvert traditional wisdom and traditional torah. I would add that the disciples thus become the "simple" (פְּתָאִים) of Proverbs who need "instruction" (מוּסָר); while the authorities become the "fools" (אֱוִילִים) who are unable to heed such instruction.

This claim about Jesus speaking in parables appears only in Matthew: "Jesus told the crowds all these things in parables; without a parable he told them nothing. This was to fulfill what had been spoken through the prophet: 'I will open my mouth to speak in parables; I will proclaim what has been hidden from the foundation of the world'" (13:34-35).

Sirach says that one job of the sage is "to penetrate the subtleties of parables and to seek out the hidden meaning of proverbs" (Sir 39:2-3). Here Jesus goes further. He reveals creational truth in his own parables, truth that can be known only by one who knows what has been hidden since the beginning of the world. We have landed squarely into the realm of wisdom.

Note also that Jesus even teaches parables from a boat in the midst of the sea (Matt 13:1-3). Just as surely as the subsequent walking on water is a calming of the storm, so also this teaching from the midst of the sea is a cosmic act. Teaching becomes a cosmological activity, and, in the process, "rabbi" or "teacher" takes on a christological air.[38]

Four additional aspects of the connection between Jesus and wisdom lead me to conclude that for Matthew, Jesus not only teaches wisdom, he is wisdom: (1) the identification of Jesus as Son of David, something greater than Solomon; (2) the extensive reference to wisdom in Matthew 11-12; (3) the correspondence with a picture of wisdom found in Sir 4:11-19; and (4) Matthew's use of the rejection theme in chapter 23.

---

[37]B. B. Scott, "Jesus as Sage: An Innovating Voice in Common Wisdom," in *The Sage in Israel and the Ancient Near East*, ed. John Gammie and Leo Purdue (Winona Lake, IN: Eisenbrauns, 1990) 399-416.

[38]Note the very interesting discussion about addressing Jesus as "rabbi" and "teacher" in Witherington, *Jesus the Sage*, 344-352.

The significance of Matthew's identification of Jesus as son of David is suggested by Ben Witherington.[39] Witherington pictures Jesus as being like Solomon, but something more. He argues that much of the significance of identifying Jesus as "son of David" comes because of the comparison with Solomon. Jesus, like any king, receives special attention at birth. Not incidentally, he is visited and recognized by foreign magi. He, like other kings, has one who prepares the way (John). And he, like Solomon, receives the gift of the Spirit. For Solomon, this spirit is identified as the spirit of wisdom (Wis 7:7). Jesus, like Solomon, is the exemplary teacher and more. Witherington notes that in Josephus and elsewhere, Solomon is also associated with miracles, cures, and exorcisms.[40] So Jesus, like Solomon, heals and performs exorcisms. All of this builds to the final comparison to Solomon made in Matt 12:42, "The queen of the South will rise up at the judgment with this generation and condemn it, because she came from the ends of the earth to listen to the wisdom of Solomon, and see, something greater than Solomon is here!"[41]

These verses bring closure to a section in Matthew that is crucial for the identification of Jesus as sophia. This section begins in chapter 11 when Jesus goes on "to teach and proclaim his message" beyond his disciples. He begins by telling his many deeds—healing, raising the dead, and bringing good news to the poor—to John's disciples. He then speaks about John, ending with these words:

> But to what shall I compare this generation? It is like children sitting in the market places and calling to their playmates,
>> 'We played the flute for you, and you did not dance;
>> we wailed, and you did not mourn.'
> For John came neither eating nor drinking, and they say, 'He has a demon'; the Son of Man came eating and drinking, and they say, 'Look, a glutton and a drunkard, a friend of tax collectors and sinners!' Yet wisdom (σοφία) is vindicated by her deeds. (Matt 11:16-19)

Much ink has been spilled over these words, trying to unravel the meaning of the last phrase. It differs from the final phrase in the parallel passage in Luke 7:35, presumably also Q, which reads, "Yet is σοφία vindicated by all her children."[42] Some would say that both versions imply that John and Jesus are wisdom's envoys, sent by her to deliver her message. Others would say that Matthew, at least, is claiming that Jesus is not an envoy, but rather wisdom herself. I side with those who say that the context settles the matter of interpretation. The list of Jesus' deeds that

[39]For what follows see Witherington, *Jesus the Sage*, 352-360.

[40]Ibid., 357.

[41]See also Matt 6:28-29, "Consider the lilies of the field, how they grow; they neither toil nor spin; yet I tell you, even Solomon in all his glory was not arrayed like one of these."

[42]What Luke does with this passage is interesting in its own right. Luke moves immediately into a banqueting scene, a meal, where Jesus typically feasts not with the deserving and the wise but with the poor and the outcast, the unclean, the undeserving, and the sinners. The banqueting and feasting imagery of woman wisdom is evoked and then turned on its head. This is rather subversive wisdom, where the invited guests are not the self-evidently righteous and wise who study torah and walk in the paths of goodness. Rather, those who end up accepting and issuing the invitation and recognizing Jesus either as wisdom or as one of wisdom's envoys (not to predetermine Luke's understanding of Jesus in this regard) become the righteous who feast at wisdom's table.

precedes this passage is clearly to be equated with wisdom's vindicating deeds. Just as Jesus is "Son of Man" in this passage, so also he is "Sophia."

After Matthew makes this identification, he moves through a series of woe oracles, not surprisingly identified by some as a wisdom form opposite the beatitude, and then comes to the following passage:

> All things have been handed over to me by my Father; and no one knows the Son except the Father, and no one knows the Father except the Son and anyone to whom the Son chooses to reveal him. Come to me, all you that are weary and are carrying heavy burdens, and I will give you rest. Take my yoke upon you, and learn from me; for I am gentle and humble in heart, and you will find rest for your souls. For my yoke is easy, and my burden is light. (11:27-30)

References to both wisdom and torah as a yoke abound. Sirach says of wisdom:

> At last you will find the rest she gives,
>   and she will be changed into joy for you.
> Then her fetters will become for you a strong defense,
>   and her collar a glorious robe.
> Her yoke is a golden ornament,
>   and her bonds are a cord of blue. (Sir 6:28-30)

And later he says: "Put your neck under her yoke, and let your souls receive instruction; it is to be found close by" (51:26). In Matthew, Jesus becomes the one who gives the restful yoke. He is identified with woman wisdom, having the same intimate relationship with God the Father; he is the same revealer of hidden wisdom and the same bestower of rest.

Some would say that the identification of Jesus and wisdom in Matthew, if present, is only a minor consideration. I have tried to show that much of the book points in this direction. In fact, a passage in Sirach strikes me as almost a programmatic statement of how Jesus is understood as wisdom in Matthew:

> Wisdom teaches her children
>   and gives help to those who seek her.
> Whoever loves her loves life,
>   and those who seek her from early morning are filled with joy.
> Whoever holds her fast inherits glory,
>   and the Lord blesses the place she [or he] enters.
> Those who serve her minister to the Holy One;
>   the Lord loves those who love her.
> Those who obey her will judge the nations,
>   and all who listen to her will live secure.
> If they remain faithful, they will inherit her;
>   their descendants will also obtain her.
> For at first she will walk with them on tortuous paths;
>   she will bring fear and dread upon them,
> and will torment them by her discipline until she trusts them,
> and she will test them with her ordinances.
> Then she will come straight back to them again and gladden them,
>   and will reveal her secrets to them.
> If they go astray she will forsake them,
>   and hand them over to their ruin.
> Watch for the opportune time, and beware of evil. (Sir 4:11-20)

This passage comes as close as any to bringing into the picture of wisdom the themes of rejection and judgment with almost apocalyptic force. One can make use of those themes without necessarily resorting to some story of wisdom's ascension. The themes are pertinent to the discussion of the final wisdom passages found at the end of Matthew 23 (again, after a series of woe-oracles):

> Therefore I send you prophets, sages, and scribes, some of whom you will kill and crucify, and some you will flog in your synagogues and pursue from town to town. (Matt 23:34)

The parallel passage in Luke 11:49 reads:

> Therefore also the Wisdom of God said, "I will send them prophets and apostles, some of whom they will kill and persecute."

I am struck by Matthew's addition of sages and scribes alongside of prophets as those who will be killed and crucified. Some have invoked a "criterion of crucifiability" in objecting to the portrayal of Jesus as sage, claiming that it is difficult to imagine a sage being guilty of anything bad enough to lead to crucifixion, because sages wouldn't be politically dangerous. But Matthew seems intent on just such an idea. Perhaps the difficulty lies both in assuming that sages do not act politically and that they are not identifiable as prophets.[43] But even more important for our purposes is the attribution to Jesus of a saying that in Luke and presumably Q is directly attributed to the "Wisdom of God." Again, it seems that Matthew is consciously identifying Jesus as wisdom. This claim is supported by the final passage in Matthew 23 in which Jesus says:

> Jerusalem, Jerusalem, the city that kills the prophets and stones those who are sent to it! How often have I desired to gather your children together as a hen gathers her brood under her wings, and you were not willing! See, your house is left to you, desolate. For I tell you, you will not see me again until you say, "Blessed is the one who comes in the name of the Lord." (Matt 23:37-39)

Not everyone is convinced that Matthew and John identify Jesus as wisdom herself. Many would stop with a less inflated claim, speaking only of similarities between the way in which Jewish tradition speaks of the figure of wisdom and the way in which Christian tradition speaks of Jesus. This approach, while certainly true, does not hear the powerful way this metaphor speaks within the tradition. My own claim is not so much historical as literary. One cannot move blithely from Matthew's and John's identification of Jesus as wisdom to historical claims about Jesus. One of the fascinating aspects of this inquiry is that even though these two books make the same claim, the manner in which the claim is made, as well as the conclusions which might be drawn, often differ. They differ in the sort of teaching they associate with Jesus as wisdom. In John the teaching is more radical theologically but less radical socially. John identifies Jesus as wisdom in basic opposition to

---

[43]Both Sirach and the Wisdom of Solomon envision a connection between prophets and sages. Note Sir 24:33 and the verse about Samuel in Sir 46:15 as well as Wis 7:27. Socrates might also be invoked as an example of a sage whose activities led to death.

torah. Matthew identifies Jesus as wisdom both as fulfillment of torah and as a greater manifestation than torah.

III. THE QUEST FOR JESUS

The time has come to ask what these two gospel portraits of Jesus as wisdom have to do with the quest for Jesus and the Christian faith. Is this identification a central issue or a peripheral one? Is a wisdom christology always gnostic or, at best, pre-gnostic and therefore to be regarded with suspicion? Every aspect of christology has its potential heresy, of course. If we eliminate all christological pronouncements for fear of their extremes, we are left with nothing.

Somewhere in the midst of this identification we do find some association between the historical Jesus and wisdom. Our options are finite: (1) Jesus was, in fact, some sort of a wisdom teacher; (2) Jesus was and/or considered himself to be one of wisdom's special prophets or envoys;[44] (3) Jesus was and/or considered himself to be wisdom incarnate.[45]

A number of questions present themselves in relation to the first option, that Jesus was some sort of wisdom teacher. What sort of wisdom teacher? A number of scholars have suggested that Jesus might be more a Cynic than a hellenized Jewish wisdom teacher. I would agree with those who reject this option.[46] For one thing, the picture of the Cynic doesn't really fit; second, Jesus was, in fact, a Jew; and third, as I think I have made clear, one need not go outside the hellenistic Jewish wisdom tradition to make a case.

Other questions are more significant. For example, what is the relationship between wisdom and apocalyptic or wisdom and prophecy? What is the relationship between Jesus as wisdom personified and Jesus as Son of Man? For many the picture of Jesus as wisdom is rejected on the grounds that Jesus was an apocalyptic prophet. But recently, von Rad's early thesis that apocalyptic is a child of wisdom rather than prophecy is enjoying a renaissance.[47] Even if this is not accepted entirely, the relationship between wisdom and apocalyptic is being understood as more complicated, allowing for complementarity and intertwining rather than strict opposition. What is to prevent us from thinking of Jesus as a Jewish prophetic sage with apocalyptic leanings? Part of the difficulty of categorizing Jesus is that combinations don't fit neatly into our predetermined categories. I myself rather like this description.

The second possibility, that Jesus was and/or considered himself to be one of wisdom's special prophets or envoys, raises an obvious question. Do we know or

---

[44]So Elisabeth Schüssler Fiorenza, *Jesus: Miriam's Child, Sophia's Prophet* (New York: Continuum, 1995).

[45]Witherington, *Jesus the Sage,* 204-205, speculates that Jesus believed himself to be wisdom, a living *mashal,* the embodiment of the ultimate kingdom parable.

[46]N. T. Wright, *Jesus and the Victory of God,* vol. 2 of *Christian Origins and the Question of God* (Minneapolis: Fortress, 1996) 66-74; Witherington, *Jesus the Sage,* 117-145.

[47]See John J. Collins, "Wisdom, Apocalypticism, and Generic Compatibility," in *In Search of Wisdom: Essays in Memory of John G. Gammie,* ed. Leo Purdue, Bernard Brandon Scott, and William J. Wiseman (Louisville: Westminster/John Knox, 1993) 165-186.

can we suggest with some certainty that hellenized Jewish wisdom speculation gave birth to such an idea or at least contained seeds that naturally blossomed in response to the life, teachings, death, and resurrection of Jesus? Here I am not certain. The texts used to support this idea are scanty. Still we do have before us the texts in Matthew and Luke that suggest that sophia did indeed send prophets and others who were persecuted and killed. This text perhaps suggests that both John and Jesus were among those sent. Still, one would then have to work out what differentiates Jesus from John. Problems abound.

The last possibility, that Jesus was and/or considered himself to be wisdom incarnate, is the most radical and the trickiest. Different versions of this idea are possible. One could center such speculation only on the teaching of Jesus. This option would emphasize that what gave Jesus such authority as a teacher was precisely his self-understanding or the reality of his being incarnate wisdom.

But the heart of this speculation lies elsewhere. It centers on the vindication pattern spoken of in relationship to John but applied as well to Matthew—the pattern that has Jesus as wisdom descending from heaven, living on earth for a time, being rejected, and then ascending back to heaven to deliver weal and woe and perhaps to come again. Some speculate the presence of a full blown pre-Christian wisdom myth which contained these elements. I find such a suggestion highly unlikely. But relevant here are some comments by Elisabeth Schüssler Fiorenza:

> "Reflective mythology" is not a living myth but is rather a form of theology appropriating mythical language, material, and patterns from different myths and using these patterns, motifs, and configurations for its own theological concerns. Such a theology is not interested in reproducing the myth itself or the mythic materials as they stand, but rather in taking up and adapting the various mythical elements to its own theological goal and theoretical concerns.[48]

At issue is this: The immediate followers of Jesus were presented with certain facts. Jesus, their teacher, was crucified, had died, and was buried. He then appeared again on earth, living not dead. How were they to make sense of this? Perhaps extant speculation about woman wisdom had just enough already in place to allow the community to use this figure to explain in a satisfactory and uplifting way exactly what happened. Perhaps this very understanding is reflected in the earliest hymns. The truth is, I don't know.

Yet even in my ignorance, I am prepared to suggest some ways that the identification of wisdom and Jesus feed Christian faith.

Minimally this identification provides a way for us to take more seriously Jesus' role as teacher. That is, when "rabbi" or "teacher" as a form of address implies "*the* Rabbi" or "*the* Teacher," then what Jesus *says* has a place alongside of what Jesus *did* in our christology. That is, we have a faithful reason for attending to what Jesus said, and we do not rob Jesus of speech as we do in the creeds. In claiming this, I am, in some ways though not in others, disagreeing with Mary Knutsen's assessment in this collection that Jesus is unique only as revealed and

---

[48]Elisabeth Schüssler Fiorenza, "Wisdom Mythology," 29.

not as revealer. If Jesus is wisdom, then his words are true. This claim is still, of course, replete with historical difficulties. We cannot finally distinguish between what Jesus actually said and what the gospels say he said. Moreover, most of what Jesus said or is purported to have said has parallels elsewhere. Does this fact lessen our portrait of Jesus as wisdom? Is uniqueness to be equated with truth? That what Jesus, true wisdom, said is like unto what is said elsewhere, both within the tradition and outside of it, can be considered cause for rejoicing. God's wisdom knows no boundaries. Still, within the New Testament, the center of Jesus' teaching is about himself and the kingdom.[49] Particular claims are being made. The appropriate balance between the universal and the particular is, as always, a deep challenge.

Maximally, we have a pregnant metaphor which offers a way of thinking about preexistence, incarnation, teaching, healing, rejection, and resurrection in a consistent and profound manner.

In between we are offered other gifts. Jesus as wisdom helps us to see a connection between Jesus and creation, a connection sorely needed by both church and world. Jesus as wisdom becomes a fruitful path for exploring attitudes towards the law, towards torah, in the New Testament. Jesus as wisdom provides a way to underline the countercultural, world-redefining nature of Jesus as both teacher and crucified savior by both drawing on tradition and turning it on its head.

Jesus as wisdom provides us with a new opportunity to explore the place and character of the Spirit. And, finally, among the most complicated and important of gifts that the identification of wisdom and Jesus brings is the impact and importance of the feminine when speaking of divine and earthly realities. Some would say that gender has no role in the discussion (Ben Witherington). Others would claim that the feminine aspect of wisdom is perhaps her most important characteristic (Elisabeth Schüssler Fiorenza, Elizabeth Johnson). I am interested in the actual effect that the feminine character of wisdom has, in fact, had on the contemporary church. The reactions range from accusations of heresy to experiences of liberation. Both extremes catch me off guard. But I am particularly pleased whenever Christians can reach out to those who find the church to be irredeemable and overly authoritarian—in this case, secular and, indeed, Christian, feminists. To these, Jesus as wisdom offers new insights and possibilities for finding life in Christ. ⊕

---

[49]It is worth noting that the gospel which has the "highest" wisdom christology, i.e., John, also makes the most particular claims about Jesus and is said to be the least historical.

Word & World
Supplement Series 3
1997

The Trial and Death of the Historical Jesus

Donald H. Juel

Princeton Theological Seminary
Princeton, New Jersey

I. A Few Preliminaries

SEARCHING AFTER THE HISTORICAL JESUS IS ONE OF THE FEW ACADEMIC VEN-tures in which the wider public has shown interest. One reason is perhaps fascination with the sensational; another may be a sense that something important is at stake. I happen to agree that the enterprise is not trivial. The Christian tradition has a considerable investment in the particularity of God's saving work. We do not worship a generic but a specific God, with a name and a history of involvement with the world that comes to focus on Jesus of Nazareth. To sever the proclaimed Christ from the Jesus of history would be fatal to the Christian faith.

We should be clear, however, what we are after. To ask about the "historical Jesus" may involve little more than knowing something about the circumstances of his ministry. It may involve, in other words, locating Jesus in a particular social and historical setting that may or may not be accurately represented by the gospels.

Few people would be satisfied with such a quest. More commonly, people are interested to come to know Jesus "as a person." They might hope for an insider's glimpse at what it must have been like to be such a person in such an historical setting. Kazantzakis and Mailer, for example, seem interested in such an encounter. What must have been the experience of one who knew himself to be more than an ordinary man? What must it have felt like? While such investigations may be entertaining, they offer little historical promise—and they reveal the degree to which much of modern culture collapses human experience into psychological categories, as Wrede complained almost a century ago.

It is not only popular works on Jesus that suffer from the disease. Much that passes for contemporary historical scholarship betrays similar views, if expressed in more sophisticated form. One still hears the dominant themes of the romantic movement, with its interest in minds and personalities and intentions. To know the historical Jesus, according to such a view, would be to know his intentions—and to use these intentions as a critical point of departure for interpreting and evaluating the New Testament and the tradition of the church. I must confess that I find such notions largely bankrupt and hope for more among interpreters of the tradition. My colleague Patrick Keifert has been helpful in providing some clear diagnosis of the situation as well as some fruitful suggestions. [1]

II. The Task

My assignment is to offer some historical assessment of the stories of Jesus' trial and death. That the stories are crucial is clear from their place in the gospel narratives and in the tradition of the church. The last climactic days of Jesus' career occupy an inordinately large portion of the accounts of his career. One might say that, for Paul, these events are almost the only things about Jesus that matter. What can we say about the historical reliability of the traditions narrating Jesus' arrest, trial, and execution? It is perfectly appropriate to ask the simple question, "What really happened?"

Answering the question is far from simple if we understand that we are playing in an arena where believers in Jesus do not set the rules and where arguments, not pronouncements, will be convincing. There is apparently enough question about the reliability of the passion tradition to justify in the eyes of some scholars outright dismissal of the entire passion tradition as lacking in historical value.[2] I find such views unconvincing, often bordering on the outrageous—but pronouncements about one's own opinions do not constitute arguments. I shall try to make a case about a particular historical reconstruction that will include specu-lation about Jesus' own views of those events that brought his ministry to a dramatic and violent conclusion.

Not every aspect of the stories merits our attention; others may be worthy of attention but offer little promise of yielding up their secrets. We shall never be able to make more than guesses, for example, about the young man in Mark 14 who runs away naked. There is not enough information to know if this is a story about a real person and, if so, about whom. Similarly, we will probably never know more about Alexander and Rufus other than that they were sons of Simon of Cyrene, who—according to Mark—carried Jesus' cross. And while the grim history of Christian persecution of Jews as so-called "Christ-killers" makes the question of the role of the Jewish leaders important, there is still uncertainty among the experts

---

[1]Patrick Keifert, "Mind Reader and Maestro: Models for Understanding Biblical Interpreters," *WW* 1/2 (1981) 153-168.

[2]John Dominic Crossan, *The Cross that Spoke: The Origins of the Passion Narrative* (San Francisco: Harper and Row, 1988).

in the field about the nature of the group our gospels call the sanhedrin and its precise legal competence.[3]

In a brief paper, drastic choices must be made from a vast range of important issues.[4] For reasons I hope will become clear, I have chosen to focus on two issues. The first is the extensive use of Old Testament language in the account of Jesus' trial and death. So pervasive and fundamental is the language in these narratives that some have suggested the stories have no historical value. They are, as John Crossan argues, prophecy historicized. The Bible has provided a "script" for the events. Our inquiries, according to this view, lead us no farther back than the script.

The claim is a serious one. The only access we have to historical events leads through our written evidence back through reconstructed histories of tradition. I would like to examine with some care precisely what passages have been chosen to tell the story and to ask, in view of their place in other post-biblical Jewish scriptural tradition, how just these passages might have come to their present place in the story. Drawing historical conclusions on the basis of the gospel narratives requires taking responsibility for constructing such a history of tradition. What are the forces that shape this biblical interpretation, and what historical inferences might be drawn?

The second matter is the consistent use of royal language in narrating the story of Jesus' trial and death. Jesus is crucified, according to all the gospel writers, as "the King of the Jews." He is mocked by Romans as a would-be king. Jewish leaders speak of him as "the Christ," "the Christ, the King of Israel," and "the Christ, the Son of the Blessed One." With Jews and non-Jews alike, the language of kingship dominates the story.

This issue has not been as obviously crucial in New Testament scholarship. There are reasons for this, most of them having to do with a lack of familiarity with Jewish tradition. I will argue that the story of Jesus the crucified king, told with the language of Israel's scriptures, is so contrary to Jewish visions and dreams of the future, so unprecedented in the heritage of scriptural interpretation known from apocryphal writings, the Dead Sea Scrolls, and the rabbinic writings, that the basic facts of the story must be true: Jesus was executed by Pontius Pilate as a would-be king.

One need not appeal to Jewish tradition to make the case that Jesus' royal death requires some attention. Even within the context of the gospel narratives

---

[3]I agree with the majority of scholars that the accounts of Jesus trial before the Jewish court are so heavily influenced by church tradition that they have little historical value other than indicating that the Jewish leadership had a role in handing Jesus over to the Roman authorities. That Jesus was executed as a political criminal by Roman officials seems beyond dispute. Issues related to the competence of the Jewish authorities are exhaustively discussed (with a full bibliography) in Raymond Brown, *The Death of the Messiah* (New York: Doubleday, 1994); see also E. P. Sanders, *Jesus and Judaism* (Philadelphia: Fortress, 1985), and *Jewish Law from Jesus to Mishnah* (London: SCM, 1990); and Ellis Rivkin, *What Crucified Jesus?* (Nashville: Abingdon, 1985).

[4]The issue is covered in breadth and depth in Raymond Brown's massive two-volume work on *The Death of the Messiah* and the more-than-adequate bibliography he provides.

themselves there is something peculiar and unprecedented about the accusations that Jesus is a would-be king. Nothing in his public ministry suggests such a view. Jesus appears to his contemporaries as a holy man, a teacher, a wonder-worker, or a prophet. What then is the source of the charge that he is a would-be "King of the Jews"? The question is important exegetically and, I will suggest, historically.

III. THE MESSIAH

My point of departure is the particular language the gospels use to speak of Jesus. While no less a scholar than E. P. Sanders can still speak of Jesus as having been condemned as an "eschatological prophet," the gospels are very precise in their reporting of Jesus' trial and execution: he was executed on a cross by the Roman prefect as a would-be "King of the Jews." Two others were executed with him, according to all the gospel accounts. They are called "bandits" (Matthew and Mark), or "wrongdoers" (Luke), not would-be kings. Soldiers cast lots for Jesus' clothing—a detail reported with words from Psalm 22 in which a "righteous sufferer" takes his case to God in a lament. Jesus is not a paradigmatic sufferer, however. He is tried, taunted, and executed as "king."

This kingship is variously expressed. For Jews, the language is shaped by their scriptural heritage. Kingship has religious as well as political dimensions. They speak of "the Christ, the Son of the Blessed [God]" (Mark 14:61, Matt 26:63); "the Christ, the King of Israel" (Mark 15:32); "the King of Israel" (Matt 27:42); "the Christ" (Luke 22:67; 23:39); "the Christ, a king" [or "an anointed king"] (Luke 23:2); "the Christ of God" (Luke 23:35). For Romans, the expression is "the King of the Jews." The differences appropriately reflect the vantage points of the speakers. The people of Israel do not refer to themselves as "Jews," a term employed by non-Jews (Romans). "The King of the Jews" reflects the interests and concerns of Roman officials, for whom the claim is political. In both cases, however, it is clear that Jesus is tried and executed as a would-be king.

The story is particular. It tells not only how Jesus was tried and executed as king; it offers from the perspective of the participants a sense of the messianic claim. In the eyes of all those who should know—the religious and political leaders responsible for interpreting as well as carrying out the religious and political laws—the claim that Jesus is a king is absurd. The claim to be "the Christ, the Son of the Blessed One" gets Jesus condemned for blasphemy, according to Mark. His prophecy that "you will see the Son of Man..." (Mark 14:62) is an occasion for mockery. Roman soldiers find the idea that Jesus is a king an opportunity for public ridicule. They put a cloak and a crown on him and give him a mock investiture: "Hail, King of the Jews." As he hangs on the cross, he is taunted by Jews who insist that if he is the Christ, the King of Israel, he should come down. That he does not—that he dies abandoned by the mobs, his followers, even by God—is proof that he is a pretender.

This particular feature of the story is all the more important when viewed in the context of each of the gospel narratives. There is nothing royal about Jesus' public ministry, the more striking when each of the gospel writers tells us at some point that Jesus is the Christ. In Luke, Mary is told by the angel that her son "will be called Son of the Most High, the Lord God will give to him the throne of his father, David, and he will reign over the house of Jacob forever" (Luke 1:32-33). In Matthew, magi come seeking the one born "King of the Jews," whose star they have seen. Yet Jesus' ministry is played out with a notable absence of royal categories. In Matthew and Mark, the only suggestion that Jesus is the Christ comes from Peter—and in Matthew Jesus says explicitly that "flesh and blood has not revealed this to you but my Father who is in heaven" (Matt 16:17). Further, whatever Peter believes he knows, he is unable to hold together his new insight into Jesus' identity with Jesus' promise of what lies ahead. For Peter, there is something irreconcilable about the claim that Jesus is Christ and the prediction of his rejection, suffering, and death. The gospel writers want us to know that even for the disciples, there is something profoundly inappropriate about claiming messiahship for one who dies on a cross. Paul, who should know about such things, expresses it well in his letter to the Corinthians: "but we proclaim Christ crucified, a stumbling block to Jews and foolishness to Gentiles" (1 Cor 1:23).

This feature of the story demands explanation. Albert Schweitzer was one who saw the problem. The central issue in reconstructing an historical Jesus, he insisted, was the gap between a non-messianic ministry of Jesus and his messianic death. Where does the legal charge come from? There is nothing in Jewish tradition, Schweitzer insists, that would lead anyone to view Jesus' teaching and actions as messianic.[5] Those who do not attend to the particulars of the gospel stories are perhaps not impressed by the question. But the gospels themselves highlight the problem: calling Jesus "the Christ" in view of his humiliating death does not make sense. And in view of the imagery employed in the story, it is unnecessary as well as inappropriate. The crowds apparently suggested that Jesus is a prophet, perhaps the prophet like Moses or Elijah (Mark 8:27-28). That would seem both adequate and appropriate to Jesus' ministry of teaching and performing "signs and wonders." Why is Jesus executed as Messiah—and subsequently confessed as Messiah by his followers—when other biblical evaluations were available?

IV. POST-BIBLICAL JEWISH VISIONS AND DREAMS

Posing such a question invites attention to an enormous corpus of literature from which we must reconstruct the first-century context within which to locate the New Testament writings. The literature is far too vast for any one person to master, so we make choices, and our appreciation of some aspect of the biblical witness is heightened, based on our tiny realm of expertise. At this point, however, we are obliged to attend to the Jewish setting within which the story is set, since the story of Jesus is about an Israelite whose ministry is principally among the people of Israel and whose story is told within the context of Israel's scriptural heritage. Language used to speak of Jesus is the language of Israel's Bible.

---

[5]Albert Schweitzer, *The Quest of the Historical Jesus* (New York: Macmillan, 1947). John's Gospel is an exception, where the notion of king and prophet are interwoven in a singular fashion, reminiscent perhaps of Samaritan notions. See W. Meeks, *The Prophet-King* (Leiden: Brill, 1967).

For those who knew Israel's scriptures within their setting in post-biblical tradition, what would it have meant that Jesus is tried, executed, and later confessed as "the Christ"? What difference does it make to our appreciation of the story if we know some of the alternatives available to those whose visions and dreams of God's future had been shaped by the scriptures and their interpretation?

I shall deal with this question by referring to a massive study of the question at a 1987 conference on "Messianism" at Princeton Seminary. The conference gathered scholars from Old Testament, Hebrew Bible, intertestamental literature, Qumran studies, New Testament studies, and rabbinics to ask what it would have meant to call someone "the Messiah (or the Christ)" in the first century. While the training and interests of those present varied, the results of the 24 papers were remarkably consistent.[6] Let me offer a brief summary.

1. The title "the Messiah," without modifiers, is not a biblical (Old Testament) term but represents a post-biblical development.

2. While in the Old Testament priests and prophets could be spoken of as "anointed," in the New Testament—and in later rabbinic writings—"the anointed one" refers to a royal figure from the line of David.

3. Among the wide variety of Jewish groups there was a corresponding variety of visions and dreams of the future. Some expected a prophetic figure like Moses to appear as deliverer (e.g., the Samaritans); others seemed invested in a priestly figure (the Testament of Levi). The sectarians at Qumran seem to have had room in their visions for several players in the final drama, including two "anointed ones" (a priest and a royal figure). Some Jews apparently anticipated the day when God alone would judge. There was among these varied visions no one "normative" view. All drew on the scriptures, but the selection of passages and their configuration varied enormously.

4. "The Messiah" from the line of David was a figure in only some of the visions of what God had in store. He was by no means the most significant, as the Qumran Scrolls indicate, where the priestly figure is granted priority. While there were royalists among the visionaries, as reflected in *Psalms of Solomon* 17, even where there were expectations of such a figure, there was no uniformity.

5. The one consistent feature is that "the Messiah" is a royal figure whose career is portrayed in categories appropriate to royalty. The coming king would rule. That could mean defeating Israel's enemies, purifying the country, or insuring justice. The clarity of vocation is indicated in the constellation of Old Testament passages that tend to recur: 2 Sam 7:14; Psalm 2; Isaiah 11; Zechariah 6, Gen 49:8-10; and Num 24:17 ("A star shall come out of Jacob"). Notably absent are passages that speak of healing and teaching. Such vocations are more appropriate to prophets, who like Moses and Elijah, perform "signs and wonders."

The literature suggests, in other words, that Jesus' followers did not have to speak of him as "Christ" in order to make a statement about his significance. The

---

[6]James H. Charlesworth et al., eds., *The Messiah: Developments in Earliest Judaism and Christianity* (Minneapolis: Fortress, 1992).

estimate of the common people seems far more appropriate in view of Jesus' public ministry: he is a prophet (Mark 8:27 par). And if "the Christ" means the king from the line of David, we can understand Schweitzer's difficulty. The only "royal" act seems to be the triumphal entry into Jerusalem on a donkey. And we can understand the view of the chief priests: as a would-be king Jesus is a threat, but in view of the collapse of his movement, it is absurd to imagine that he is the promised king for whose coming some longed. Jesus is depicted as "king" ("Christ") in the gospel narratives at the point where the language seems least fitting. Of all the language available from Jewish tradition, in fact, it would seem that "Messiah" is the least appropriate to speak of Jesus in view of what he does (and does not do).

Our survey of Jewish tradition thus confirms exegetical observations—and simply poses the question more forcefully: What led anyone to imagine that Jesus was the Messiah? And why did his followers come to confess him as "the Christ"?

V. In Accordance with the Scriptures

The story of Jesus' trial and death, as already noted, is narrated with words and sentences from Israel's scriptures (not the "Hebrew Bible" in this case but the Greek Septuagint). While there are citations in the Fourth Gospel, in the synoptics allusions are more common, the most obvious to the Psalms:

> Ps 22:18 (Mark 15:24, Matt 27:35, Luke 23:34; quoted in John 19:24)
> Ps 22:8 (Mark 15:29-30; more extensive allusion in Matt 27:43)
> Ps 22:1 (Mark 15:34; Matt 27:46)
> Ps 69:21 (Mark 15:36; Matt 27:48; John 19:28?)
> Ps 31:5 (Luke 23:46)

Of particular interest is the use of Ps 22:18 in both the Fourth Gospel and the synoptic gospels, the more striking in view of the considerable differences between the synoptic and the Johannine versions of the passion. Lacking any convincing theory of literary dependence, the agreement may suggest that Psalm 22 had an early place in the passion tradition.

There is less agreement about "echoes" and allusions to passages from Isaiah, particularly to the now-familiar "servant song" in Isa 52:13-53:12. I have come to regard alleged allusions in the passion story as highly suspect, but that is a matter for another time.[7] For the moment I am willing to grant the possibility that in the account of Jesus' humiliating trial and death there are echoes of the famous passage from Isaiah.

The biblical words and sentences are so intimately bound up with the story that it is difficult to imagine a passion narrative without them. Some have in fact argued that biblical material provided the "script" for the passion story from the outset, with Psalm 22 as perhaps the first primitive narrative.[8] That the strands of the present narrative cannot be disentangled from the biblical wording is easily

---

[7]Donald Juel, *Messianic Exegesis: Christological Interpretation of the Old Testament in Early Christianity* (Minneapolis: Fortress, 1988) 119-135.

[8]E.g., Hartmut Gese, "Psalm 22 und das Neue Testament: Der älteste Bericht vom Tode Jesu und die Entstehung des Herrenmahles," *ZTK* 65 (1968) 1-22.

demonstrable. In Mark's account, the last words of Jesus from the cross ("My God, my God, why have you forsaken me") are misunderstood by the crowd: they believe he is calling Elijah (Mark 15:34-36). The misunderstanding, appropriate within the larger context of Mark's story, is completely dependent upon the words that Jesus speaks (in Aramaic!) which come from the psalm. While it might be possible to argue that Jesus did in fact speak such words, thus making the first connection with Psalm 22, there is no way to make the case convincingly when it is as possible that the psalm has itself generated narrative. The proposal that Jesus actually spoke words from Psalm 22 would also have to account for the absence of these words of Jesus in Luke and John, while both evangelists include allusions to other portions of the psalm.

Particularly striking, then, is the absence of "messianic" texts as defined by Jewish tradition. The allusions are to passages from the psalms that are not royal in the sense that they were so understood by prior tradition. Even if we consider allusions to Isaiah 53 likely, this is another passage that is not read as messianic among Jewish interpreters.[9]

One explanation of the presence of this particular biblical material is that the first stories of Jesus' death depicted him as a paradigmatic sufferer, thus drawing on laments. Such a view must then explain, however, where the royal features of the story come from. At what point is the story of Jesus the righteous sufferer transformed into a story of the crucified Messiah? It is sufficient here to note that Jesus' messianic identity does not arise from any of the biblical texts employed to tell the story of his death. The contrast between non-messianic passages and a royal story is as pronounced as the contrast between Jesus' non-messianic ministry and his royal death, noted above. An explanation is required.

VI. THE ORIGIN OF THE CONFESSION[10]

The thesis I am arguing is deceptively simple: the story of Jesus is told as the story of the crucified Messiah because Jesus was in fact executed as "the King of the Jews."[11] The biblical passages employed to tell the story, while certainly shaping the narrative, do not provide a reasonable explanation for the specifically royal character of the story. A more reasonable explanation is that Jesus' followers turned to the scriptures to find language appropriate to the story of the crucified Messiah, thus enlisting passages that may never have been part of messianic tradition in telling the new and surprising story of Jesus the Messiah.

Other observations add weight to such arguments. The charge against Jesus, according to all the gospels, is that he claimed to be "King of the Jews." The

---

[9]Juel, *Messianic Exegesis*, 121-124. The exception is the *Targum of Isaiah*, the final edition of which may be as late as the seventh century, in which the "servant" is identified as the Messiah. In this creative rendition of the passage, however, it is not the Messiah who suffers but the enemies of God.

[10]For a fuller discussion, see my *Messianic Exegesis*, 5-29, and "The Origin of Mark's Christology," in Charlesworth, *The Messiah*, 449-460.

[11]The suggestion, made by Julius Wellhausen, has been developed in an important essay by Nils A. Dahl: "The Crucified Messiah," in *Jesus the Christ*, ed. Donald Juel (Minneapolis: Fortress, 1991) 27-48.

phrasing is not biblical and it is not Jewish. It is only attested in Josephus, where it is used to speak of Herod. Arguing that the royal features have been retrojected into a story in which Jesus was first depicted merely as a typical biblical figure would in this case require assuming that, after first appropriating Jewish royal terminology for Jesus, narrators then invented language appropriate to Romans. It is less cumbersome to argue that the non-biblical language is primary and has been interpreted in light of Jewish tradition. In either case, one must still determine on what basis the "messianic" conviction arises. Attempts to derive "messianic" beliefs from known traditions about messianic figures are unconvincing. In fact, the more we have learned about Jewish tradition, the more unlikely the explanation becomes.

Some scholars have argued that the confession would have arisen with Jesus' resurrection: as the one raised from the dead, Jesus is the Christ.[12] Because no one expected the Messiah to suffer and die, however, there is little reason to believe that a resurrection would have convinced anyone that Jesus was the Messiah. He could have been identified more appropriately as a vindicated prophet (Elijah, who was carried into heaven) or might simply have been known as the "living Jesus" (the *Gospel of Thomas*). There had to be another reason to confess Jesus as the crucified and risen king.

What does the New Testament allow us to say? The reason the risen Jesus was confessed as the Christ is because he was executed as "the King of the Jews." When God raised him from the dead, his disciples spoke of him—had to speak of him—as the crucified and risen King of the Jews (= Christ). It makes sense that they would have turned to the scriptures to understand the "surprise," employing all the interpretive skills they had as Jews, but now using them to understand how it could be that Jesus was the one toward whom the promise had been pointing.

There is no precedent in Jewish tradition for a crucified Messiah; thus, there is no way to account for the royal imagery in the story except to agree that it is historical. That Jesus was executed by Pilate as "King of the Jews" is the most reasonable explanation for the data incorporated into the gospel (and epistolary) accounts.

VII. THE MIND OF CHRIST

It is inevitable that we press the question further: If what we know about Jesus is that he died as King of the Jews—and, in the view of his followers, God vindicated him by raising him from the dead—what do the accounts permit us to say about Jesus' own ideas? Was he the source of New Testament christology?

One explanation for the confession of Jesus as Messiah is that he knew himself to be the promised king from the line of David and so instructed his followers. "Messianism" would finally be traced to Jesus himself and to a "messianic self-consciousness." The major difficulty with such proposals is that they must presume insight into Jesus' own consciousness that the gospel narratives do

---

[12]One such scholar is Barnabas Lindars, *New Testament Apologetic* (London: SCM, 1961) 32.

not permit. And to the degree that we are able to read Jesus' intentions from his actions, there is little indication of a messianic self-consciousness. Another problem is the use of anachronisms. Arguing that Jesus reinterpreted the notion of Messiah, for example, in light of Isaiah's servant not only must presume Jesus' reflections to which we no longer have access; it must also assume there was such a notion as "the servant." I have argued elsewhere that such notions are largely the product of modern scholarship and were not available within the culture.[13] If Jesus not only reckoned with the possibility of his death but offered a "messianic" interpretation of it in light of the scriptures, he would have done something utterly without precedent that neither his followers nor anyone else could understand. This is a serious violation of Schweitzer's old insistence that any portrait of an historical Jesus must be conceivable within the world of which he was a part.

There is greater validity in claiming that Jesus' actions reveal a sense of unprecedented authority. "Not like the scribes" is a regular refrain in the gospel stories, even if Jesus' actions and teachings are not as unprecedented within Judaism as many have claimed.[14] It would be inaccurate to speak of such notions as an "implied christology," however. There is no reason these authority claims should take concrete form in a confession of Jesus as Messiah. They could as well be expressed in the crowd's notion that Jesus was a prophet—perhaps *the* prophet like Moses. They might well have resulted in something like the *Gospel of Thomas's* "living Jesus."

Others, with E. P. Sanders, have tried to derive the messianic claim from Jesus' preaching about the kingdom of God.

> I do not think it worthwhile to quibble very much about terms. Let us grant that Jesus did not call himself "Messiah." We must still take into account the indisputable or almost indisputable facts outlined above. These focus on "king" rather than "Messiah," but they explain why "Messiah" was *ever* thought to be an appropriate title. If Jesus said to the disciples only "there will be a kingdom," and "you will have a role in it," and "I will share the banquet of the new kingdom with you," the disciples would naturally have been as willing as the Romans to think that he considered himself "King," and they would equally naturally have found the title "Messiah" an appropriate one....The point which remains unsolved is *just* how Jesus conceived his own role. I must confess that I have no answer to the question of precisely how Jesus saw the relationship between himself, the Son of man, and the Father.[15]

The stubborn fact remains that the New Testament does not speak of Jesus' messiahship (kingship) in the context of the kingdom of God. Sanders' view, like others, must rely on inferences from silence. His view is possible, but it does not adequately account for the concentration of royal imagery in the context of Jesus' trial and death.

---

[13]See especially, Juel, *Messianic Exegesis*, 119-134.

[14]Locating Jesus' ministry within the context of Jewish tradition is one of the major contributions of E. P. Sanders, *Jesus and Judaism*; see also G. Vermes, *Jesus the Jew* (Philadelphia: Fortress, 1981) and *Jesus and the World of Judaism* (Philadelphia: Fortress, 1983).

[15]Sanders, *Jesus and Judaism*, 307-308.

The reason Jesus' followers came to confess him as Messiah (Christ) is that he was executed as "King of the Jews," and when he was vindicated by God on the third day, he was proclaimed as the crucified and risen King (Messiah). His identity—particularly his identity as Christ—is tied intimately to his trial and death, not to his preaching about the kingdom.

We proceed behind that event with little evidence. As Schweitzer noted long ago, one could not in Jesus' day and cannot now deduce from his teaching and activity that he understood himself as God's anointed king from the line of David. That his followers may have come to suspect he was the king is characterized in the gospels as an insight possible only through "inspiration," and the accounts likewise indicate that the disciples did not see any connection between messiahship and death.

One clearly royal moment in Jesus' ministry is his entrance into Jerusalem. Did Jesus ride into Jerusalem on a donkey, clearly imitating royal precedent? That the gospel writers so understand the event is clear. Separating later views from historical events at this point, however, is probably impossible. Had his entry signaled a messianic claim, it is inconceivable that he would not have been arrested immediately, together with his followers.[16] That Jesus alone was arrested suggests his movement was viewed as something less than a political threat. Such arguments do not rule out the possibility that Jesus made some symbolic gesture for his followers, but they make it move beyond "possible" to "probable."

The messianic claim must have come from somewhere. The question remains where. Did Jesus know himself to be the Messiah, and is that self-consciousness the source of his arrest? Or did others suggest the possibility, so that the accusation is as much the function of an out-of-control rumor as a response to a claim? Either explanation could fit the facts. It seems a bit unlikely that Jesus' followers would have chosen a title for Jesus that was utterly contrary to all that he stood for and one which he personally opposed. Perhaps such reasoning is enough to argue, with Nils Dahl, that there is reason to accept what the gospels say: at the critical moment of his life, when Jesus was asked if he was the Messiah, he did not deny it, and his response was understood as accepting the title.

> The contradiction between Jesus' nonmessianic public appearances and his messiahship is to be explained neither from the nature of Jewish messianic ideas nor by the tension between historical facts and the conceptions of the evangelists....The real explanation, however, is to be sought in the historical event itself; the inconsistency stems from Jesus' crucifixion as the Messiah, although he never made an express messianic claim. He did not deny the accusation that he acted the role of Messiah when it was raised against him. This fact had a determinative significance for the Christian kerygma and thus for the ideas of the evangelists. The end of Jesus' life stands at the heart of the gospel; the historical Jesus, like the kerygmatic Christ, is the crucified Messiah.[17]

More than that cannot be argued convincingly.

---

[16]Ibid., 307-308.
[17]Dahl, "The Crucified Messiah," 44.

What can be said with more confidence is that Jesus' followers reflected on his death as king—as Messiah—and of that reflection there is a substantial deposit in our written New Testament. Israel's scriptures were reread from the perspective of the resurrection of the crucified Messiah. The most reasonable accounting we can give of the development of "messianic" interpretation of Israel's scriptures must take its point of departure from the confession of Jesus as the crucified and risen Christ. The trial and death of Jesus thus remain at the heart of the confession of Jesus as Messiah.

If there is anything historical we can know about Jesus, it is that he was executed as "King of the Jews" by Pontius Pilate. Such an assessment best makes sense of the development of a tradition that has left its deposit in our New Testament. Some may wish to dispute the claims of the tradition. When such disputations take their point of departure from reconstructions that seek to disqualify the passion tradition by historical argument, they will remain unconvincing. More appropriate—and potentially more interesting—would be a theological argument that seeks to commend a "wisdom" theology over against a "theology of the cross." There are good reasons to question the history of Christian interpretation and practice. Such a theological argument, however, will involve something quite different from historical reconstruction.

VIII. SOME IMPLICATIONS

One implication should be clear: the Christian gospel is not an idea in search of narrative embodiment. It is unreasonable to argue that it is, and historical argument must first of all be reasonable. The idea of a crucified Messiah is not only unprecedented within Jewish tradition; it is so contrary to the whole notion of a deliverer from the line of David, so out of harmony with the constellation of biblical texts we can identify from various Jewish sources that catalyzed around the royal figure later known as "the Christ," that terms like "scandal" and "foolishness" are the only appropriate responses. Irony is the only means of telling such a story, because it is so counterintuitive. The accounts of Jesus' trial and death, therefore, are most reasonably understood as reflections on actual events—specifically, the execution of Jesus of Nazareth as "the King of the Jews" under the procuratorship of Pontius Pilate—rather than as "prophecy historicized." A view such as Crossan's will be compelling only to those unfamiliar with the tradition of Jewish scriptural interpretation. That many have found it compelling suggests to me the continuation of a long-standing tradition of studying Christian origins in which the voices of our Jewish colleagues remain silenced, to our own detriment and impoverishment.

Further, such reflections indicate the degree to which we speak appropriately of the work of God as genuinely historical. The shape of the Christian tradition owes a great deal to Pontius Pilate who formulated a charge against Jesus. If he had chosen different words, who knows how we might be called?

Finally, such historical reflection can suggest that the church has not been misguided in concentrating, as do the gospels, on those dramatic events that marked the climax of Jesus' career. While there appears to have been enough in Jesus' public ministry to give rise to various interpretations of his career, the New Testament—and the "Christian" tradition—have chosen to view that ministry through the lens of the cross: whatever else Jesus may have said and done must make sense in light of those events that marked the climax of his confrontation with the religious and political establishment. The historical Jesus finished his ministry a failure and a disappointment, hanging from a Roman cross as "King of the Jews." The central question is what God accomplished on and through the cross. While our interpretation of that work of God may leave much to be desired, historical study should not undermine our conviction that this is the crucial matter after all. ⊕

Word & World
Supplement Series 3
1997

Jesus and the Manifest Power of God

DAVID L. TIEDE

Luther Seminary
St. Paul, Minnesota

WHEN JOHN THE BAPTIST'S MESSENGERS DEPARTED, JESUS, ALLUDING TO MALACHI 3, asked the crowds:

> What did you go out into the wilderness to look at? A reed shaken by the wind? What then did you go out to see? Someone dressed in soft robes? Look, those who put on fine clothing and live in luxury are in royal palaces. A prophet? Yes, I tell you, and more than a prophet. This is the one about whom it is written, "See I am sending my messenger ahead of you, who will prepare your way before you." I tell you, among those born of women no one is greater than John; yet the least in the kingdom of God is greater than he. (Luke 7:24-28)

And when the Greeks who had come to festival worship approached Philip, they said, "Sir, we wish to see Jesus!" (John 12:21). What did they hope to see?

What is the purpose of our quest for Jesus? Some stand in the long line from Reimarus to Wrede, honing critical methods to move behind the church's faith to make their own rational judgment concerning the "historical Jesus."[1] Some comb the sources to seek Jesus the peasant liberator or Jesus the sage or Jesus the spiritual guide. One might be a secret Nicodemus yearning for new birth, for restoration of the promises. Others are on a post-Christian journey, a search for a thoroughly human Jesus. The quests of the last three centuries are replete with companions on all these forms of pilgrimage.[2]

Terms like "quest" and "pilgrimage" still reflect religious or spiritual purposes, but their force needs to be understood anew in each circumstance. In earlier

---

[1]Albert Schweitzer, *The Quest of the Historical Jesus: A Critical Study of its Progress from Reimarus to Wrede* (1906; reprint, London: A. & C. Black, 1954).

[2]For a concise summary, see Paul Rhodes Eddy, "Jesus as Diogenes? Reflections on the Cynic Jesus Thesis," *JBL* 115 (1996) 449-469.

times, Christian Europe proudly exhibited the splendor of its churches and universities, and the theological faculties reigned as "queen of the sciences" of human knowledge. Intellectual inquiry was lively, and a quest for Jesus could have been an enterprise of the Christian faith seeking understanding and finally seeking God. In later years, the rationalistic sciences of the enlightenment wrested the universities from the church, and the quest for the historical Jesus was caught up in the efforts of the intellectual estate to free Jesus from the shackles of church dogma. This was also a quest for Jesus, but increasingly ambivalent about the biblical God.

The so-called "second quest" was the effort of Christian scholars who survived the second world war. Their pilgrimage led to the earliest Christian memories and oral traditions about Jesus.[3] Here they encountered a thoroughly Jewish Jesus announcing the kingdom of God. They abandoned the effort to get behind these early sources, all of them infused with Christian faith but still differing significantly. They were seeking to see Jesus as much as possible through the eyes of his earliest followers and from there to understand how the many presentations of Jesus developed over time. This quest also sought to apprehend the experience and revelation of God which the earliest Christians knew through their encounter with Jesus in his words and works, then crucified and raised.

The "third quest" is a post-modern enterprise, both in the sense of its simple acceptance of the relativity of all historical research and in its confidence in the human "construction of reality" as reality. Here the quest is unapologetic in its effort to construe the past. John Dominic Crossan contends, "If you cannot believe in something produced by reconstruction, you may have nothing left to believe in."[4] Historical work must be carefully pursued because these efforts undergird the legitimacy of its reconstruction, and great attention is paid to the poetry (ποίημα: anything made or done). This is also a quest for god, because god is a human fabrication.

"We would see Jesus." What did you come out to see?

Do you seek healing? Have you brought a sick child, a disabling condition, a deep grief, a soul disturbed by evil inclinations? Are you deprived of justice, hungry, dispossessed? The affluent and elite seldom regarded desperate human quests as legitimate reasons to look for Jesus. The rulers of Israel along with Jesus' disciples found them disquieting. Profound, urgent need disturbs religious systems which those who carefully contrived them defend righteously.

Then what about our "Quest for Jesus and the Christian Faith"? We who are engaged in sophisticated historical and theological discussion may also be embarrassed by empassioned pleas. Most of the so-called miracle stories have also been ignored or dismissed by modern scholarship, although they fill page after page of the gospels. Apparently Jesus was not put off by intense human need.

[3]See Günther Bornkamm, *Jesus of Nazareth* (original 1956; trans., New York: Harper and Row, 1960).

[4]John Dominic Crossan, *The Historical Jesus: The Life of a Mediterranean Jewish Peasant* (San Francisco: HarperSanFrancisco, 1991) 426.

My assignment in this essay is to deal with the Jesus traditions of healing, exorcism, and wonders. In part, this may be my penance for no longer teaching regularly in the scripture division at Luther Seminary.[5] My goal is to influence the reader's quest, emphasizing that we cannot see or meet Jesus for the first or any other time without encountering the presence of God's mighty rule. If we go out into the wilderness or into the seminar room or somewhere else in an honest effort to encounter Jesus, that quest will inevitably expose our own convictions about God, the world, and ourselves.

Furthermore, we cannot do historical justice to Jesus unless we understand him within his thoroughly Jewish, first-century context. When the Christian creeds confess that Jesus was "born of the virgin Mary and crucified under Pontius Pilate," they acknowledge that no Christ of faith or spiritual Jesus exists apart from this historical figure. Whether our quest for Jesus is that of Christian faith or of human spirituality, the path is thoroughly historical, and Jesus the first-century Jew will point us to his God, the God of Israel, like it or not.

This is a journey of the mind, but let no one feign dispassion. We quest in order to find something. The quest for Jesus is also a matter of heart and soul, even for those who would rescue Jesus from the Christian tradition. Research into what we can know about Jesus from the miracle stories soon encounters witness to the manifest power of God. Quite properly, this quest leads to faith in God, understanding Jesus as Messiah, and obeying the Holy Spirit.

I. FAITH IN GOD: I BELIEVE IN THE RESURRECTION OF THE BODY

A. Theological convictions count: "Nothing is impossible with God"

About 20 years ago, I was laboring in my office on a summer day, writing an article. It was hot. The window and the door were propped open to catch the breeze, and public radio was on. My colleague Marc Kolden stuck his head in the door and declared, "I see you don't believe in the New Testament miracles!"

To say I was dumbfounded would be an understatement.

"You are a student of Rudolph Bultmann," he teased. "Bultmann argued that anyone who has heard a radio no longer believes in the miracles."

I'm a little slow on the uptake, but two decades later I have an answer: "Anyone who believes in the resurrection of the body can cope with the miracles!" Or to raise the horizon one more time, anyone who believes in the triune God can hope for the resurrection of the body. What's more, the radio was developed in a period of mechanical science, with little knowledge of the dynamic indeterminacy of the world of space, time, waves, particles, energy, and matter in the new physics.

Let me state three convictions about resurrection before returning to miracles.

---

[5]The project of my doctoral dissertation is now again attracting interest as the third stage of the scholarly quest focuses on the deeds of Jesus: David L. Tiede, *The Charismatic Figure as Miracle Worker*, SBLDS 1 (Missoula, MT: Society of Biblical Literature, 1972).

1. Belief in the resurrection of the body does not qualify someone as an historian, but neither does it disqualify. At this stage, it is about being respectful and honest to the historical testimony of our sources. The chief priests and Pharisees in Matt 27:62-66, who petitioned Pilate to set a guard on the tomb, feared the disciples of Jesus the impostor (πλάνος) would "steal him away, and tell the people, 'He has been raised from the dead,' and the last deception (πλάνη) would be worse than the first." Matthew's report is more surprising with respect to the Pharisees, who otherwise were thought to believe in bodily resurrection (see Acts 23:1-11),[6] but less so with the chief priests, who were seen by Jesus' followers as having much to protect (see John 11:45-53).

Those who deny the possibility of the resurrection of the body must disallow both the historical testimony and the faith of the New Testament. John Dominic Crossan asserts that Jesus' body was dug up and eaten by wild dogs, although no source mentions even the fear of such a possibility. Gerd Luedemann, writing as a Christian, holds that the body decayed in the tomb: "The literal statements about the resurrection...have lost their literal meaning with the revolution in the scientific picture of the world."[7] Then by his own literal "scientific picture of the world," Lüdemann simply claims to have "explained away" the consistent New Testament witness to resurrection.

2. Belief in the resurrection does not mean an ability to explain what happened in my personal frame of reference, my standard for the truth. Paul resists just such presumptions: "But someone will ask," says Paul (1 Corinthians 15), "'How are the dead raised? With what kind of body do they come?' Fool!...Listen, I will tell you a mystery!...For this perishable body must put on imperishability, and this mortal body must put on immortality."

3. The resurrection of the body is an eschatological event, a signal of the last judgment, an apocalypse of God's agency. This is exactly why it is so confounding to those who want Jesus in their control. As Paul put it, "None of the rulers of this age understood this; for if they had they would not have crucified the Lord of glory" (1 Cor 2:8). The resurrection is no mere message of existential significance, declaring that Jesus died but Christ rose in the church's preaching. The early Christians knew how to venerate a martyr like Stephen, but the sources consistently show they were unprepared for the manifest power of God displayed in Jesus' resurrection. The resurrection is God's vindication of Jesus, placing all of Jesus' works and words in a new light for his followers and adversaries alike.

The Bible's wonders, signs, mighty acts, and displays of power, which moderns call "miracles," were astonishing and inexplicable in the ancient world too. That was just the point of telling about them. But the force of these stories was felt quite differently in diverse cultures or traditions of interpretation in the first century as people sought to understand or make sense of events beyond their knowledge or experience.

---

[6]See also Josephus, *Ant.* 18.12-17 and *War* 2.163-166.

[7]Gerd Luedemann, *The Resurrection of Jesus* (Philadelphia: Fortress, 1994) 180. Cf. John Dominic Crossan, *Who Killed Jesus?* (San Francisco: HarperSanFrancisco, 1995).

The apostle Paul cites the proverb, "Jews demand signs and Greeks seek wisdom" (1 Cor 1:22). At the risk of separating Jerusalem too far from Athens,[8] it is noteworthy that the scriptural vocabulary for "signs," "wonders," and "mighty acts" expresses Israel's convictions about God. The interpretation of the inexplicable lies in the prophecies, scriptural testimony, or story of what God has done in Israel's history. Jews demanded signs because their standard of truth and meaning was scriptural and theological.

The broader hellenistic quest for wisdom, on the other hand, is also reflected in its distinctive vocabulary for "miracles," reflecting a differing epistemology. The language of "magic," "impossibilities" (ἀδύαντα), "thaumaturgy," and "paradoxography" (a literary genre in itself) reflects this more philosophic signification. The eventual dominance of this intellectual and cultural tradition in Christendom caused scriptural signs, wonders, and mighty acts to be measured by the standard of "natural law."[9] Then the scientific rationalism of the western enlightenment all but foreclosed the possibility of miracles by defining these phenomena in terms that were categorically impossible.

The confidence, indeed the arrogance, of this closed metaphysical model of the universe has been challenged profoundly elsewhere—which is not to say that the miracles are any more comprehensible than before, surely not explicable except by the scriptural standard of truth. But perhaps the theological testimony of the scriptures may be heard without being shouted down summarily as "impossible."

Those who would see Jesus within his own world and understand the claim he represents would do well to listen to Mary's testimony in Luke 1:37, which is itself a scriptural echo of the word of the Lord to Sarah in Gen 18:14: "nothing will be impossible with God" (οὐκ ἀδυνατήσει παρὰ τοῦ θεοῦ πᾶν ῥῆμα).

B. The sources are abundant: "Many have undertaken to set down an orderly account!"

When they come to study such figures as Socrates, Alexander the Great, or Caesar Augustus, historians would be delighted to have a fraction of the datable sources we have for Jesus. Even the canonical gospels suggest a surfeit of accounts and an inexhaustible treasury of stories (Luke 1:1-2; John 21:24-25). The scholarship of the last two centuries has produced incredibly detailed and industrious efforts to identify and explore the pre-literary and literary sources that lie behind the canonical gospels. In the last forty years, sources and texts which were once regarded as apocryphal or late and heretical have attracted immense interest on the chance that they may contain early materials which by-passed the Christian community's collection and canonization of the fourfold gospels.

This meticulous attention to diverse sources is an historical enterprise, but it is never neutral. As Mary Knutsen observed, the Jesus tradition has become the livelihood of a generation of scholars in institutions which are legally aloof, if not

---

[8]See John J. Collins, *Between Athens and Jerusalem: Jewish Identity in the Hellenistic Diaspora* (New York: Crossroad, 1983). Martin Hengel, *Judaism and Hellenism* (Philadephia: Fortress, 1974.) For an exemplary encounter between these two worldviews, see Origen, *Contra Celsum.*

[9]See Robert M. Grant, *Miracle and Natural Law in Graeco-Roman and Early Christian Thought* (Amsterdam: North Holland, 1952).

culturally hostile to the Christian faith.[10] This scholarship needs a non-canonical Jesus tradition, and it has produced a very successful industry.

Even when dealing with the gospels in the New Testament, this historical research is driven alternatively by either a *suspicion* or a *concern*, depending on the prior commitments of the investigator. The suspicion is generally that the canonical gospels were so intent on proclaiming faith in the risen Christ that they neglected or misrepresented the historical Jesus. Here the "criterion of dissimilarity" reigns supreme in efforts to liberate Jesus from his perceived ecclesiastical captivity, ancient and modern. The suspicion seeks to construct a portrait of Jesus from the few details that cannot be discredited because they serve the faith of Jesus' followers. Think about what an odd exercise this is for an historian; it is guaranteed to produce a peculiar Jesus. Each generation of scholars again dons the guise of the investigative reporter for a fresh verdict.

The popular appeal of the "I-Team" regularly feeds upon discrediting any official interpretation of emotionally powerful events. The Zapruder film of President Kennedy's assassination and the murder of Lee Harvey Oswald before millions of live television viewers only intensified the question, "Who killed JFK?" Surely the FBI is hiding something. Or in Robert Funk's language, "The religious establishment has not allowed the intelligence of high scholarship to pass through pastors and priests to a hungry laity."[11] This interpretation from suspicion must itself be held accountable.

The historical research driven by *concern*, however, also seeks to understand the building blocks of the Jesus tradition as they were assembled in the Christian gospels. Genuinely interested in identifying earlier historical strata or sources, this research constantly seeks to glean what it may from the more adversarial inquisition of suspicion. The concern is not to disabuse, but to understand the testimony of the sources as addressed in distinct forms in diverse contexts. In this more comprehensive enterprise, the limits of the criterion of dissimilarity also become evident. As Nils Dahl put it, "We know Jesus only as the disciples remembered him."[12] But what can be discerned of Jesus' agency or force as identified within his historical context and as traced through a complex development in memory and manuscript?

Helmut Koester's 1968 essay, "One Jesus and Four Primitive Gospels,"[13] was a monumental achievement in three senses of the word. First, it marked the culmination of over a century of source criticism in its identification of the genre and plausible community uses of pre-canonical sayings sources, apocalyptic oracles, collections of miracles, and narratives concerning Jesus' cross and resurrection.

[10]See Mary Knutsen's essay in this volume, pp. 13-32.

[11]See the citation of Funk's keynote address at the opening of the Jesus Seminar in 1985 in Richard B. Hays, "The Corrected Jesus," *First Things* (May, 1994) 47-48. The analogy to Crossan's title, *Who Killed Jesus?* or even to the soap-opera fiction "Who shot JR?" should not be missed.

[12]Nils A. Dahl, "The Problem of the Historical Jesus," in *Jesus the Christ*, ed. Donald H. Juel (Minneapolis: Fortress, 1991) 94.

[13]Helmut Koester, "One Jesus and Four Primitive Gospels," *HTR* 61 (1968) 203-247.

Secondly, this essay pointed researchers to paths around the canonical gospels from the diverse early collections, which Koester called the "primitive gospels," to the para- and post-canonical sources, traditionally called apocryphal gospels. Koester's essay demonstrated how thoroughly the canonical gospels had gathered divergent portraits of Jesus as sage, miracle worker, and apocalyptic prophet into the early Christian confession of him as crucified and vindicated. But the very possibility of these pre-canonical or primitive "gospels" also suggested an alternative way back to Jesus, evading the normative Christian traditions. Perhaps, the gnostic scribes in Nag Hammadi did not merely pervert canonical sources. Surely they had spiritual ancestors among the opponents of Paul. Could they also have had "gospels" or collections of Jesus' sayings that were like those possessed by Paul's opponents before the canonical gospels were composed? *If so,* then the sayings of Jesus could again be cut free from the cross-resurrection narrative which Mark "invented" to proclaim the εὐαγγέλιον.[14]

Thirdly, Koester's essay set up a monument directing broadly divergent modern perspectives toward compatible understandings and claims upon Jesus in the first centuries of the common era. His work, published along with that of James Robinson,[15] spawned a generation of doctoral dissertations on the future of early Christianity,[16] including my own thesis against the θεῖος ἀνήρ (divine man) as a category for the way those who recited Jesus' miracles understood him.[17]

Koester's approach both aids and poses deep problems for our concern. He highlighted the intent of the canonical gospels to interpret Jesus' sayings, acts, and prophetic oracles in the light of his crucifixion. Jesus' execution is the most documented datum of Jesus' history, arguably the most profound memory of his disciples, and essential to faith in the resurrection of the body.

But the possibility that the late, divergent, and apocryphal gospels had pre-canonical prototypes also gave free rein to renewed quests for Jesus as guru, spiritual guide, or bandit, evading the foolishness or stumbling block of a crucified Messiah.[18] Furthermore, pressing Jesus so thoroughly into the religious conflicts and milieu of the broader Greco-Roman world has made him less historically comprehensible within his local Galilean setting prior to the Roman destruction of the second temple.

C. *Jesus was engaged in the restoration of Israel: "Lord will you now restore the kingdom to Israel?"*

It is not possible to develop a comprehensive approach to these issues in the confines of this essay. In my efforts to guide our quest for Jesus, I have refused to dismiss the miracles as historically impossible. I have emphasized the scriptural

---

[14]See Willi Marxsen, *Mark the Evangelist* (Nashville: Abingdon, 1969).

[15]James Robinson, *Trajectories through Early Christianity* (Philadelphia: Fortress, 1971).

[16]See the essays in Koester's honor, published under this title, *The Future of Early Christianity*, ed. Birger A. Pearson (Minneapolis: Augsburg, 1991).

[17]Tiede, *Charismatic Figure.*

[18]The centrality of this ignominious death in Paul (1 Cor 1:23) indicates this to be the central point where history and faith meet (even historically and theologically prior to Jesus' resurrection).

signification of Jesus' mighty acts, and I have pressed back into the datable first-century canonical gospels in order to direct the quest for Jesus to the Roman provinces of Galilee and Judea. My understanding of the hellenization of Galilee fits more with that of Sean Freyne and Eric Meyers (i.e., a culture still more Jewish than Greek) and less with those who propose the garb of a Cynic sage for Jesus.[19] The reader will also observe my dependence upon our two most comprehensive and historiographic late first-century Jewish and/or Christian writers, Josephus and the author of Luke-Acts.

My historical proposal fits closely with that of E. P. Sanders. It also involves a theological judgment as to the character of Jesus' mission, including his mighty acts. According to Sanders:

> As we proceed to the study of other material, we must bear in mind the most secure conclusions: Jesus expected the kingdom in the near future, he awaited the rebuilding of the temple, he called the "twelve" to symbolize the restoration of Israel, and his disciples thought about the kingdom concretely enough to ask about their place in it. Thus we cannot shift the normal expectations of Jewish restoration theology to the periphery.[20]

As I have written earlier:

> The critical question for all Israel was how God would fulfill the scriptural promises of salvation and restoration. Jesus took a distinctive position on this central hope....This Galilean prophet and sage stood out among the teachers of Israel's hope, but he can only be understood as one of them. [21]

II. UNDERSTANDING JESUS: THE KINGDOM OF GOD HAS COME UPON YOU!

The following passage from Luke was composed from traditions also shared with Mark and Matthew:

> Now he was casting out a demon that was mute; when the demon had gone out, the one who had been mute spoke, and the crowds were amazed. But some of them said, "He casts out demons by Beelzebul, the ruler of the demons." Others, to test him, kept demanding from him a sign from heaven. But he knew what they were thinking and said to them, "Every kingdom divided against itself becomes a desert, and house falls on house. If Satan also is divided against himself, how will his kingdom stand?—for you say that I cast out the demons by Beelzebul. Now if I cast out the demons by Beelzebul, by whom do your exorcists cast them out? Therefore they will be your judges. But if it is by the finger of God that I cast out the demons, then the kingdom of God has come to you. When a strong man, fully armed, guards his castle, his property is safe. But when one stronger than he attacks him and overpowers him, he takes away his armor in which he trusted and divides his plunder. Whoever is not with me is against me, and whoever does not gather with me scatters." (Luke 11:14-23 NRSV)

These powerful declarations of Jesus about himself and Beelzebul are attested in all three synoptic gospels and probably in the "sayings source." As

---

[19]See the discussion in the essay in this volume by Walter Taylor, Jr., pp. 49-71.

[20]E. P. Sanders, *Jesus and Judaism* (Philadelphia: Fortress, 1985) 156.

[21]David Tiede, *Jesus and the Future* (New York: Cambridge University, 1990) 38.

Sanders observes, "In broad terms, there is not much dispute about what Jesus thought. He thought that the kingdom would come in the near future and that God was at work in a special way in his own ministry."[22] But how was it special? The problem quickly becomes not the wonders, but the wonder-worker.

Probably John the Baptist, Honi the Circle Drawer, and Theudas the revolutionary shared the general thoughts that the kingdom would come in the near future and that God was at work in a special way in them. So we are right in seeking to understand Jesus within this cadre of teachers or "action prophets," leading toward what N. T. Wright calls the "reconstitution of Israel."[23] But in Jesus' thought and action, what was the "special way" that God was at work toward this reconstitution or restoration? Can we say more about Jesus' self-presentation or how he was interpreted in Israel's faith?

A. Jesus enacted and proclaimed the word of God

It is difficult to identify the exact points at which particular scriptural interpretations of Jesus' words and actions enter the tradition, but the sources portray Jesus himself as actively engaged in the process. Not only is it surprising that the evangelists would report that Jesus was accused of being in league with Beelzebul, his sabbath healings put him in direct conflict with the interpreters of the law. Would such action not put God to the test? In Mark 3:4 Jesus confronts such views directly with a word that summarizes the conflict in classical Pharisaic terms: "Is it lawful on the sabbath to do good or to do harm, to save a life or to kill?"[24]

In Luke 7:11-17, when Jesus raised the widow's son, he was hailed as a great prophet like Elijah and a visitation of God. Could Jesus have consciously imitated Elijah, as John the Baptist apparently did? Clearly the evangelist saw this action as an incursion of God's reign.

When in Luke 11:20 Jesus refers to casting out demons by "the finger of God" (see Matt 12:28: "by the Spirit of God"), the allusion is clearly to Exod 8:19 where Pharaoh's magicians recognized God's true power at work in Moses and Aaron. But did this scriptural signification originate with Jesus or the tradition or with the evangelist's efforts to identify Jesus as "the prophet like Moses" (see Acts 3:22; 7:37; Deut 18:15)? When did Jesus' use of the kingdom prophecies of Isa 61:1-2 and Isa 35:5-6 enter the tradition to identify his healings as fulfillments of God's promises (Luke 4:16-30; 7:22)?

The question returns repeatedly as Jesus' mighty works are linked with the fulfillment of scriptural testimonies concerning God's agency or the appearance of God's reign, always within Israel's history. By comparing and contrasting these accounts concerning Jesus with those we have about other figures, Jesus' identity with other Jewish prophets becomes evident and his distinctive profile begins to emerge.

---

[22]Sanders, *Jesus and Judaism*, 155.

[23]See N. T. Wright , *Jesus and the Victory of God*, vol. 2 of *Christian Origins and the Question of God* (Minneapolis: Fortress, 1996) 168-169.

[24]See *Aboth de Rabbi Nathan*, 31.

Geza Vermes places Jesus within the select company of "first-century charismatic Judaism," as one of the hasidim or "holy ones," the men of deed or miracle workers (see Luke 24:19: "a prophet mighty in deed and word"). Honi the Circle Drawer and Hanina ben Dosa fit this pattern. Vermes cites David Flusser's observation of "the inevitable tension between charismatic miracles and institutional Judaism."[25] Later tradition claims that a first-century B.C. leader of the Pharisees wanted to excommunicate Honi, but dared not. Upon healing someone at a distance, the first-century A.D. Hanina was asked, "Are you a prophet?"[26] Vermes argues that these "charismatic miracle workers" caused offense by their being less scrupulous in their religious observance than some officials desired, and they provoked opposition because of their popularity.

The Jewish historian Josephus also tells of a first-century figure named Theudas, who is also mentioned by Gamaliel in Acts 5:36 as "claiming to be somebody." Theudas "persuaded the majority of the masses to take up their possessions and follow him to the Jordan River. He stated that he was a prophet and that at his command the river would be parted and would provide them an easy passage."[27] Although Josephus regards him a fraud (γόης) and reports his easy execution by the Romans, Theudas is a self-proclaimed prophet whose intended wonder-working was a scriptural re-enactment of the miraculous crossing of the Jordan in Joshua's conquest (Joshua 3).

Josephus also tells of several prophetic figures in the midst of the siege and destruction of Jerusalem. He refers to "deceivers and imposters" who led the masses into the wilderness where God would show them "signs of deliverance" (σημεῖα ἐλευθηερίας) and of an Egyptian who "passed himself off as a prophet," rallying the people for an assault on the city, promising the walls would fall down at his command, an act that would do Joshua proud.[28]

According to Josephus, a "rude peasant," "Jesus, son of Ananias," was moved, like Jeremiah, to cry out a prophecy of doom on the city for "seven years and five months," in spite of repeated beatings by the authorities: "Woe to Jerusalem!" "He neither cursed any of those who beat him from day to day, nor blessed those who offered him food: to all men that melancholy presage was his one reply. His cries were loudest at the festivals." Then finally in besieged Jerusalem, says Josephus, this Jesus "added a last word, 'And woe to me also'" as a stone from a catapult hit and killed him.[29]

These accounts are examples of wonder-workers and charismatic figures, prophets from Galilee and Judea in approximately the same era as Jesus. They identify themselves as or are called "prophets," and their deeds display the presence and power of divine activity. All with scriptural prototypes, they provoke

---

[25]Geza Vermes, *Jesus the Jew* (Philadelphia: Fortress, 1973) 79-80.

[26]Ibid., 81, with citations on 243. These sources are much more difficult to assess historically than the canonical gospels.

[27]Josephus, *Ant.* 20.97-98. See also Tiede, *Charismatic Figure*, 178-240.

[28]Josephus, *War* 2.258-263, and *Ant.* 20.169-170.

[29]Josephus, *War* 6.301-309.

conflict over divergent proposals for Israel's salvation or restoration. Even Josephus, who regarded himself as a prophet, appealed to the "records of the ancient prophets" and cried out to besieged Jerusalem, offering restoration of the temple sacrifices and salvation for the city by relying on Roman virtue.[30]

All Israel had the scriptures. All Israel hoped for God's salvation. But how would God's manifest power accomplish restoration? Israel was divided.

Surely the tradition and the canonical evangelists amplified and further identified how Jesus' words and deeds constituted the fulfillment of the scriptures (see the formula quotations in Matthew). Careful study of individual stories and elements of the tradition will demonstrate the ways the tradition amplified faint scriptural echoes or implied allusions. Further insight will be gained by correlating such traditions with the ascription of Jesus' titles as Son of God, Son of Man, Lord, Savior, prophet, and Messiah. But the practice of other Galilean prophets demonstrates that Jesus himself also infused his deeds and words with scriptural precedents. This is how he, like any other prophet, marked the "special way" that his works and words inaugurated the fulfillment of God's promised restoration of Israel.

B. Jesus confronted his adversaries with mighty deeds

Jesus of Nazareth was embedded in Israel's history. He was "a prophet mighty in deed and word before God and all the people." He was "crucified under Pontius Pilate," like many of his compatriots. "But," say the travelers to Emmaus, "we had hoped he was the one to redeem Israel" (Luke 24:19-21).

Although he contended with the powers of "waterless places," Jesus was not an ascetic who withdrew to the wilderness, either to eat locusts and wild honey by the Jordan or to write tracts among the Dead Sea sectarians against the wicked priest in Jerusalem. That was not his program of restoration. He was schooled in the synagogue, but he refused the kingdom of the strict observance of the Pharisees. He did move to cleanse the temple and grieved its fate, but he was no pretender to the restoration of the office of the high priest or the temple bureaucracy with its links with the occupation forces. He was executed with probable bandits and revolutionaries, but he did not raise up a force or seek to accomplish a restoration of the kingdom to Israel through the holy warfare of Joshua.

Jesus' disciples remembered his signs, wonders, and mighty acts as manifesting the "special way" God was at work toward Israel's restoration. He not only healed the sick, but he did so on the sabbath, showing messianic license in his interpretation of sabbath observance. He exorcized demonic powers, a display of God's mercy to the afflicted and a gauntlet laid down to those who rejected his program of restoration. He touched the unclean, was touched by the desperate, and transgressed the boundaries of ritual pollution of the dead. He tamed the sea, like Moses of old, and he presented himself as the sign of Jonah, calling for a return to God in accepting his mission.

Jesus' works and words prompted questions of his identity—scriptural ques-

---

[30]Josephus, *War* 6.96-117.

tions: "Are you the one who is to come or are we to wait for another?" (Luke 7:20); expectations from those who were "looking for the redemption of Jerusalem" (Luke 2:38) or "waiting for the kingdom of God" (Luke 23:51); questions of the future: "Lord, is this the time when you will restore the kingdom to Israel?" (Acts 1:6); truth questions: even unto the present, his disciples have "examined the scriptures daily to see whether these things were so" (Acts 17:11).

It is now impossible to know exactly what Jesus thought of himself as distinguished from what he prompted others to think of him. His first followers saw him on an intentional mission, not to be deterred, and his mighty acts fit his goal. "Listen, I am performing cures today and tomorrow, and on the third day I finish my work. Yet today, tomorrow, and the next day I must be on my way, because it is impossible for a prophet to be killed outside of Jerusalem" (Luke 13:32-33). All four of the canonical gospels testify to the "necessity" or scriptural and divine design of Jesus' mission: showing forth the manifest power of God in signs, wonders, and mighty acts, leading to death by crucifixion. Jesus the Galilean prophet knew he was on his way to die. Surely it was predictable, if not inevitable. His mission of restoration was an act of obedience, requiring God's action to be completed. "God has made him both Lord and Messiah," declares Acts, "this Jesus whom you crucified."

Now this is the manifest power of God: "If it is by the finger of God that I cast out the demons, then the kingdom of God has come to you!"

If our quest is to see Jesus, we will encounter the manifest power of God as Jesus enacted God's distinctive restoration of the kingdom to Israel. This is the same Jesus God raised up, vindicating his words and deeds and sustaining the merciful mission of restoration in his name to all the earth.

III. OBEDIENCE TO THE SPIRIT: YOU SHALL BE MY WITNESSES

Almost a century ago, Albert Schweitzer wrote:

> He comes to us as One unknown, without a name, as of old, by the lake-side, He came to those men who knew Him not. He speaks to us the same word; "Follow thou me!" and sets us to the tasks which He has to fulfil for our time. He commands. And to those who obey Him, whether they be wise or simple, He will reveal Himself in the toils, the conflicts, the sufferings which they shall pass through in His fellowship, and, as an ineffable mystery, they shall learn in their own experience, Who He is.[31]

This is a calling worthy of a lifetime. At his leprosarium on the Zambezi River, Schweitzer saw the Jesus whose love for the outcasts offended the righteous. We can glimpse Jesus' alternative reign of mercy in the humble tasks and toils of our time. Jesus' holy life can teach our souls to forsake self-interest. If we yearn to experience this wonderful fellowship, we will come and see Jesus.

But Jesus is not done with us. He is no longer where they laid him. Jesus' holy life, his wisdom of mercy, his mighty acts of love, his suffering and death will

[31]Albert Schweitzer, *The Quest of the Historical Jesus* (1906; trans., New York: Macmillan, 1961) 403.

restore our souls and the world, because in him the fullness of God dwells. God raised him to be Messiah and sent the Holy Spirit that we may serve his reign on earth as in heaven. The ineffable mystery is deeper than we dreamed. Our quest for Jesus will end, finally, in God. ⊕

Word & World
Supplement Series 3
1997

What Is the Saving Work
of Christ?

SARAH HENRICH

Luther Seminary
St. Paul, Minnesota

THIS TITLE ASKS A QUESTION THAT KNOWS NO BOUNDS. WOMEN AND MEN HAVE been pondering and answering this question in various ways and from various angles of approach for centuries. One who confesses that Jesus of Nazareth is the Christ could answer one way. But the approach would be different were one to ask the question from a more general "historical" perspective. How in the first century might one (anyone) be understood to be God's Christ, and what role would the work of such a one play in his (or her) designation as such? In this essay I will limit the question in two ways. I will pursue it, first, in the context of an interest in the historical Jesus. In that setting, we turn not to systematic theology, but to the biblical witness and the work of historians who ask about Jesus of Nazareth. (I will discuss in a moment whether this enterprise—thinking about the saving work of Christ in relation to Jesus of Nazareth—is worth carrying out.)

I will confine my work primarily to the witness to Jesus of Nazareth in the New Testament. Because our question concerns the saving work of *Christ*, however, we must consider the New Testament witness along with other Jewish witnesses up through the first century A.D. "Christ" is neither a name nor a clear and self-explanatory title. Its content stems from its tradition: Jewish belief, practice, and scripture. Jon Levenson is not alone when he refers to the "heated apocalyptic Judaism that served as the matrix of Christianity."[1]

---

[1]Jon D. Levenson, *The Death and Resurrection of the Beloved Son: The Transformation of Child Sacrifice in Judaism and Christianity* (New Haven: Yale University, 1993) 209. This is also the view of many others. Among the most articulate exemplars are Paula Fredriksen, "What You See is What You Get: Context and Content in Current Research on the Historical Jesus," *TToday* 52 (1995) 75-97; Richard Hays, *Echoes of Scripture in the Letters of Paul* (New Haven: Yale University, 1989); N. T. Wright, *The New Testament and the People of God*, vol. 1 of *Christian Origins and the Question of God* (Minneapolis: Fortress, 1992).

In a second limitation, I will concentrate within the New Testament on Luke-Acts. This decision is a somewhat arbitrary way to limit the material, but, in fact, Luke makes abundant use of and shows great interest in "salvation" in connection with the work of Jesus of Nazareth. Furthermore we benefit from the book of Acts, Luke's own reflection on his gospel.

I. Is History Possible?

To begin: Is the question about the saving work of the Messiah worth asking in relation to Jesus of Nazareth, given our sources? One of my colleagues says quite simply, "There is no historical Jesus." He puts straightforwardly what is ultimately both true and not true. Few of us seek detailed knowledge of Jesus and imagine that we know the man or his messiahship from such details. We acknowledge that every Jesus we meet is a Jesus interpreted from as much evidence as we can bring to bear, including our own experience of the living Lord. Wayne Meeks suggests that "history is also a constructed narrative, not experimentally corrigible like the fictions of the natural sciences."[2] To construct a narrative, particularly an ongoing one, is to imagine connections between episodes and actors, to discern at least some elements of a plot that continues. Precisely because we believe that the "plot" of this story continues and that some of the "characters" in it continue to be involved in our own dramas, we need to do the best job we can in exercising our historical imaginations. Because I will never know my husband or parents fully in the present, let alone in the past, does not mean that their history is of no importance as I seek to know better their present. Nor does it suggest that *any* "constructed narrative" will do to deepen my sense of who they are.

What is to be gained by deepening our sense of who Jesus of Nazareth was and how he understood himself (or was understood) to be related to the Christ of Israel's God? The simplest response stems from the fact that "the Gospel is the proclamation that certain events *happened* and wrought a fundamental transformation in our relationship to God."[3] Saving was considered to be an historical event. As Paula Fredriksen says, "Modern Christianity's continuing commitment to a theology of the Incarnation is thus expressed in its quest for the Jesus of history. The church, by claiming faith in Jesus as the unique occasion of divine revelation, thus lays upon itself the obligation to do history."[4] Luke T. Johnson, in a strong argument against reconstructions of the historical Jesus, insists, "It is not the facts of Jesus' life that can find new expression in the lives of others, but rather the pattern of his existence. Jesus' existence as one of radical obedience toward God and self-disposing service toward others forms a pattern for all humanity that can

---

[2]Wayne Meeks, review of *Rediscovering Paul: Philemon and the Sociology of Paul's Narrative World*, by Norman Petersen, in *JBL* 106 (1987) 558. Meeks begins this sentence with an "if," but leaves little doubt in his review that he thinks this is so.

[3]Richard Hays, in a review of recent literature on the "third quest," in *First Things* 64 (1996) 44-46.

[4]Paula Fredriksen, *From Jesus to Christ: The Origins of the New Testament Images of Jesus* (New Haven: Yale University, 1988) 214-15. Her argument is undergirded by the need to do good history. Bad history, she insists, "results in bad theology, the subtle Docetism of anachronism."

be written in the heart by the Holy Spirit."[5] Such a pattern is formed and revealed in narrative about the public ministry of Jesus and his death. No part of these stories can stand alone and tell us all we need to know. But, if no part of these narratives corresponds to any of the "certain events" that *happened*, how can we talk about a "fundamental transformation in our relationship to God"? If Jesus bears God among us, how does God look? If Jesus is Messiah, how does that look? How do we know that he is not the anointed of Isis or Baal? Why are the Jews unpersuaded? This interest in history, then, is theological, as both Ernst Käsemann and N. T. Wright argue, suggesting that our failure to seek to know Jesus as well as we can puts us at the mercy of various constructions of Jesus that may come from anywhere.

Something is to be gained. To be sure, it is "interpretation all the way down." Still, knowing that history is itself a fictive process does not mean that we can make no statement about Jesus of Nazareth that may help us think about how his saving work may have been conceived in his own day. Jesus himself interpreted the traditions of his people and the circumstances of his day. He was, in turn, interpreted by those around him, just as he has been interpreted by the evangelists and countless others since that time. But the fact that all history is interpretation does not mean there is no history—only that we must be modest in our claims to know it.

Using narratives like the third gospel and Acts as resources for thinking about history is a complex task. It can, however, yield some degree of confidence about how Luke-Acts presents the saving work of Christ and some degree of confidence about what a first-century audience was imagined to know for that presentation to "work." Using what we can best formulate about first-century audiences and first-century Judaism, together with what it seems we can most clearly say about Jesus, we may draw some tentative conclusions about the saving work of the Messiah and Jesus of Nazareth. This last step is the most speculative, but none the less interesting for that.[6]

Even the most basic narrative always includes two levels of interaction.[7] Within the narrative there is dialogue among the characters. At the same time, the narrative is a dialogue between the audience and the author, who may be at some distance in time and/or space from the characters in the story. In order to understand a narrative, interpretation must take seriously the dialogue within the narra-

---

[5]Luke Timothy Johnson, *The Real Jesus: The Misguided Quest for the Historical Jesus and the Truth of the Traditional Gospels* (San Francisco: HarperSanFrancisco, 1996) 149.

[6]See Paula Fredriksen, "What You See Is What You Get," 77: "The quest for the historical Jesus requires the reconstruction of Jesus' message and, to the degree that we can get at it, his motives and goals. This effort at reconstruction, in turn, requires getting a fix on Jesus' religious, social and political context. The reconstructed context requires that we analyze material presented in the Gospels before we can assess, historically and critically, their—and in some sense, Jesus'—content. This effort can land us in the proverbial hermeneutical circle." But there are "other fixed points by which we can measure whether we write, and read, good history or bad."

[7]For an eloquent discussion of this kind of analysis, see Susan R. Garrett, *The Demise of the Devil: Magic and the Demonic in Luke's Writings* (Minneapolis: Fortress, 1989) 6-7.

tive itself. The context for interpretation of a narrative is, first of all, the "narrative world." The context for interpretation of the dialogue between audience and author is the culture presumed by the author. These two levels overlap significantly as the author, the evangelist in this case, expects that an audience knows certain things in order to fill in the inevitable gaps in the story—the things the author must simply take for granted.

Consider what kinds of information you would need to know to make sense of the following sentence: She came tearing down the road hoping to catch up with the mustang (Mustang?) only to be stopped dead by a red light at the corner. Interpreting this sentence is difficult because of its metaphors, the uncertainty of capitalization, an uncertainty of pronunciation (was she weeping or moving fast down that road?), and our potential lack of clarity about the nature of a particular object and its power (What is a red light? How can it stop someone? Can it kill?). I assume that present readers can make sense of this admittedly odd sentence very quickly by filling in the gaps in accord with culturally provided information.

Our question about the saving work of Christ is gap-laden. The process of considering the saving work of Christ will be twofold: first, we will consider "saving" in Luke-Acts as a part of the narrative itself; secondly, we will consider what weight or resonance these terms for saving (and related themes) might have had in the larger first-century world. Our questions will be the following:

Where and how does Luke use the term salvation?

How does he connect this complex of meaning with the Messiah or Christ?

What we can say about this, if anything, historically?

The saving work of Jesus is of high significance in Luke-Acts. In this paper we are focusing on Greek words connected with the roots σωζ- and σωτ-. This particular vocabulary of salvation occurs frequently and at critical points.[8] Not only does Luke retain "save" and its cognates in most of his parallels with Mark, the terms also appear frequently in Luke's own redactional material in the gospel.[9] All the places where "save" occurs in Acts are, as far as we know, Luke's work and therefore offer excellent opportunities for study. Texts in which "saving" activity is explicitly connected with "Messiah" or "anoint" are most important for this paper. Words that are used as alternatives to Messiah (e.g., the Righteous One) and saving (e.g., redeem) will also be given some attention.

II. SALVATION IN LUKE'S GOSPEL

1. "Saving" frames the gospel: The beginning

Luke's gospel is framed with references to saving. In Luke 1:47, 69, 71, and 77, in the responses of Mary and Zechariah to the news of the impending birth of Jesus, God the savior sends a savior to save the people. Mary praises "God my

---

[8]See σωτήρ in Luke 1:47; 2:11; Acts 5:31; 13:23; σωτηρία in Luke 1:69, 71, 77; 19:9; Acts 4:12; 7:25; 13:26, 47; 16:17; 27:34; σωτήριον in Luke 2:30; 3:6; Acts 28:28; σώζω in Luke 6:9; 7:50; 8:12, 36, 48, 50; 9:24, 56; 13:23; 17:19; 18:26, 42; 19:10; 23:35, 37, 39; Acts 2:21, 40, 47; 4:9, 12; 11:14; 14:9; 15:1, 11; 16:30, 31; 27:20, 31.

[9]With a majority of New Testament scholars I assume a two-source theory for Luke's gospel.

savior" at the beginning of the magnificat, and then goes on to describe those saving acts and God's motivation for them. While she begins by naming God "*my* savior" and blessing God's mercies to *her*, she then shifts to laud God whose mercy is on those (plural) who fear him and finally on God's servant Israel (1:54). God remembers God's promise to Abraham and acts to save (i.e., free) Israel from oppression and keep the promises made to Abraham. Mary does not go into detail about those promises. Luke will spell them out in Acts 3:20-26 in ways that might surprise Mary as she sings of Jesus so early in the gospel.

Mary's words are reinforced by those of Zechariah's canticle when his mouth is unstopped. Zechariah speaks of the Lord God of Israel who looked favorably on his people, redeemed them, and raised up a "horn of salvation for us" (1:67-69). In verse 71 the savior's task is to save the people from enemies and oppressors in order that God might be found faithful and the people worship without fear forever. Freedom from the hand of the oppressor for the sake of worship has echoes of Moses' urging of Pharaoh to let the people go in order to worship God. Luke, however, explicitly connects these promises to Abraham and the oath that God swore to him. Does Zechariah speak of Jesus even at his own son's circumcision party? Yes, he does. Zechariah addresses John only in verse 76, after he has praised God for the work God has already begun in the yet-to-be-born Jesus. John's task will be to give knowledge of salvation to God's people by forgiveness of their sins. According to Luke, after the death of John forgiveness of sins becomes available only through the work of Jesus Messiah.

Mary and Zechariah are both trustworthy characters as they sing in these verses. Both prophesy in the power of the Spirit (Zechariah in 1:67; Mary in 1:35). They prophesy through passages of scripture (the Septuagint). We hear a pastiche of promises that firmly connects Jesus with God's saving activity, making Jesus a savior. God's saving activity will be to keep God's ancient promises to Israel. There are echoes of rescue and liberation as in the exodus. There are explicit references to God's keeping the promises made to Abraham.[10] In addition, there are implied references to messiahship or the choice of an anointed one. For example, Psalm 132:17 (LXX 131:17), quoted in Luke 1: 69, refers to God's causing a "horn to spout up from David." And what is this horn? It is the "anointed one," who will be crowned when God has cared for the inhabitants of Zion.[11] In these first few verses, Luke tells his audience of a saving God whose work of salvation includes the liberation of God's people through a savior who will be the anointed one and will bring to pass for Israel the promises God made to Abraham.

Luke does not specify the content of the promises to Abraham. Luke's readers are expected to understand that these are good promises. It also seems likely

[10]Note that promises are made to "Abraham and his seed forever" in Luke 1:55, a passage that echoes 2 Sam 22:51(LXX) in which promises are made "to David and his seed forever." This alteration suggests the importance of Abraham's promise from God in Luke's understanding.

[11]Psalm 132 (LXX 131): 15-18: "I will abundantly bless its provisions; I will satisfy its poor with bread. Its priests I will clothe with salvation and its faithful will shout for joy. There I will cause a horn to sprout up for David; I have prepared a lamp for my anointed one. His enemies I will clothe with disgrace but on him, his crown will gleam."

that the readers are to relate the promises to Abraham to God's other freeing activity, as detailed in the canticles—although feeding the poor and dethroning the mighty are not specifically Abrahamic promises in scripture. The non-specificity of the promises creates a gap that accounts for much of the misperception at work throughout Jesus' ministry, death, and resurrection, as we shall see. Another gap is created right at the beginning of the gospel between two different understandings of the beneficiaries of God's saving work. In the canticles it is clear that Israel, the children of Abraham, are to receive the covenant blessings at last.[12] But other characters name another element of the Abrahamic promise that is important for Luke. Both the angels and Simeon (Luke 2:10-11 and 30-32, respectively) expand the locus of God's mercy to include the gentiles. This is in accord with the promise to Abraham that Luke records in Acts 3:25. The promises of God to Israel for her salvation include, as Luke sees it, promises to enable Israel to fulfill her calling to be salvific for all persons. Luke is careful to include representatives of Jews and gentiles among those who reject Jesus' saving work as well as among those who accept it.

2. "Saving" frames the gospel: The end

From these prophecies of Jesus as savior, the one who was to carry out God's work of saving and blessing Israel, we move to the passion scene. Luke 23:35, 37, and 39 all revolve around Jesus as savior and Christ. He is challenged to carry out the very task for which he seemed to have been destined in Acts 1 and 2. Here the tone is mocking and cruel, not hopeful and trusting that God will keep promises. While the speakers understand themselves to be mocking Jesus, it is clear that Luke understands that they mock themselves. Their self-deceit will be revealed by the outcome of the story, which will attest to Jesus' ability to save. More pertinently, within the gospel we grasp the nature of mockery by noting who it is that mocks Jesus. In 23:35 the people have grown silent: it is the leaders (οἱ ἀρχοντες) who mock Jesus. Their line is found in each synoptic gospel, "He has saved others, let him save himself." Luke follows Mark in connecting this saving activity to Jesus as Messiah.[13] According to literary convention, because the words are put into the hostile mouths of those who do not believe them, they can be regarded as true. It is precisely the truth of these words that the scoffers miss, as they have done and will continue to do throughout Luke's work. Simeon's prophecy about the rising and falling of many in Israel is borne out by this sort of misperception.

Luke, in distinction from the other evangelists, speaks twice more of saving. It is not only the leaders of the people, but also the soldiers, that is, the Romans, who mock Jesus. They call him "King of the Jews" and exhort him to "save" himself. Finally, even the criminals charge Jesus to save himself and them, if he is the Christ. It is Jesus as Messiah who is challenged to do saving work. For all these characters, saving has to do with overcoming the power of oppressive and un-

---

[12]Luke 1:16, 32-33, 54, 67-75, 77.

[13]Mark explicitly calls the Messiah the "King of Israel," while Luke here names Jesus the "Christ of God, God's chosen one."

godly persons, as in Luke 1 and 2. It also seems to be true for Luke, at least, that the one who is Messiah should be able to save people from such experiences.[14] Jesus has already saved persons from death, demonic possession, deadly illness. At the end, he can't even save himself from the death-dealing oppression of ungodly persons.[15] What power does he have to save the people, that is, carry out his mission as Messiah? Acts 10:38 suggests a similar expectation of saving and messianic mission (although it does not use the word, "save"), telling "how God anointed (ἔχρισεν) Jesus of Nazareth with the Holy Spirit and with power; how he went about doing good and healing all who were oppressed by the devil, for God was with him." "Doing good" and "healing" are synonyms for saving that make the connection between God's anointing and the kind of saving that is expected in Luke 1 and 2. Here, though, we note that the prophecies from those early chapters seem quite doomed in the mockeries of Luke 23. If one had hoped that God by memory, mercy, and might would set wrong right and enable worship, one would be likely to give up that hope when the "savior" is found hanging on a cross.

It is of utmost importance, however, that these two passages bracket a story whose brunt it has been to delegitimate the speech of those who mock Jesus the savior at his end. Steadfast misperception of Jesus' saving activity has been the hallmark of his enemies. The question of who says what about saving provides the would-be historian with an interesting conundrum. The wrong-headed ones actually offer a "normal" or "right" scenario for a saving Messiah. Their grasp of the meaning of Messiah is much in tune with the hopes of the canticles. Their perceptions, although incorrect, are natural and to be expected among many first-century Jews. In Luke's Gospel, everyone agrees about the saving work of God's Messiah. Even Jesus' own followers agree that his death marks his failure to save, not his success in so doing: "We had hoped that he would be the one to redeem Israel" (Luke 24:21). Yet we dare not trust even these disciples' idea of saving, for we know that they, too, have misperceived Jesus. They are, after all, walking right next to him and remain unable to recognize him.

How has saving been defined within the gospel itself in such a way that the audience understands the references in Luke 23:35, 37, 39 to be ironic? The failure to perceive that remaining on the cross is saving work—were it not so, the irony would not make sense—occurs close to the end of the gospel. At the start, characters spoke of saving with different sensibilities. Instead of serving as God's mighty arm raised on their behalf, as the characters had imagined, Jesus, the anointed one, submitted to other, mightier arms. None of his followers seem safe or saved. Yet, if God's angels do not lie, and the assumption is that they do not,[16] then Jesus is in fact saving himself and others no matter how it looks. The audience knows that

---

[14]See Luke 1:51-54, 69-72.

[15]This is firmly associated for Luke with the power of the devil. The devil is clearly at work in Luke 4:2-13; 13:16; 22:2. See Acts 10:38, where Peter sums up Jesus' activity over against the devil. See also Susan R. Garrett, "The Meaning of Jesus' Death in Luke," WW 12 (1992) 11-16.

[16]See Luke 1:19, 26; 2:9, 13. Gabriel's self-identification to Zechariah in 1:19 is specifically offered to obviate any possibility of error or deceit.

Jesus is saving and saved, though the participants in the drama do not. Where do we see what saving means so we can make sense of this? It is not only in the stories of the resurrection, crucial as they are, but within the gospel story as well.

3. "Saving" within Luke's Gospel

Saving, sometimes translated as "curing" or "making well," is what Jesus does in many texts, including Luke 8:12, 36, 48, and 50. Most of this material is found also in Mark and/or Matthew, but Luke adds "saving" in several places where the other evangelists do not mention it. In Luke 8:12, it is Satan's work not only to snatch up the seed that has been sown but to do it so that persons might "not trust and be saved." So Satan is clearly the enemy against whom God acts to save. With that in mind, Luke 8:36 tells us that the Gerasene demoniac was saved or cured (while neither Matthew nor Mark use the word). Here is what "saving" looks like for the one who trusts Jesus. Jesus, the anointed one, expels the demons, Satan's minions, and restores to health.[17] (One is reminded of Acts 10:38.) In 8:47, the woman with the flow of blood was healed (ἰάθη), an experience which is then described by Luke, along with Mark and Matthew, as having been saved (σέσωκέν). Finally in 8:50, Luke (alone of the three evangelists who tell this story) promises that the little girl shall be "saved" if her father trusts Jesus. He does, and she is restored from death. A similar pattern is seen in Luke 18:42, also parallel to stories in Matthew and Mark, where Jesus heals the blind man at the man's own request. Luke follows Mark in Jesus' declaration that the blind man's trust has "saved" him.

Chapter 8 in Luke clearly sets saving in opposition to the work of Satan. It is the work of the Messiah and his disciples[18] to heal by casting out demons. This healing returns life and wellness to the one saved. It is certainly possible to translate the forms of σωζ- in these chapters as "healed" or "cured." It is legitimate to highlight the word's usage here, since Luke adds it to Mark's text and since it has been presented as the work that Jesus will do in the birth canticles. It is also useful to imagine that "saved" is not different from "cured," although it is not limited by it. The term is of great importance to Luke as he describes the mission of Jesus to heal and to restore to community as saving work.[19]

Who can be saved is at issue in two other Lukan narratives. In the first, 13:22-30, the question is put to Jesus, "Will only a few be saved?" Jesus answers in a passage that is similar to Matt 7:13-14 but placed in a very different setting. In Matthew the response is part of the sermon on the mount and not distinguished from other material in that sermon in regard to location or audience. In Luke the

[17]See also *Jubilees* 10:7-14 for a description of the prince of spirits, Mastema, and how a tenth of his evil spirits were allowed to remain and be subject to Satan upon earth. These spirits were the cause of all kinds of illness and "seductions."

[18]See Luke 9:1-2 where Jesus sends the disciples to heal diseases by virtue of the authority they are given over all the δαιμόνια. See also Luke 10:17, 19, where the returning disciples rejoice because they were able to command δαιμόνια in Jesus' name and where Jesus says once again, "I have given you authority to trample upon snakes and scorpions and upon all the power of the enemy."

[19]Healing accompanies proclamation of God's kingdom in Luke 6:18-20, for example. This is also the case when the twelve and then the 72 are sent out (9:6; 10:9).

question is specifically put as Jesus and his disciples journey to Jerusalem (13:22). He exhorts his hearers to enter by the narrow gate and tells the story of the stern householder who will not recognize those who knock at his door. Going to Jerusalem is surely entering by the narrow door for Jesus. Jesus is just as surely among those being saved; indeed, he is on his way to be saved and to be saving. Here is an early signal that perishing in Jerusalem (13:33) is not equivalent to not being saved. For Jesus, the narrow door will be the way of *not* coming down from the cross (Luke 23). It is the lot of a prophet to be destroyed by those he would heal, exorcise, and gather (vv. 32, 34).

Jesus answers the query in a way that clarifies what is necessary for salvation and provides an image of it. The image of a householder's banquet is suggestive of salvation. Who will sit at table with Jacob, Isaac, and Abraham? Only one who is not a doer of unrighteousness. Abraham's name is significant in this parable. In the parable of the rich man and Lazarus (Luke 16:19-31), Abraham presides over benefits (or blessings) received in the afterlife. To recline in the bosom of Abraham, that is, to be one of his children or a member of his household, is to be saved from torment. The blessings promised to Abraham and his descendants (those who bear fruits!) will come in this life or the next. We will look below at the connection of Abraham and the saving work of the anointed one.

The longer saving narrative begins in Luke 18:24-26 and runs through the story of Zacchaeus in 19:1-10. In Luke 18:24-26 we hear how hard it will be for the rich to be saved, and we see that entering the kingdom of God (like entering the householder's house in 13:28-29) is being saved. What does this mean? Has the blind man, now saved (18:42), entered the kingdom of God? Jesus says that he has been saved. He glorifies God and all who see him praise God. Here we find wholeness restored, trust that wholeness is God's will for humans, and trust that God can do God's own will. Consistently throughout Luke's Gospel and Acts, persons who experience some sort of salvation rejoice and praise God.

When Zacchaeus is introduced as a rich tax collector, the audience is put into some tension. Tax collectors, while clearly unloved by the general population in Luke's Gospel, receive good treatment from Jesus. He has fraternized with tax collectors throughout the gospel. Jesus tells a parable in which a tax collector rather than a Pharisee prays with appropriate humility and is rewarded (18:10-14). But Jesus has also indicated that rich people are likely to have problems being saved (18: 25-26). Zacchaeus becomes a prime exhibit of the truth that "with God all things are possible" (18:27). Jesus announces at the end of this story that "salvation has come today to this house" (19:9). Is Jesus himself salvation or has he brought it? He follows this with the rationale: "because [Zaccheus] too is a son of Abraham." Zacchaeus is a doer of justice (cf. 13:27) and will sit at table with Abraham. It is not clear whether being acknowledged as a son of Abraham *is* salvation or whether salvation has come *because* Zacchaeus is a son of Abraham. Zacchaeus is able to enter the kingdom of God, that is, be saved (18:24-26). He welcomes his salvation with joy (19:6).

4. Saving the children of Abraham

In Luke 3:8, John the Baptist tells the crowds who have come seeking baptism that "God can raise up children for Abraham from these stones." John warns that when God's judgment comes no one dare claim safety on the basis of being a child of Abraham, but on the basis of fruits suitable for such a child (cf. Luke 13:27). John disallows the saving power of religious or ethnic identity. He does, however, retain "children of Abraham" as the description of those who will receive the blessing God promised to Abraham. In the case of Zaccheus, he is pronounced a son of Abraham and need not fear the "wrath to come" (Luke 3:7). The crowds were wrong about him. Salvation has come in the interaction of Zaccheus and Jesus according to a model that permeates the corpus of Luke-Acts.[20] At the least, salvation means being restored to the people of God, a fact that explains Jesus' announcement to the murmuring crowd at the end of the story when he switches to the third person and speaks about Zaccheus. Jesus makes the decision about restoration, not the crowd. The saving work of Jesus is to judge fruits and to restore or not. In some cases, "fruits" seem to be trust that Jesus wields the power of God as well as trust that God desires to restore.

For the bent-over woman (Luke 13:16), being a daughter of Abraham was reason enough that she be freed from the bonds of Satan, even on the sabbath. In this story the blessings of being a child of Abraham take precedence over keeping the law of Moses. God's promise to Abraham is the saving promise that is at stake for Luke's Jesus. It is the work of Jesus to seek and save the lost, to prepare a people to receive the blessings of Abraham (1:55, 73), and to administer those blessings. Often, as the gospel goes on, we see that the work of Satan stands in opposition to the blessings; it is, therefore, at least part of the saving work of God's Messiah to defeat Satan's power.

5. Testing, Abraham, Satan, and the Messiah

To restore a people who will receive the blessings promised to Abraham, Jesus, as Messiah, is forced to defeat Satan. Jesus does so by remaining faithful to God during the most difficult testing. Jesus expects such faithfulness and obedience from his disciples as well. "Testing" is an important theme in Luke-Acts and is connected to the Messiah's saving work. We will look at the occurrences of this word and seek to discern the response of Jesus to testing, his sense of the reward for remaining faithful during testing, and the connection of these to Satan. We will see that the crucifixion is important because it is a final and unjust test that Jesus endures faithfully, thus leading God to raise him. Finally we will ask whether there

---

[20]Three verbs describing three related activities mark Luke's sense of mission and the way in which God is made present to people. The three activities are: enter, welcome, remain (εἰσέρχομαι, δέχομαι, and μένω, sometimes in compound form). Notice the confluence of these verbs in the mission instructions Jesus gives in Luke 9:4-6; 10:5-8. Notice his practice of these three in Luke 19:1-10; 24:28-32. These instructions shaped the mission practice of the disciples in, for example, Acts 10:21-23, 27-48; 11:3; 16:15; they occasioned the need for the apostolic council in Acts 15, since, as Luke saw it, entering and remaining with gentiles was not acceptable for Jews (Acts 10:28).

is a connection with Abraham, his testing and his faithful endurance of the test, with the promised reward of blessing from God.

"Test" and its cognate forms[21] play a significant role in the description of Jesus' messianic work. The words are used frequently and at important points. The term marks the opening and closing of the temptation account (Luke 4:1-13), in which Jesus encountered and bested Satan. A petition to avoid testing is part of the prayer Jesus gives his disciples (11:4), and the term is used almost immediately thereafter to describe the purpose of the challengers in the Beelzebul controversy (11:16). Three times the noun shows up in Luke 22, where Jesus proclaims that his disciples have stood by him during his testings and will be rewarded. In Gethsemane he twice adjures his disciples to pray that they might not come into a time of testing.

Testing marks the beginning and ending of Jesus' earthly ministry. That Jesus underwent testing is common to the synoptics. Matthew and Luke develop this story with the same three tests. Luke, however, structures his tests differently and in such a way that "testing" is itself highlighted. He puts last the devil's dare that Jesus throw himself from the temple. Thus, Jesus' last word in Luke's story is a recitation of Deut 6:16, "You shall not test the Lord your God." The sequence builds towards Jesus' proclamation of his relationship with God. This understanding will shape Jesus' ministry and death throughout the gospel. At the very end of this passage, Luke provides an epilogue that reminds his audience that this was a test and that it is not over, even though Jesus has emerged the victor in this skirmish. Luke uses words for testing three times (to Matthew's single use). That Jesus met the devil and did not yield to behavior that would "test" God is his most important qualification for beginning ministry.

When his ministry is about to end with crucifixion, Luke's Jesus declares that the disciples have continued with him "in my trials." The reward for this enduring loyalty is, for the disciples as for Jesus, a kingdom. A literal translation of 22:28-30 makes the point: "You are the ones who have continued with me in my trials; and I appoint for you, just as he appointed for me, my father, a kingdom so that you will eat and drink at my table in my kingdom and you will sit on the thrones, and judge the twelve tribes of Israel." Jesus is going through the narrow door, and his disciples will do the same.[22] It is this narrow door of endurance through testing that bests the devil and empowers the stronger person to seize the kingdom and oust the enemy (11:21-22). This is the saving work of the Messiah to which Jesus' other acts of healing and restoration attest.

Jon Levenson points out the extraordinary power of God's naming Jesus "the beloved son" at his baptism and at the transfiguration.[23] This title puts Jesus in a

---

[21]Verbs are formed from the Greek πειράζειν. The noun is πειρασμός. For Luke's usage of πειράζειν, see: Luke 4:2; 11:16; Acts 5:9; 9:26; 15:10; 16:7; 24:6; πειρασμός: Luke 4:13; 8:13; 11:4; 22:28, 40, 46; Acts 20:19. The verb in Acts 9:26; 16:7; 24:6 means to "make an attempt," "try." See also ἐκπειράζειν in Luke 10:25.

[22]Jesus recognizes that some who hear God's word will fall away in a "time of testing"; he does not take faithful obedience for granted (see Luke 8:13).

[23]Jon D. Levenson, *The Beloved Son*, 200.

group with Isaac and others, who die or come near death for the sake of the people. In Jewish exegesis, Isaac was taken to foreshadow also the paschal lamb and what its death heralded.[24] In Gen 22:1 (LXX) we hear that God tested (ἐπείραζεν) Abraham. The test was revealed in God's command, "Take your son, the beloved one whom you love, Isaac, and go to the mountain." The test was passed in 22:12, "For now I know that you fear God and will not withhold your son, the beloved one from me." The promises to Abraham—the keeping of which serves to define the task of God's Messiah for Luke—follow as God's reward to Abraham for his obedience and devotion to God. In *Jubilees* 17:15-18 we hear that it is the plot of Mastema (the "chief of the spirits") to test Abraham. God tests Abraham at Prince Mastema's instigation. Prince Mastema is finally "shamed" by Abraham's willingness to sacrifice Isaac (18:12). This is the same Mastema who gets to keep one-tenth of his spirits unbound to serve Satan on earth by causing illnesses and other human woes. As in Luke's gospel, illness, possession, and death, as well as testing, were in the hands of Satan and his minions.

The saving work of the Messiah, as Luke sees it, is obedience to God through all testing, the reward for which will be enthronement in God's kingdom and, as Acts suggests, administration of the Spirit. Levenson says, "Abraham's willingness to sacrifice Isaac has become a foundational act, indeed the essential foundational act for the existence and destiny of the people Israel."[25] Jesus' similar faithful obedience is his saving work as Messiah. The saving work of the Messiah is revealed in his acceptance of such a test in which he, as beloved son, will finally be the offering. The blessings promised Abraham will accrue to his children after the testing of the beloved son when he proves himself stronger than the devil. This he does during the temptations and on the cross.

In Luke the Holy Spirit leads Jesus out to be tested after his baptism. The Spirit fills Jesus, who is able to continue in utmost obedience to God. The Messiah himself will distribute this same Spirit to his followers, empowering them to continue with him in obedience to God.[26] Jesus will be the only one who is perfectly obedient to God through all testing. He alone will fully manifest within the gospel narrative what the "good soil" shows in that parable: holding fast with an honest and good heart and bearing fruit with patient endurance.

III. SALVATION IN ACTS

Saving continues as an important theme in Acts. The language of saving again frames the book in a way that suggests a move to redefine saving. The Messiah now pours out the Spirit, the agent of incorporation into the people of God, and he awaits the opportune time to return for final restoration and judgment.

---

[24]See *Jubilees* 17:15-18:19, and Levenson, *The Beloved Son*, 201. Levenson connects the suffering servant with Isaac and with early Christian exegesis.

[25]Levenson, *The Beloved Son*, 212.

[26]Note that in Luke 22:31-32 Satan has demanded to sift all the disciples like wheat, that is, to test them. It will be Peter's task to strengthen the disciples when Jesus returns to God.

1. "Saving" frames Acts: The beginning

Acts begins with a question about salvation, although the σωζ- and σωτ-words are not used. When the disciples of Jesus ask, "Lord, is this the time when you will restore the kingdom to Israel?" (Acts 1:6), they are asking about salvation.[27] Salvation is to be understood as the restoration of Israel—perhaps in the sense of liberation: Israel is freed from domination in such a way that they can be God's people. The exodus provides numerous images for this, some of which are important in Luke-Acts. Salvation can also be a return from exile. Isaiah, to name just one whom Luke quotes abundantly, is a source of images for this.[28]

Saving terminology does appear in Acts 2 and again near the end of the book. In Acts 2:21, after the descent of the Spirit, Peter speaks with the Jews assembled in Jerusalem at the time of Pentecost. His first sermon has to do with a redefinition of being saved. As Peter interprets Joel's prophecy, the day of judgment is upon the people. He exhorts them to repent, to call upon the name of the Lord, for the sake of their salvation. In its own context, Joel's prophecy tells of the restoration of the land and people of Israel and the judgment of God upon the nations. For Peter, the resurrection of Jesus, his ascension, and, most important at this point, the pouring out of the Spirit, are taken as signs that this day is about to dawn. If this Jesus is the Lord whom David predicted, then God will put God's enemies under his feet (Acts 2:35; Ps 110:1). God has done this by raising Jesus. The enemies that have been overcome, however, do not seem to be the Romans or any Jewish opposition. Luke raises the messianic ante: the devil has been overcome, the same devil who had entered Judas. On that basis, Jesus is understood to be Lord and Messiah. The time has come. The Messiah is acting. No wonder the people ask what to do next (Acts 2:37).

"Save yourselves from this crooked generation," Peter says to the Jews gathered in Jerusalem. "Be baptized." By baptism one is saved, incorporated into the rebuilt and blessed people of God. An elegant inclusio clarifies salvation in Acts 2:40 and 47.[29] These two verses suggest that the first step in saving has to do with being baptized, incorporated into those whose sins have been forgiven. A second inclusio is nested within the first (vv. 42 and 46). It shows that the saved have a particular kind of life together in which attention to apostolic teaching, commu-

---

[27]This is a question about salvation, although it is not always so understood. When the disciples of Jesus ask about the restoration of the kingdom to Israel (Acts 1:6), they are asking about salvation of a people. "Restoration" here is related to the term used in 3:21 to refer to the promised universal restoration. In 3:21, the restoration is in the future; no time for its inauguration is given. On "salvation" from first-century Jewish perspectives, see N. T. Wright, *The New Testament and the People of God*, 334-338.

[28]Ibid. Consider the following vocabulary of salvation: ἀποκαθηιστανεις in Luke 6:10 and Acts 1:6 (referring to restoration of a hand and of a people); ἀποκαταστασις in Acts 3:21; λυτρωσις in Luke 1:68; 2:38; λυτρωτης in Acts 7:35; ῥυομαι in Luke 1:74.

[29]This speech and description, framed by a concern for salvation (vv. 40, 47), takes place among Jews alone. The complexities of being a people of God that will include gentiles have not yet arisen. But those complexities will be understood in light of salvation as it is here presented (see also Luke 9:1-6; 10:1-9).

nity, breaking of bread, and prayer hold central place.[30] At the very heart of this passage are verses 43-45, which speak of two things at the heart of the community: the many signs and wonders (often in reference to healing) done through the apostles; and life without need. Both are signs of eschatological existence, of living in God's kingdom. This life of salvation is an experience of the "times of refreshing" and a taste of "universal restoration" (Acts 3:20-21). The work of the Messiah Jesus has been to usher in and provide the first and to come again to initiate the second. The Messiah saves by pouring out the Spirit upon those who turn to God and are baptized. He will judge in the age to come.

2. "Saving" frames Acts: The end

At the very end of Acts, salvation appears once more. In 28:28 the announcement is made by Paul that the salvation of God has been sent to the gentiles. It is a peculiar and inconclusive ending. To explain the reaction of some Jews to the gospel Paul "quotes" the Holy Spirit, who spoke through the prophet Isaiah. The reader of Acts knows that there is division among the Jews: some hear and some do not (see, e.g., 28:24). The reader knows that among the gentiles, some listen and some do not. But it is clear that Paul's hope at the end of Acts—hope based in the words of the Holy Spirit (always reliable) and the prophet Isaiah whom Jesus quoted (Luke 8:10)—is that the salvation promised in Luke 1 will be extended to those gentiles who will hear it. Salvation will have a slightly different shape than Zechariah and Mary anticipated, but it will be much as Simeon declared in Luke 2:29-32 and Peter in Acts 3:25.

Acts 27:20 and 31 use forms of the σωζ-, σωτ- family to speak of saving from shipwreck. While these meanings seem different from the "save" that appears in more overtly theological contexts, it is the same word and provides an instance where the power of God, poured out by Christ, does indeed "save" Paul and those with him. There is not a qualitative difference in the meaning of this word. The God of Israel and numerous gods and goddesses were designated as "savior" on the basis of rescuing and preserving their devotees, not least from death at sea. It is an act of God's saving power that Paul and his companions live. It is also an act of God's saving power that Paul arrives in Rome alive to preach this saving God unhindered. So the end of Acts provides an experience of "saving" for one who repented and was baptized in the name of the Lord Jesus.

3. "Saving" within Acts

a. "Saving" Jews

Richard Hays points out that Luke's careful attention to audience-appropriate speech makes his use of language for and among Jews quite possibly the oldest

---

[30]For a pre-ascension experience of such a gathering, see Luke 24:13-49. In Acts 2, see verses 42 and 46. In verse 46 breaking bread at home and eating with glad and joyous hearts mark table fellowship and community. That all are gathered together (another sign of a saved community) in the temple provides the location of prayer and possibly of teaching as well. Note that the same description of the saved ones is also provided by a repetition of προσκαρτεροῦντες (devoting themselves) in 42 and 46.

tradition he knows about Jesus.[31] In their address to the temple authorities after the healing of the man born lame (Acts 3:1-4:22), Peter and John refer to the healing they have performed in Jesus' name and by his power as "saving."[32] Moreover, when the two disciples head back to their own circle to debrief their encounter with the authorities, they begin with a prayer addressed to God who "anointed" God's "holy servant Jesus to do whatever your hand and your plan had predestined to take place."[33] That predestination is described in Acts 3:17-26. The work of the Messiah, Jesus (3:20), is to be the source of the "times of refreshing" and to come again at the time of "universal restoration." Israel's role is to recognize the Messiah and to find blessing in order that it may be the source of blessing for all nations, according to God's promise to Abraham. Recognition of the Messiah, referred to as the Righteous One, is difficult for Israel. This Righteous One was martyred by his own people and raised by God. This section suggests a two-step model of salvation. In the first step, the "times of refreshing" are experienced by those who turn to God's Messiah, Jesus, and receive the power of the Holy Spirit. The Messiah brings salvation to the Jews. In step two, the Messiah will come as judge at the time of universal restoration, a promise which Peter's quotation of Joel had evoked earlier for the Jews in Jerusalem. Some will be judged for their rejection of the Messiah or his disciples, just as they rejected the prophets. Such rejections constitute a rejection of God.

The rejection of prophets, God, and God's Messiah—which is also rejection of salvation[34]—is a major theme in two additional long speeches to Jewish audiences: Stephen's address in Acts 7:2-60 and Paul's speech in Acts 13. Stephen is an absolutely credible speaker. In Acts 6:8 he is described as "full of grace and power," one who does "signs and wonders." In 6:15 he is seen even by his enemies to have the "face of an angel." Before his death he is given a vision of the ascended Lord, and his death imitates Jesus' own. Stephen begins his speech with Abraham, telling a detailed story of promise and warning from God. God warned Abraham (and his descendants) that, though it might seem as if the covenant would not be kept, God had foreseen the difficulties. Even God's action in bringing the people out of Egypt was in accord with the promise made to Abraham (7:17).

The brunt of the speech focuses on Moses (7:20-44). In Moses we see a kind of prototype of Jesus. Like Jesus, Moses was powerful in words and deeds (v. 22); he supposed that his kinsfolk would understand that God through him was rescuing them (giving them salvation), but they did not understand (v. 25). Moses tried to intervene among quarreling Jews, as did Jesus. Moses fled, was called, and re-

---

[31]Richard Hays, "The Righteous One as an Eschatological Deliverer: A Case Study in Pauline Apocalyptic Hermeneutics," in *Apocalyptic and the New Testament: Esssays in Honor of J. Louis Martyn,* ed. Joel Marcus and Marion Soards (Sheffield: JSOT, 1989) 197.

[32]In Lystra (Acts 14:9) Luke says that the crippled man is "saved" when he is able to get up and walk.

[33]Notice that they raised their voices together: ὁμοθυμαδον expresses the perfect concord of a community in the Spirit. See Acts 1:14; 2:46; 5:12, in addition to 4:24. For groups united by spirits other than the Holy Spirit, see 7:57; 12:20; 18:12; 19:29.

[34]This is also a theme throughout Luke's gospel; see, e.g., Luke 10:8-16.

turned to his people. He returned as ruler and liberator, performed wonders and signs, and promised that God would raise up a prophet from the people, just as God had raised Moses. Here Stephen describes the pattern followed by the Jews in relation to Jesus (of internal dissent and resistance to what God offers).[35] In this speech, Davidic promises are played down; it is the coming of the Righteous One (v. 52) that is anticipated. This Righteous One dies a martyr's death in this passage as in Acts 3.[36] This is Jesus, who presumably has been called by God to intervene among a quarreling people and "give salvation" to them. The liberation is to turn the people again to the worship of God (see v. 42) and true keeping of the law (v. 53).[37]

Saving has a high profile in Paul's speech in Pisidian Antioch (Acts 13). Forms of σωζ-, σωτ- are found in verses 23, 26, and 47. The speech begins with an address designed to create good will among the listeners (13:16).[38] In the first section Paul mentions God's leading of the people out of Egypt, but highlights God's promise to David and his descendants (13:22-23). From David's posterity God brought to Israel a savior, Jesus (13:23). The message of salvation was sent to "Abraham's family" (v. 26). Luke shows again his interest in what God had promised Abraham. Delivering on that promise is surely the work of the Messiah: "what God promised to our ancestors he has fulfilled for us, their children, by raising Jesus" (vv. 32-33). By the resurrected Jesus people are set free from sins from which they could not be freed by the law of Moses (vv. 38-39). The gentiles were pleased to hear this, of course, since they did not live according to the law of Moses and could not be freed from anything by it. In fact, Paul and Silas take on themselves the mission to the gentiles given by God to Israel in Isaiah 49:6. Simeon quoted that same verse in reference to Jesus. Simeon saw that Jesus was the salvation that would be taken to the ends of the earth. In this identification, the saving work of Jesus is the saving work of the Messiah.

It is not only gentiles who require a forgiveness of sins that comes independently of the law of Moses. Acts 15:1 and 11 use the words save and salvation in the context of Jewish believers who debate the inclusion of the gentiles among God's saved people. Some were teaching that the gentile brothers could not be saved without circumcision according to the "custom" (ἔθει) of Moses (15:1). In response, believers gather in Jerusalem; testimony to the work of God among gentiles is given by Peter, Paul, and Barnabas; and James closes the discussion with interpretation of scripture. Peter's speech (15:7-11), summed up by James, talks about salvation of both Jews and gentiles, using the word "saved": "But through

---

[35]On Luke's presentation of Moses as a type of Jesus, see Luke T. Johnson, *The Acts of the Apostles*, ed. Daniel J. Harrington (Collegeville, MN: Liturgical, 1992) 135-138.

[36]The connection of the Righteous One (ὁ δίκαιος) with the Messiah is discussed by Richard Hays, "The Righteous One," 191-215. See especially pp. 193-194 and notes.

[37]Recall that Jesus comments on the keeping of the law in Luke's Gospel, not least in 10:25-28; 16:29-31.

[38]This is a good example of *captatio benevolentiae*, in standard rhetorical terminology.

the grace of the Lord Jesus we trust that we shall be saved, in the same way as they also [will be]" (v. 11).

Peter suggests provocatively that Jews will be saved in the same way as gentiles rather than the other way around. He undoes the question about keeping the custom of Moses and declares that the grace of Jesus will suffice for Jews, even as for gentiles. Saving happens to Jews and gentiles through the same savior. James' speech, following Peter's, clarifies the meaning of this word: God visits (ἐπεσκέψατο) to take from the nations a people for God's name.[39] This same term is used in Luke 1:68 to describe God's action in raising up the horn of salvation: God will visit and redeem (λύτρωσιν). The crowd recognizes such a visitation when Jesus raises from death the widow's son (Luke 7:11-17, no parallels). Through a "great prophet" God has visited to restore one even from death to the living people of God. This is salvation. The understanding of Peter and James is in accord with the prophets. God will build up once again what was in ruins—the people Israel—in order that all nations and the rest of humankind will call on the name of the Lord (Acts 15:16-17, quoting Jer 12:16 and Amos 9:11 LXX). God is building a people through this prophet raised up from among the people. He will save Israel by building it up again and returning its vocation. This is exactly what Jesus does. Though not all Israel becomes a beacon to the gentiles, some return to the Lord, are purified by trust in the savior's way, and summon others into this same people.

b. "Saving" gentiles

Two tales about salvation are told to and about gentiles in Acts 16. Though Cornelius was the first clear case of the baptism of a non-Jew and non-proselyte (Acts 10), salvation is particularly emphasized in the stories of the slave girl with the pythian spirit (16:16-18) and of the jailer who becomes a believer (16:28-34). The pythian spirit knows what many others do not, that Paul and Silas, servants of the most high God, are proclaiming a way of salvation; and the jailer asks, "What must I do to be saved?" (16:30).[40] In neither story is salvation explicitly connected to Jesus as Messiah. It is connected to the "Lord Jesus" in Acts 16:31, a concept much more intelligible among non-Jewish peoples. Paul does, however, adjure the pythian spirit by the name of Jesus Christ, successfully calling it out of the young slave girl (16:18). The non-Jews understand that salvation is not in tune with their

---

[39]Jesus and the disciples also carry out such visitation with the power and authority of God. The mission instructions in Luke 9 and 10, as well as Jesus' interpretation of what happens in those "visits," describe this kind of saving. For additional uses of ἐπισκέπτομαι, see Luke 1:68, 78; 7:16; Acts 6:3; 7:23; 15:36. There are only four non-Lukan uses of this word in the New Testament.

[40]How does he know himself to be in such a state that saving is required? Surely the fact that Paul and Silas were praying and singing hymns to God at the time of the earthquake is associated with the jailer's awe. To be both servant and served by such a power leads him to ask for the same. It is good to have that kind of power on one's side. The jailer, we presume, had no scriptural background from which to form his sensibility about salvation, nor are we told that any biblical images are used to convey it to him. Saving was not an activity unique to Jews or their God. Evidence of a god's power and goodwill, especially as the first enacted the second, were understood as saving (and that god/dess as savior) throughout the ancient world. Indeed, humans who combined power and goodwill were also heralded as savior. That Jesus is Messiah is not mentioned in this story, but only that he is Lord, a term quite intelligible in non-Jewish circles.

regular practices; it involves a change in custom, perhaps a change in how one is part of a people. Ironically, the behavior of Paul and Silas is attributed to their being Jews, a claim denied by many Jews in earlier and later chapters of Acts.

IV. The Saving Work of Christ

"Saving work" is a phrase that evokes two questions about the Messiah's task. One question concerns what the Messiah does and how it is salvific: How does someone designated Messiah spend his time among the people he is anointed to serve? A second question has to do with the crucifixion of the Messiah: Is this crucifixion connected with his saving work? If so, how? We ask, then, about the way the work of the Messiah is salvific. In addition we seek to grapple as best we can with the question of whether the historical Jesus did this work. It is clear that questions of Messiah and Jesus are utterly intertwined in New Testament sources. Other Jewish literature will help us think about what a messiah might do to save his people; historical literature reminds us that others were deemed, at least for a while, to have been messiahs. Such material helps us see what first-century people hoped and longed for and how they did or did not understand Jesus of Nazareth to be Messiah.[41]

Luke-Acts presents the saving work of the Messiah in a three-step process. Although each step is distinctive, they also overlap. First, the gospel describes Luke's version of "all the time that the Lord Jesus went in and out among us, beginning from the baptism of John until the day when he was taken up from us" (Acts 1:21-22).[42] During this time people are saved from the depredations of the evil one, Satan, and his minions as they are restored to full participation in the covenant people of God. This is salvation from those forces that would disrupt God's coming reign or limit it. Secondly, in Acts Jesus almost immediately ascends to the side of God where he pours out the Holy Spirit on his baptized followers and thus enables them to live with bold trust (πίστις) and confidence (παρρησία),[43] as he did. This he continues to do, as the presence of the Spirit and baptism in the name of Jesus are inextricably woven together (Acts 2:33 and 19:1-7). At this stage the "times of refreshing" are bestowed upon the communities of believers and the great sign is joy. Lastly, Jesus will be sent again from heaven to inaugurate the final restoration.

There are distinctions between the saving work of stage one and that of stage two. In the gospel, Jesus bore the very presence of God among the people and empowered his disciples to do the same. Salvation and saving work have to do with besting the devil in a variety of ways. Jesus exorcizes demons, heals illness,

---

[41]See Donald Juel's essay in this volume (pp. 94-106).

[42]This stage is also summarized in several passages in Acts, most notably Acts 10:34-43. See also 13:22-33.

[43]All uses of παρρησία and παρρησιάζομαι occur in Acts. See Acts 2:29; 4:13, 29, 31; and 28:31 for παρρησία and Acts 9:27, 28; 13:46; 14:3; 18:26; 19:8; 26:26 for παρρησιάζομαι. The verb παρρησιάζομαι is used only two more times in the New Testament, suggesting that it was of particular and peculiar importance to Luke.

raises from death, and restores to community. He begins to share the blessings promised to Abraham's children, even to those who might not have been deemed Abraham's children (e.g., the slave of the centurion in Luke 7:1-10). Such sharing is, of course, part of the blessing, for God states that through Abraham's descendants all nations will be blessed.[44] Jesus also names those who are children of Abraham, as in the story of Zacchaeus, challenging local perceptions of status.

In Acts, Jesus' disciples are the bearers of this presence; they gather communities that live by the Spirit. Concrete acts that bring about human well-being are salvific. Although Jesus no longer does the saving work that he did in the gospel, the same kind of work does take place. All this is the work of the Messiah. Does such work cohere with any historic pictures of Messiah, or is this work messianic only because the Jesus who did it was raised from the dead? That question is debated.[45]

The third step in Christ's saving work is clearly yet to be. It is the least historically sensible. At the end of Luke's story the Romans remain in power in Israel and in Rome. The promises of God to bring down the mighty from their thrones and fill the hungry have not been met. In spite of his successful messianic activity, Jesus speaks of a delay in God's promise-keeping and the fulfillment of his messianic work (Luke 13:22-30; 21:5-36). No timeline is given, however, and it is not immediately clear how very far apart these two aspects of messianic saving will be. In Acts 3:19-26 we hear more explicitly about the future sending of the Messiah that will initiate the universal restoration, but it is in the unknown future.

Both N. T. Wright and Paula Fredriksen point out that messianic claims of salvation in the face of no restoration would have struck most Jews as patently absurd.[46] We must consider now this and other historical factors that are likely to have led Luke to shape his story of Jesus as the Messiah of the God of the Jews in the way he does. We need to refresh our sense of the historical milieu of Luke's dialogue with his audience (Garrett's second level of interpretation). Part of that milieu is the set of constructs about saving that circulated in first-century Judaism.

If, as most scholars agree, Luke's Gospel and Acts were written in that order for a second or third generation of believers (75-95 A.D.), then a number of things have already taken place that control Luke's interpretation of scripture and the questions his work seeks to answer. Most significant, the temple and much of Jerusalem were destroyed in 70 A.D. by Vespasian. This destruction was but the culmination of a long siege in which territory around Jerusalem and any population that showed resistance to Roman rule was decimated.[47] Moreover, by Luke's time more gentiles than Jews seem to have become believers. Some Jews, it seems,

[44]This is also in accord with the promises from Isaiah so dear to Luke. For a quick review of this topic, see James A. Sanders, "Isaiah in Luke," *Int* 36 (1982) 144-55.

[45]Again, see Donald Juel's essay (pp. 102-105).

[46]Paula Fredriksen, *From Jesus to Christ*, 123, 167-168; see also her discussion of "Jewish restoration theology," ibid., 77-81. N. T. Wright, *Jesus and the Victory of God*, vol. 2 of *Christian Origins and the Question of God* (Minneapolis: Fortress, 1996) 202-209, 223, 271.

[47]For a concise description of the Roman subduing of Jerusalem, see Robert M. Grant, *Augustus to Constantine* (New York: Harper and Row, 1970) 21-39.

continued to hope for salvation from other messiahs right up until the destruction of the temple. Further, Jesus the Messiah had not yet returned by Luke's day to establish the restoration of all things. This postponement of the ultimate saving work is likely to have been at odds with much of the expectation of early believers. Additionally, many people, styled by themselves or others as messiah, rose and fell again in first-century Jewish circles. How was Jesus different? How was his work more "saving" than anyone else's?

Such questions can be confronted only by filling the gap in our knowledge of what messiahs were imagined to be about in the first century.[48] It is fair to say that Jewish messianic hope, in whatever form, was about the liberation of God's people to worship God without fear. This hope often involved the restoration of the land to Israel, a renewed, holy temple and priesthood, harmony among Jews, and freedom from want. Since God was creator of all the universe, God would have to deal with the gentiles at some point. A number of scenarios for God's reign include gentiles who come to worship God—either because or in spite of Israel. In some cases gentiles were slated for a severe comeuppance and would not enjoy the blessings of God's reign.[49] In some cases, by the first century, God's reign includes the resurrection of the dead and the vindication of the righteous.[50] In no case was the Messiah portrayed as one who would die and be raised again, although there are a number of traditions that could be combined (as the New Testament indicates!) to make this a possible scenario.

Meanwhile, if Levenson is only half right, and he is at least that, about the "heated apocalyptic Judaism" of the second quarter of the first century in Judea, Jesus did make his appearance, carry out his ministry, and die at a time when martyrdom for the sake of faithful obedience to God or for seeking the kingdom of God could have endtime overtones. What do we know about Jesus in his time and place? At a most basic level Paula Fredriksen lists the following: "He [Jesus] preached in the Galilee. He was executed by Rome in Jerusalem around Passover. His movement relocated itself in Jerusalem. It proclaimed that he had been raised from the dead. Within a very few years, it also embraced gentiles."[51]

Luke Johnson gleans other materials from Paul's letters, which he treats as primary, non-narrative historical documents.[52] Johnson's list includes these items: Jesus was a Jew; Jesus had a mission to the Jews; he was a teacher; he prayed and suffered; he was tried and appeared before Pontius Pilate; he was crucified, buried, and appeared to witnesses after his death. Johnson thinks that Jesus seems to have

---

[48]The issue, of course, is huge. Among its parts is the question of how apocalyptic language is to be understood. Paula Fredriksen differs strongly from N. T. Wright on this point; see Fredriksen, "What You See," 86-87, and Wright, *The New Testament and the People of God*, 280-299.

[49]For good information on this, see Paula Fredriksen, *From Jesus to Christ*, 149-153, and N. T. Wright, *The New Testament and the People of God*, 259-338, especially 299-334. Both writers direct the reader to primary sources, which are numerous and diverse.

[50]See Fredriksen, *From Jesus to Christ*, 84-86, 140-142; Wright, *The New Testament and the People of God*, 307-20.

[51]Fredriksen, "What You See," 77.

[52]Johnson, *The Real Jesus*, 117-122.

interpreted his last meal with reference to his death, this point being important in consideration of Jesus' saving work.

In putting this all together, we discover that Luke's three-step process, described above, fits very well the three historical stages faced by Jesus' followers:

- the life of a Jewish Jesus (Luke's first stage)
- the lives of early believers (in Luke's day many of these would have been gentile) without Jesus but with spiritual experiences (Luke's second stage)
- the hope of those believers that God would eventually restore them as his living people (Luke's third stage)

We can imagine that, in stage one, the Jew, Jesus of Nazareth, carried out the work of saving—particularly through exorcisms, healing, and teaching about the proper interpretation of scripture—in such a way that great power was attributed to him (Luke 7:16). He is likely also to have entered Jerusalem in a way that raised the ante on his work and to have engaged temple practices in a similar way. Pilate's decision to title Jesus "King of the Jews" would have been senseless, and certainly neither ironic nor threatening, had not messianic claims been made by or on behalf of Jesus. Nor is it likely that Pilate's epigraph would have been worthy of so much interpretative activity by believers had Pilate been the only one to title Jesus in this way.

The death, resurrection, and ascension of Jesus reshape our understanding of his messianic role, as does the demise of the temple and the non-belief of most first-century Jews. The presence, growth, and power of communities formed by those who claimed to be witnesses to Jesus' resurrection must be accounted for historically. These communities are testimony to the "real Jesus" perhaps, but because they are in the process of interpreting the lack of Jesus' political (and therefore theological) success, their assessment of the historical Jesus must be used with caution. We can see that for Luke, in this second stage, when Jesus is not on earth and restoration does not occur, there is refreshment given through the presence and power of the Spirit. The need for a renewed temple disappears when God's Spirit is present among the people. The need for a particular restored land becomes absurd, because all things are to be restored through the Spirit. In this light, Acts 1:8, which sends witnesses out from Jerusalem instead of gathering the redeemed into the holy city, makes sense. Since by Luke's day there is no longer a holy city or a temple, it is also helpful to believers to be able to relocate God's presence when the eschaton is not ushered in. Hope for final restoration and the judgment of those who do not understand and participate in God's new people is deferred until an unknown time (the third stage), about which one ought not even ask.

Because this three-step process corresponds so well to the historical realities of early believers, we can dare to imagine that the first stage, that of Jesus' earthly ministry, also fit well with historical realities. Of course the story of Jesus' ministry has been transmitted by believers and for believers as they tried to understand its coherence with Jesus' death and the existence of communities who experienced

Jesus as living. Yet, the story also had to make sense to those first-century audiences who knew something of messiahs, Jews, Romans, and perhaps, Jesus himself. Dare we agree to the following? Jesus came to Galilee, was baptized by John, and undertook an itinerant ministry. He preached, taught, and healed as both call and sign of God's coming reign in which Israel would be set free from oppression. He may well, although we cannot know for sure, have understood himself to be in mortal combat for the sake of God's people against all powers opposed to God, both the devil and the Romans. It seems likely, from both the Pauline and gospel witnesses, that his energies were directed more against the former than the latter. He came to Jerusalem, probably not for the first time, to celebrate Passover. There he died at the hands of the Romans, the death attributed to his sedition, crucifixion being the punishment for such a charge (for non-Roman citizens).[53]

The saving work of Jesus was not unlike the saving work done by Tobit, the Maccabees,[54] and the prophets, as their stories have been told. It was action in accord with the will of the God of Israel, on behalf of God's people, and eventually for the restoration of that people. It was critical of current events, policies, and behaviors, powerful over hostile powers, and imbued with a sense of the imminence of God's judgment and of God's promise to save the people, even to restore them from death. It is neither difficult nor inappropriate to imagine a Jew of the first century imbued with these traditions and images of God. Such a Jew may also have been aware of the cluster of beliefs that had come to surround the story of Abraham and Isaac, including the connection of that story to Passover. This Jew was called, as prophets had long been called, to save the people. He was empowered to begin his mission. The fact that Jesus was crucified attests to his empowered saving work; a person isn't hung up as "King of the Jews" if there are no persons who would so herald him. If no one had paid attention or if Jesus had been interested only in purity of heart or in including folk who had not been there before in public worship of God, he would not have died as he did.

When he died, he may well have disappeared from history as just another would-be Messiah, but for the conviction of his followers that the "saving" was continuing and indeed would at some point be perfected. Here, however, the Jesus of history disappears from view and the saving work of the Messiah becomes other than would have been imagined. Now, believers like Luke needed to reinterpret saving in light of the destruction of the temple and of many Jews and of the failure of Jesus to return.

The claim that God's Messiah continued his work after his ascension, albeit in a different mode, makes the work of the historical Jesus very important to us. It is important to us that saving is corporate (social); that it is a matter of restoration of the people, that it entails keeping God's promises to bless Israel and through Israel

---

[53]Ibid. Paula Fredriksen, in "What You See," also develops these points, particularly in regard to the use of the Johannine chronology and its connection to Jesus' final fatal trip to Jerusalem.

[54]Tob 1:5-9, 16-20; 2:1-9; 14:5-9; 2 Macc 7:7-9, 10-11, 14, 16-17, 29, 30-38. Note the redemptive power of the Maccabean sacrifice to end the wrath of the Almighty that has justly fallen on the whole nation in verse 38.

the world; that it involves defeating powers of darkness manifest in illness, disability, outcast status, failure to use wealth properly, and idolatry.[55] For those who believe that Jesus' saving work continues and that cross, resurrection, and ascension have something to say to us about God's will to save, then the activity of Jesus that constituted the narrow door through which he entered his own resurrection dare not be underplayed. Simultaneously, the work of Jesus must be read in its own context, that of first-century Judaism, to avoid the dangers of taking Jesus as warrant for understanding Christianity simply in opposition to Judaism and for interpreting salvation as being "saved" from being God's people. Instead, Jesus' saving activity leads us into God's people, which is a way of life rather than a way of death. ⊕

---

[55]Luke does not use "salvation" speech to talk of eternal life, even in those places where he does speak of such life.

Word & World
Supplement Series 3
1997

The Word and Its Witness in John and 1 John:
A Literary and Rhetorical Study

PAUL S. BERGE

Luther Seminary
St. Paul, Minnesota

IN A RECENT ARTICLE MARIANNE MEYE THOMPSON SUMMARIZES THE CURRENT state in Johannine studies:

> Because scholars depend on the Synoptics for the materials used to reconstruct their portraits of Jesus, "the historical Jesus" is nowadays almost synonymous with "the Synoptic Jesus." John's portrait seems to be painted in such an innovative style and with such unusual technique that critics have wondered whether the portrait better captures the subject or the artist. So, whereas one studies the canvases of the Synoptic Gospels to catch a glimpse of "the historical Jesus," in the distinctive rendering of the Fourth Evangelist we have "the Johannine Christ"—almost a different subject, and certainly a unique interpretation of him. More interested in mimetic representation, the Synoptics allegedly approximate Jesus "as he really was." But John, not so interested in art imitating life, gives us "the Christ as the church confessed him."[1]

Contemporary interpretations of the New Testament gospels continue to propose and create a gulf between Jesus "as he really was" in the synoptic gospels, and Christ "as the church confessed him" in the Gospel of John. Clement of Alexandria's second-century characterization of the Gospel of John as "a spiritual gospel" continues to stand. The separation between "history" and "theology" remains, even though twentieth-century work on the gospels has shown that the difference between the synoptic and Johannine traditions is one of degree rather

---

[1]Marianne Meye Thompson, "The Historical Jesus and the Johannine Christ," in *Exploring the Gospel of John: In Honor of D. Moody Smith*, ed. R. Alan Culpepper and C. Clifton Black (Louisville: Westminster John Knox, 1996) 21.

than one of kind.[2] In light of continued attempts to interpret the gospels as litera-ture from which "the historical kernel" can be extracted from "the kerygmatic husk," we need to be reminded of the work of Martin Kähler and Albert Schweitzer a century ago.

In 1892 Martin Kähler warned:

> The historical Jesus of modern authors conceals from us the living Christ. The Jesus of the "Life-of-Jesus movement" is merely a modern example of human creativity, and not an iota better than the notorious dogmatic Christ of Byzantine Christology. One is as far removed from the real Christ as is the other. In this respect historicism is just as arbitrary, just as humanly arrogant, just as imperti-nent and "faithlessly gnostic" as that dogmatism which in its day was also considered modern.[3]

Albert Schweitzer laid to rest the nineteenth-century attempts to reconstruct the life of Jesus "as he supposedly was" in the synoptic *and* Johannine traditions:

> Formerly it was possible to book through-tickets at the supplementary-psycho-logical-knowledge office which enabled those travelling in the interests of Life-of-Jesus construction to use express trains, thus avoiding the inconvenience of having to stop at every little station, change, and run the risk of missing their connexion. This ticket office is now closed. There is a station at the end of each section of the narrative, and the connexions are not guaranteed.[4]

Günther Bornkamm, a voice of the mid-twentieth century, took the results of *Formgeschichte*, which followed Kähler and Schweitzer, and opened the way of *Redaktionsgeschichte*. Bornkamm identified the kerygmatic nature of the gospels, which expresses the inseparability of content and form, tradition and faith:

> It has increasingly become an accepted result of New Testament enquiry and a principle of all Synoptic exegesis that the Gospels must be understood and interpreted in terms of *kerygma* and not as biographies of Jesus of Nazareth, that they do not fall into any category of the history of ancient literature, but that in content and form as a whole and in matters of detail they are determined and shaped on the basis of faith in Jesus Christ. We owe the methodical establishing of this knowledge above all to form-critical research into the Gospels. This work put an end to the fiction which had for so long ruled critical investigation, that it would eventually be possible to distil from the Gospels a so-called life of Jesus, free from and untouched by any kind of 'over-painting' through the faith of the Church. Faith in Jesus Christ, the Crucified and Resurrected, is by no means a

---

[2]The distinctive historical tradition that underlies the Gospel of John was established in the work of C. H. Dodd, *Historical Tradition in the Fourth Gospel* (Cambridge: Cambridge University, 1963). The work of C. H. Dodd and Percival Gardner-Smith is noted by D. Moody Smith, *John among the Gospels: The Relationship in Twentieth-Century Research* (Minneapolis: Augsburg Fortress, 1992) 37-62.

[3]Martin Kähler, *The So-called Historical Jesus and the Historic Biblical Christ*, trans., ed., and with an introduction by Carl E. Braaten (Philadelphia: Fortress, 1964) 43. Kähler goes on to say, "Therefore, the reason we commune with the Jesus of our Gospels is because it is through them that we learn to know that same Jesus whom, with the eyes of faith and in our prayers, we meet at the right hand of God, because we know, with Luther, that God cannot be found except in his beloved Son, because he is God's revelation to us, or, more accurately and specifically, because he who once walked on earth and now is exalted is the incarnate Word of God, the image of the invisible God—because he is for us God revealed. That is what the believer seeks. This is what the church celebrates" (60-61).

[4]Albert Schweitzer, *The Quest of the Historical Jesus: A Critical Study of Its Progress from Reimarus to Wrede* (New York: Macmillan, 1959) 333.

later stratum of the tradition, but its very foundation, and the place from which it sprang and grew and from which alone it is intelligible.[5]

Twentieth-century research into questions and proposals about the life of Jesus has focused on the continuity and discontinuity between the Jesus of Nazareth and the Christ of faith.[6] The work of the Jesus Seminar draws upon this twentieth-century quest and further develops the criteria of antiquity—coherence, dissimilarity, multiple attestation, linguistic evidence—in determining what are the authentic sayings of Jesus. A multicolored text reflects their decisions, indicating red for definitely, pink for possibly, gray for unlikely, and black for definitely not. With these criteria of evidence as presuppositions, it is not surprising that not one of over 140 sayings attributed to Jesus in the Gospel of John is printed in red, and only one saying is printed in pink: "A prophet gets no respect on his own turf" (John 4:44).[7] (In their translation, Jesus comes off as the Rodney Dangerfield of the first century.) Scholarship in the gospels will express diversity over how the words and deeds of Jesus and the events of his life are to be interpreted. The methods of investigation and their use are determined by one's own presuppositions.[8]

In this last decade of the twentieth century, the ticket office that Schweitzer identified as being closed at the beginning of the century has been reopened, and the lives-of-Jesus express trains are running once again. Every engineer determines his or her own route, and, as of old, reconstructs a life of Jesus based on his or her presuppositions, criteria, and design—secular sage, peasant philosopher, Jewish Socrates, apocalyptic prophet, spirit person, wisdom teacher, healer, marginal Jew, social prophet, holy person, Jewish mystic, stand-up comic.[9]

As one assesses how the third quest for the historical Jesus relates to this study, it is helpful to refer again to Marianne Meye Thompson. Her comparative

---

[5]Günther Bornkamm, "The Stilling of the Storm in Matthew," in Günther Bornkamm, Gerhard Barth, Heinz Joachim Held, *Tradition and Interpretation in Matthew* (Philadelphia: Westminster, 1963) 52.

[6]See the survey on historical construction of Jesus research from pre-quest (before 1778) to the new quest (since 1953) in W. Barnes Tatum, *In Quest of Jesus: A Guide Book* (Atlanta: John Knox, 1982), especially 63-79; see more recently, Ben Witherington III, *The Jesus Quest: The Third Search for the Jew of Nazareth* (Downers Grove, IL: InterVarsity, 1995).

[7]Robert W. Funk et al., *The Five Gospels: The Search for the Authentic Words of Jesus* (New York: Macmillan, 1993) 412.

[8]See Rudolf Bultmann, *Existence and Faith: Shorter Writings of Rudolf Bultmann*, selected, translated, and introduced by Shubert M. Ogden (New York: Meridian, 1960) 289-296.

[9]Marcus Borg, *Jesus—A New Vision: Spirit, Culture, and the Life of Discipleship* (San Francisco: HarperSanFrancisco, 1987); *Meeting Jesus Again for the First Time: The Historical Jesus and the Heart of Contemporary Faith* (San Francisco: HarperSanFrancisco, 1994); John Dominic Crossan, *The Historical Jesus: The Life of a Mediterranean Jewish Peasant* (San Francisco: HarperSanFrancisco, 1991); *Jesus, A Revolutionary Biography* (San Francisco: HarperSanFrancisco, 1994); *Who Killed Jesus? Exposing the Roots of Anti-Semitism in the Gospel Story of the Death of Jesus* (San Francisco: HarperSanFrancisco, 1995); Robert W. Funk, *Honest to Jesus: Jesus for a New Millennium* (San Francisco: HarperSanFrancisco, 1996); Burton Mack, *A Myth of Innocence: Mark and Christian Origins* (Philadelphia: Fortress, 1988); John Meier, *A Marginal Jew: Rethinking the Historical Jesus*, 2 vols. (New York: Doubleday, 1991-1994); E. P. Sanders, *The Historical Figure of Jesus* (London and New York: Penguin, 1993); Geza Vermes, *Jesus the Jew: A Historian's Reading of the Gospel*, 2nd ed. (New York: Macmillan, 1993); Tom Wright, *Original Jesus* (Grand Rapids: Eerdmans, 1996). See also the critique by Luke Timothy Johnson, *The Real Jesus: The Misguided Quest for the Historical Jesus and the Truth of the Traditional Gospels* (San Francisco: HarperSanFrancisco, 1996).

work with the gospel traditions identifies ways in which there are "substantial similarities and considerable differences between the Synoptic and Johannine traditions" and recognizes that "the baseline against which John is measured is the Synoptic Gospels." Given these realities, there is much to be learned from the Johannine tradition, recognizing that the synoptic gospels and John reflect different approaches which "express the reality and significance of Jesus' person for those who believe." In this sense the Gospel of John is a "meaningful narration of the historical events, clearly committed to the truth of the interpretative framework in which the events are placed."[10]

This paper is a response to two contemporary issues of New Testament interpretation that have emerged from the nineteenth and twentieth centuries. The first issue centers on the continuity and discontinuity in the gospel traditions between the Jesus of Nazareth and the Christ of faith. The second issue centers on the authority of the word of God within the Christian community. These issues are at the heart of our lives in an academic community and as members of a Christian community. Both issues are directly related to the title of this book. The presupposition of this study is that Jesus Christ is the source and the subject of the tradition in the Gospel of John and in 1 John. Herein lies the continuity and authority of these writings. Access to the continuity and authority of this tradition is marked by the evangelist of the Gospel of John and the author of 1 John in their twofold confessional and instructional purpose (John 20:31; 1 John 5:13). The continuity and authority of the Johannine tradition lies not only in the literary form of the writings as a whole, but also in the rhetorical form of the instructional themes and words and in the confessional witness within the Gospel of John and 1 John. The literary continuity and rhetorical form of these writings and their authority within and for the Christian community is unique in the New Testament.

I. THE CONTINUITY OF THE WORD IN JOHN AND 1 JOHN

The relationship of the word present in Jesus and the community's witness of faith in Jesus Christ expresses the continuity and authority of these writings. In this relationship, scripture is called upon to interpret scripture, not only because this is a time-honored method, but because 1 John is a primary witness to the interpretation of the Gospel of John. The uniqueness of this literary and theological relationship offers insight into the relation between the quest for Jesus and the Christian faith.

The content and form of the Gospel of John and 1 John have been shaped on the basis of the witness of faith in Jesus Christ, the incarnate word of God and the crucified and risen Lord. These writings reflect a tradition that has its origin in the purpose of Jesus' ministry. The verb "to make known," or "to exegete" (ἐξηγέομαι), expresses this purpose in the concluding verse of the prologue of the gospel: "No one has ever seen God; the only God, who rests in the bosom of the Father, that one has made him known [exegeted him]" (John 1:18). In

---

[10]Thompson, "The Historical Jesus," 21, 26, 33, 35.

words and signs, Jesus makes known the presence of God's light in the world (John 1:19-12:50). In the form of a servant, Jesus makes known the pattern of God's love for the community's life in the world (John 13:1-17:26). In Jesus' death and resurrection, the Spirit leads the community's witness to make known the truth of the crucified and risen Lord (John 18:1-21:25). The evangelist has written the Gospel of John with a twofold purpose that is confessional and instructional: "that you may believe that, 'Jesus is the Christ, the Son of God' [confessional], and that believing you may have life in his name [instructional]" (John 20:31).

The evangelist's literary artistry draws the hearer of the gospel into the truth of this revelation. The presence of God's light and the pattern of God's love is "encamped" (ἐσκήνωσεν, John 1:14) in the person of Jesus Christ. The literary pattern of the Gospel of John is also the literary pattern of 1 John. In this artistry the truth of the gospel's message and revelation is expressed. The community's witness is "the word of life" (1 John 1:2) centered in two thematic confessions, "God is light" (1 John 1:5) and "God is love" (1 John 4:8, 16), which identify the central sections of 1 John. The concluding section, "the witness of faith" (1 John 5:6-21), identifies the witness of God and the community. Like the evangelist of the Gospel of John, the author of 1 John has written with a twofold purpose that is confessional and instructional: "I write these things to you who believe in the name of the Son of God [confessional], that you may know you have eternal life [instructional]" (1 John 5:13).

Whereas there is general consensus on the literary structure of the Gospel of John, the literary structure of 1 John has remained an enigma in the history of interpretation.[11] There is no writing in early Christian literature which reflects continuity with a Gospel tradition like 1 John. The closest parallel is in the Luke-Acts tradition where the sermons of Peter and Paul are examples of the proclamation of the gospel of Jesus Christ.

II. THE ARTISTRY OF THE WORD IN JOHN AND 1 JOHN

The literary and theological relationship between the Gospel of John and 1 John is seen most clearly when the writings are placed side by side, revealing a common chiastic or concentric literary pattern:

John	1 John
A The word became flesh 1:1-18	A The word of life 1:1-4
B The presence of God's light 1:19-12:50	B God is light 1:5-4:6
B' The pattern of God's love 13:1-17:26	B' God is love 4:7-5:5
A' The witness is true 18:1-21:25	A' The witness of faith 5:6-21

[11]See the extended discussion of the proposed divisions in Raymond E. Brown, *The Epistles of John*, AB 30 (Garden City: Doubleday, 1982) 116-130, 764. See also additional references to proposed divisions of 1 John in Georg Strecker, *The Johannine Letters: A Commentary on 1, 2, and 3 John*, Hermeneia (Minneapolis: Fortress, 1996) xiii-xliv.

The relative lengths of the corresponding sections in the two books are surprisingly similar.[12]

	John				1 John		
A	1:1-18	30 lines	1.6%	A	1:1-4	11 lines	4.3%
B	1:19-12:50	1152 lines	62.5%	B	1:5-4:6	158 lines	61.7%
B'	13:1-17:26	325 lines	17.7%	B'	4:7-5:5	50.5 lines	19.7%
A'	18:1-21:25	336 lines	18.2%	A'	5:6-21	36.5 lines	14.3%
		1843 lines	100%			256 lines	100%

In this comparison, the sums of the complementary first and fourth sections (A and A') in John and 1 John differ by slightly over one percentage point (John: 1.6% + 18.2% = 19.8%; 1 John: 4.3% + 14.3% = 18.6%), as do the sums of the complementary second and third sections (B and B') (John: 62.5% + 17.7% = 80.2%; 1 John: 61.7% + 19.7% = 81.4%). These proportional relationships are striking, especially considering the differences in the type of literature and length of writing. (The Gospel of John is over seven times the length of 1 John.) These textual and literary observations establish the basis for understanding the continuity and literary relationship between John and 1 John.[13]

1. The Literary Pattern of Chiasm in John

The fourfold literary division of the Gospel of John follows the central themes in the gospel, which are noted with slight variation by virtually all interpreters.[14] Following the prologue (1:1-18), "the book of signs" (1:19-12:50) includes the witness of John to Jesus, the confessional identifications of Jesus by the first followers, and the teachings and signs of Jesus. The next two major sections (13:1-17:26 and 18:1-21:25) are referred to as "the book of glory." The first section begins with Jesus' final meal (13:1-20) and the announcement of Judas' betrayal and Peter's denial (13:21-38). Jesus' farewell discourse follows (14:1-16:33), and the section concludes with his prayer for the community (17:1-26). The second section includes the passion and resurrection narratives (18:1-20:29), which are followed by the evangelist's witness and purpose (20:30-31). Jesus' final appearance to his

[12]In the 27th edition of the Nestle-Aland *Novum Testamentum Graece*, John 1:1-21:25 comprises 1843 lines of text and 1 John 1:1-5:21 comprises 256 lines of text. The total in the Gospel of John does not include 7:53-8:11. Even if 21:1-25 is considered as an epilogue, it is integral to the literary structure and theology of the gospel. Thus, it is included here.

[13]This study does not force the form of chiasm on the Gospel of John and 1 John. The critique of such structures, when imposed, is rightly taken. See the new preface in Nils W. Lund, *Chiasmus in the New Testament: A Study in the Form and Function of Chiastic Structures* (1942; reprint, Peabody, MA: Hendrickson, 1992) vii-xxi, which critiques this methodology but also emphasizes the importance of chiasm in biblical writings.

[14]See the fourfold outline in Raymond E. Brown, *The Gospel According to John*, AB 29 (Garden City: Doubleday, 1966) cxxxviii-cxliv: I. Prologue (1:1-18); II. The Book of Signs (1:19-12:50); III. The Book of Glory (13:1-20:31); IV. The Epilogue (21:1-25). See also the fourfold outline in Robert Kysar, *John*, ACNT (Minneapolis: Augsburg, 1986) 21-25: I. Introduction: Beginnings (1:1-51); II. Jesus Reveals Glory (2:1-12:50); III. Jesus Receives Glory (13:1-20:29); IV. Conclusion: Endings (20:30-21:25).

A THE WORD BECAME FLESH John 1:1-18

B THE PRESENCE OF GOD'S LIGHT John 1:19-12:50

    a Revelation of Jesus and Passover sign 1:19-2:25

        b Humanity's darkness and God's light 3:1-4:54

            c Sabbath healing and Passover feeding 5:1-6:71

            c' Festival of Booths and presence of God 7:1-8:59

        b' Sabbath blindness and Festival of Lights 9:1-10:42

    a' Resurrection of Lazarus and final Passover 11:1-12:50

B' THE PATTERN OF GOD'S LOVE John 13:1-17:26
    a Pattern of the servant Jesus 13:1-20
      b Betrayal and denial of Jesus 13:21-38
        c Presence of the Paraclete 14:1-31
          d Identity of the community 15:1-17
        c' Presence of the Paraclete 15:18-16:15
      b' Pain and joy of the community 16:16-33
    a' Prayer of Jesus for the community 17:1-26

A' THE WITNESS IS TRUE John 18:1-21:25
    a Crucifixion of Jesus on the day of preparation 18:1-19:42
      b Resurrection of Jesus on the first day of the week 20:1-29
        c Twofold purpose of the witness 20:30-31
      b' Appearance of Jesus by the Sea of Tiberias 21:1-23
        c' "This is the disciple who is bearing witness" 21:24-25

---

disciples (21:1-23) is concluded with the witness of the disciple and the community and reference to Jesus' further deeds (21:24-25).

A working outline of the gospel follows the evangelist's artistry, which is seen in the literary pattern of chiasm (A word, B light, B' love, A' witness). In this pattern the prologue (1:1-18) and the passion and resurrection narratives and concluding witness (18:1-21:25) enclose the complementary central sections (1:19-12:50 and 13:1-17:26). Jesus' final words to his disciples in 16:28, which are themselves in the form of a chiasm (A Father, B world, B' world, A' Father), identify that the one who is the source of the Father's word in the world is the one who is the subject of the word of God in the gospel:

John 16:28	The Gospel of John
A I came from the Father	A The word became flesh 1:1-18
B and I have come into the world	B The presence of God's light 1:19-12:50
B' again, I am leaving the world	B' The pattern of God's love 13:1-17:26
A' and I am going to the Father	A' The witness is true 18:1-21:25

2. The Literary Pattern of Chiasm in 1 John

Jesus is the source and the subject of a tradition that is the identifying mark of this community. Because the continuation of this tradition is seen most clearly in 1 John, it is not surprising to see that the literary artistry of the Gospel of John is also evidenced in the continuity of the fourfold literary structure of 1 John (A word, B light, B' love, A' witness):

John	1 John
A The word became flesh 1:1-18	A The word of life 1:1-4
B The presence of God's light 1:19-12:50	B God is light 1:5-4:6
B' The pattern of God's love 13:1-17:26	B' God is love 4:7-5:5
A' The witness is true 18:1-21:25	A' The witness of faith 5:6-21

Corresponding to the prologue in the Gospel of John (John 1:1-18), 1 John begins with a prologue focusing on the word and witness of the community: "the word of life" (1 John 1:1-4).[15] Corresponding to Jesus' revelation of the presence of God's light (John 1:19-12:50), 1 John expresses the confessional witness of the community: "God is light" (1 John 1:5-4:6).[16] Corresponding to Jesus' revelation of the pattern of God's love (John 13:1-17:26), 1 John expresses the confessional witness of the community: "God is love" (1 John 4:7-5:5).[17] Corresponding to the witness of Jesus' death and resurrection (John 18:1-21:25), 1 John concludes with the witness of God to his Son and the community's witness to God's gift of eternal

---

[15]The prologue of 1 John includes eleven verbs in the first person plural confessional style, "we." These verbs express the community's continuity with the Gospel of John and the source of that tradition, Jesus Christ. In the prologue of the Gospel of John, Jesus Christ is "the Word" (ὁ λόγος) who was "in the beginning with God" (John 1:1-2). In the prologue of 1 John, Jesus Christ is "the word of life" (ὁ λόγος τῆσ ζωῆς) who was "from the beginning," a beginning present in the gospel in his words, signs, death, and resurrection.

[16]The word "light" (φῶς) occurs twenty-three times in the Gospel of John, all within the prologue (1:1-18) and the section "the presence of God's light" (1:19-12:50). In a complementary way, the word "light" (φῶς) occurs six times in 1 John, all within the section "God is light" (1:5-4:6).

[17]Twenty-five of the thirty-seven occurrences of the verb "to love" (ἀγαπάω) and six of the seven occurrences of the noun "love" (ἀγάπη) in the Gospel of John are in the section "the pattern of God's love" (13:1-17:26). In a complementary way, nineteen of the twenty-eight occurrences of the verb "to love" (ἀγαπάω) and thirteen of the eighteen occurrences of the noun "love" (ἀγάπη) in 1 John are in the section "God is love" (4:7-5:5).

A THE WORD OF LIFE 1 John 1:1-4

B GOD IS LIGHT 1 John 1:5-4:6

a Jesus Christ is a Paraclete with the Father 1:5-2:2

b God's commandment is light in the darkness 2:3-17

c Anointing of Christ and coming of antichrists 2:18-27

d Children of God and children of the devil 2:28-3:10

c' Children of Christ's compassion 3:11-18

b' Children of God's commandment 3:19-24

a' Children of the Spirit's confession 4:1-6

B' GOD IS LOVE 1 John 4:7-5:5
a Sending of God's Son 4:7-10
b Giving of God's Spirit 4:11-14
c Perfection of God's love 4:15-18
b' Commandment of love 4:19-21
a' Triumph of our faith 5:1-5

A' THE WITNESS OF FAITH 1 John 5:6-21
a "This is the one who came by water and blood, Jesus Christ" 5:6-8
b "This is the witness of God" 5:9-12
c Twofold purpose of the witness 5:13
b' "This is the confidence we have with God" 5:14-17
a' "This is the true God and eternal life" 5:18-20
c' Exhortation against idols 5:21

life in his Son: "the witness of faith" (1 John 5:6-21).[18] In following the literary and structural pattern of the gospel, the author of 1 John expresses the truth of the "announcement" (ἀγγελία, in 1:5; 3:11) of the Gospel of John for the present time and context.

[18]Both the verb "to witness" (μαρτυρέω) and the noun "witness" (μαρτυρία) occur at the cross (19:35) and in the concluding words of the disciple and community (21:24) in the final section of the Gospel of John, "the witness is true" (18:1-21:25). Four of the six occurrences of the verb "to witness" (μαρτυρέω) and all six of the occurrences of the noun "witness" (μαρτυρία) are in the final section of 1 John, "the witness of faith" (5:6-21).

151

Like the Gospel of John, 1 John is a masterful artistic creation. The theme of the prologue in the Gospel of John, "the word became flesh" (1:1-18), and the witness of the community in the prologue in 1 John, "the word of life" (1:1-4), express the centrality of Jesus Christ in whom the word of God is present. 1 John instructs the community in the word of life, which is centered in the one who is the source and the subject of the gospel tradition.

As the literary structure of John indicates, Israel's festival days are the context in which Jesus' words and signs reveal the Father. The first half (1:19-6:71) of the section, "the presence of God's light" (1:19-12:50), leads to the confrontation of God and the devil in Peter's identification of Jesus, "You are the Holy One of God" (6:69), and Jesus' identification of Judas as the devil and the one who will betray him (6:70-71). From this center point, the second half (7:1-12:50) of this section begins with the Festival of Booths (7:2). Jesus leaves Galilee and goes to Judea, where his works will reveal him "openly" (παρρησία, in 7:4). The section concludes with Jesus' entry into Jerusalem at the time of Passover with the acclamation, "the King of Israel" (12:13), and his announcement that the hour has come for the Father's glorification of the Son of Man and the casting out of the ruler of this world (12:23-34).

In 1 John, the first half (1:5-3:10) of the corresponding section, "God is light" (1:5-4:6), identifies the community's anointing from "the Holy One" (2:20) and the confrontation of God and the devil, now expressed in the community's conflict with their opponents: "In this it is clear who are the children of God and the children of the devil" (3:10). From this center point, the second half (3:11-4:6) expresses the threefold identity of the community, as children of Christ's compassion (3:11-18), children of God's commandment (3:19-24), and children of the Spirit's confession (4:1-6). The section concludes: "From this we know the Spirit of truth and the spirit of deceit" (4:6).

In the Gospel of John, the center point of the section "the pattern of God's love" (13:1-17:26) is in the "identity of the community" (15:1-17) and expressed in Jesus' word: "This is my commandment, that you love one another just as I loved you" (15:12). This section is concluded with Jesus' final words to the disciples, "I have triumphed over (νικάω, 16:33) the world," and his prayer to the Father for the community's life in the world (17:1-26).

In 1 John the center point of the corresponding section "God is love" (4:7-5:5), is in the "perfection of God's love" (4:15-18), where the noun "love" (ἀγάπη) occurs seven times. In the unit that follows, "commandment of love" (4:19-21), the verb "to love" (ἀγαπάω) occurs seven times, which brings to perfection the community's identity in God's love. This section is concluded on the triumphing (νικάω, 5:4 [twice], 5) faith (πίστις, 5:4) of the community in the Son of God; in him there is the victory (νική, 5:4) that triumphs over the world.

The passion and resurrection narrative in the Gospel of John, "the witness is true" (18:1-21:25), is framed by the identifications of Jesus: the "I am" (ἐγώ εἰμι) self-identification of Jesus in the garden (18:5, 6, 8) and the confession of Thomas, "My Lord and my God" (20:28). Following the lancing of Jesus' side, from which flows blood and water, a confessional witness is spoken: "And the one who has seen has given witness, and his witness is true, and he knows that what he says is true, that you also may believe" (19:35).

The corresponding section in 1 John, "the witness of faith" (5:6-21), is framed by the community's witness to Jesus. "This is the one who came by water and blood, Jesus Christ" (5:6) introduces this section, which recalls the flow of blood and water from Jesus' side and the witness (John 19:34b-35). "This is the true God and eternal life" (5:20) concludes this section, which recalls Jesus' prayer to the Father: "This is eternal life, that they know you, the only true God, and him whom you have sent, Jesus Christ" (John 17:3).

III. THE AUTHORITY OF THE WITNESS IN JOHN AND 1 JOHN

The continuity and authority of the Gospel of John and 1 John are in the witness of the Son to the Father, the Father to the Son, and the Spirit-led community to the Father and the Son. The literary and rhetorical artistry of the Gospel of John and 1 John expresses this continuity and authority (see the charts on pp. 157-159, which compare the two writings). The confessional and instructional purpose of these writings (John 20:31; 1 John 5:13) is identified in the instructional themes and words and the confessional witness of the community. In the Gospel of John, "this is" (αὕτη ἐστίν) statements identify the instructional themes, and "in this" (ἐν τούτῳ) phrases identify the instructional words and confessional witness (see chart on p. 157).[19] The final "in this" (ἐν τούτῳ) phrase, in John 16:30, introduces the confessional witness of the disciples in the Gospel of John, which serves as the pattern for the confessional witness of the community in 1 John. In 1 John, "is this/this is" (ἔστιν αὕτη/αὕτη ἐστίν) statements identify the instructional themes, and "in this" (ἐν τούτῳ) phrases and a single "from this" (ἐκ τούτου) phrase identify the confessional witness of the community.[20]

[19]The confessional witness of Jesus and by Jesus in the Gospel of John is identified in the "this is/is this?" (οὗτός ἐστιν/ἐστιν οὗτός) confessions and questions addressed of Jesus, the "you are/are you?" (σὺ εἶ/εἶ σύ), confessions and questions addressed of Jesus, and Jesus' self-identification in the "I am" (ἐγώ εἰμι) statements. Of these three forms of witness, only the "this is" (οὗτός ἐστιν) confession of Jesus is present in 1 John 5:6, 20, framing the concluding section of 1 John. These confessional forms appear extensively throughout the Gospel of John; however, it is beyond the scope of this study to consider them: "this is/is this?" (οὗτός ἐστιν/ἐστιν οὗτός) in 1:30, 33, 34; 4:29, 42; 6:14, 42, 50, 58; 7:18, 25, 26, 40, 41; 12:34; 21:24; "you are/are you?" (σὺ εἶ/εἶ σύ) in 1:49 (twice); 4:19; 6:69; 10:24; 11:27; 18:33, 37; "I am" (ἐγώ εἰμι) in 4:26; 6:20, 35, 48, 51; 8:12, 18, 23 (twice), 24, 28, 58; (9:5); 10:7, 9, 11, 14; 11:25; 13:19; 14:6; 15:1, 5; 18:5, 6, 8. I have dealt with these confessional forms extensively in an unpublished manuscript.

[20]The "from this" (ἐκ τούτου) phrase occurs twice in the Gospel of John. In chapter six the phrase expresses the offense of the disciples to Jesus' words that his "flesh is true food" and his "blood is true drink" (John 6:55): "From this (ἐκ τούτου) [Jesus' word] many of his disciples drew back and no longer went about with him" (John 6:66). In the passion narrative the phrase expresses the response of Pilate to Jesus' testimony on kingship and truth (John 18:33-38a) and authority from above (John 19:11): "From this (ἐκ τούτου [Jesus' witness] Pilate sought to release him" (John 19:12). The two instances in the gospel come at the conclusion of Jesus' words and teaching and witness to the truth. The single occurrence of the "from this" phrase in 1 John is placed at a point that concludes the words and witness of Jesus from the first "is this" (ἔστιν αὕτη) announcement in 1 John: "And the announcement is this, which we have heard from him [Jesus], and we are announcing to you: 'God is light and in him there is no darkness at all'" (1 John 1:5).

The chiastic pattern (a1, b1, b1', a1') of the four "this is" (αὕτη ἐστίν) instructional themes in John 1:19; 3:19; 15:12; and 17:3, and the chiastic pattern (a2, b2, b2', a2') of the four "in this" (ἐν τούτῳ) instructional words in John 4:37; 9:30; 13:35; and 15:8 are based on the chiastic pattern (A, B, B', A') in John 16:28. As noted above, the fifth and final "in this" phrase in John 16:30 (c2) identifies the confessional witness of the disciples' response to Jesus' revelation of the Father in John 16:28. In this verse, Jesus identifies how the pattern of his life openly announces (παρρησία and ἀπαγγέλλω, in John 16:25) his revelation of the Father. As noted previously, these words also express the chiastic pattern and structure of the gospel itself (A, B, B', A'), a gospel that has its focus in Jesus' making known/exegeting (ἐξηγέομαι) his Father's presence in the world: "No one has ever seen God; the only God, who rests in the bosom of the Father, that one has made him known" (John 1:18):

John 16:28	The Gospel of John
A I came from the Father	A The word became flesh 1:1-18
B and I have come into the world	B The presence of God's light 1:19-12:50
B' again, I am leaving the world	B' The pattern of God's love 13:1-17:26
A' and I am going to the Father	A' The witness is true 18:1-21:25

All four "this is" (αὕτη ἐστίν) instructional themes are within the two central sections of the Gospel of John and identify the fourfold pattern in John 16:28, expressed in the chiasm of Jesus' coming from the Father and coming into the world, and his leaving the world and going to the Father:

a1 This is the Witness (1:19) Jesus is the one who *"came from the Father."* John is the one sent by God (1:6) to bear witness to the one who comes after him (1:15, 30) to make the Father known (1:18)

b1 This is the Judgment (3:19) Jesus is the one who has *"come into the world,"* bringing the judgment of God's light, a light which illumines the darkness of this world and human deeds

b1' This is my Commandment (15:12) In *"leaving the world,"* Jesus' words express the commandment of love, which calls the community to love one another as they have been loved

a1' This is Eternal Life (17:3) In *"going to the Father,"* Jesus' prayer to his Father is that the discipleship community may know eternal life in the only true God and the one whom he has sent, Jesus Christ

Likewise all four "in this" (ἐν τούτῳ) instructional words and the single "in this" (ἐν τούτῳ) confessional witness are within the two central sections of the Gospel of John. The instructional words also identify the fourfold pattern in John 16:28, expressed in the chiasm of Jesus' coming from the Father and coming into the world, and his leaving the world and going to the Father:

a2 In this the word is true (4:37)   As the word who *"came from the Father,"* Jesus' first teaching of the disciples is about the sowing of the word of God, a true word that comes from the Father in Jesus Christ

 b2 In this the work is marvelous (9:30)   As the one who has *"come into the world"* from the Father, Jesus has come as the light of the world, revealing the work of God in restoring a man's sight

 b2' In this everyone will know (13:35)   As the one who is *"leaving the world,"* Jesus' final words identify how all will know the community to be his disciples, as they live in love with one another

a2' In this my Father is glorified (15:8)   As the one who is *"going to the Father,"* Jesus' death glorifies the Father, who is also glorified in the fruit-bearing lives of the community in the world

The fifth and final "in this" (ἐν τούτῳ) phrase in John 16:30 (c2) takes the form of a confessional witness of the disciples to the instructive themes and words which Jesus has spoken to the community. As the one who has come from the Father into the world, his leaving the world and going to the Father will take place in his death, resurrection, and ascension. To Jesus' words spoken "openly and not in any figure" (16:29), the disciples respond:

> "Now *we know* that you know all things, and do not need anyone to question you; *in this we believe you came from God.*" (16:30; emphasis added)

This is the only time in the gospel where the "in this" phrase is used with first person plural confessional verbs—"we know" and "we believe." The final "in this" (ἐν τούτῳ) phrase in the Gospel of John expresses the continuity with the instructional and confessional tradition of the community in 1 John.

The Gospel of John is the literary pattern and rhetorical form upon which 1 John is based and the source of the community's word of witness. Throughout the Gospel of John, Jesus is the one who "makes known/exegetes" (John 1:18) God's living presence in the world. Jesus' words announce God's word and his signs enact God's presence. Centered in Jesus' words, signs, death, resurrection, and ascension, and empowered by the Holy Spirit, the community announces God's living presence in Jesus Christ.

A word group that focuses the continuity of the Gospel of John and 1 John is found in the verbs "to announce" and the noun "announcement":

ἀναγγέλλω	John 4:25; 5:15; 16:13, 14, 15	1 John 1:5
ἀπαγγέλλω	John 16:25	1 John 1:2, 3
ἀγγέλλω	John 20:18	
ἀγγελία		1 John 1:5; 3:11

The verbs, "to announce" (ἀναγγέλλω and ἀπαγγέλλω), which identify the work of the Spirit of truth (John 16:13, 14, 15) and Jesus (John 16:25) in the farewell words, express the continuity and confessional witness of the community in the opening verses of 1 John (1:2, 3, 5). The verb, "to announce" (ἀγγέλλω), in John 20:18 expresses Mary Magdalene's witness of the risen Christ to the disciples. The noun, "announcement" (ἀγγελία), occurs only twice in the New Testament and identifies two instructional themes in 1 John (1:5; 3:11).

Following the prologue on the theme "the word of life" (1:1-4), the introductory "is this" (ἔστιν αὕτη) and nine "this is" (αὕτη ἐστίν) themes in 1 John continue the instructional pattern of the Gospel of John (see chart on pp. 158-159). The fourteen occurrences of the "in this" (ἐν τούτῳ) phrase and the single occurrence of the "from this" (ἐκ τούτου) phrase in 1 John continue the confessional pattern initiated in the Gospel of John. The instructional themes and the confessional witness of the community are in a balanced relationship with one another, yet the patterns of this relationship vary in each section of 1 John.

The first two themes introduce and identify the instructional tradition in 1:5-3:10: "the announcement is this" (1:5) and "this is the promise" (2:25). Four of the five "in this" confessions (2:3, 4, 5a, 5b) in 1:5-3:10 are clustered between the two themes, and the fifth "in this" confession concludes the first half of the section entitled "God is light" (1:5-4:6): "In this it is evident who are the children of God and the children of the devil" (3:10).

The second two themes introduce and identify the instructional tradition in 3:11-4:6: "this is the announcement" (3:11) and "this is his commandment" (3:23). Two "in this" confessions (3:16, 19) follow the first theme, and two "in this" confessions (3:24; 4:2) follow the second theme in 3:11-4:6. The single occurrence of the "from this" confession concludes the second half of the section entitled "God is light" (1:5-4:6): "From this we know the Spirit of truth and the spirit of deceit" (4:6).

Five "in this" confessions (4:9, 10, 13, 17; 5:2) identify the confessional tradition in 4:7-5:5. The final confession in 5:2 concludes the teaching in 1 John on the verb "to love." Two instructional themes conclude this section entitled "God is love" (4:7-5:5): "this is the love of God" (5:3) and "this is the triumph/victory that triumphed over the world, our faith" (5:4).

Framed by two confessions of Christ (5:6, 20), the final section of 1 John, entitled "the witness of faith" (5:6-21), includes three instructional themes which identify the community's witness. The first theme identifies the witness of God: "For this is the witness of God, that he has borne witness to his Son" (5:9). The second theme identifies God's gift of life: "And this is the witness, that God gave us eternal life, and this life is in his Son" (5:11). The final theme identifies the confidence of the community in the presence of God: "And this is the confidence which we have with him" (5:14).

A THE WORD BECAME FLESH John 1:1-18

B THE PRESENCE OF GOD'S LIGHT John 1:19-12:50

a1   And **this is** (καὶ αὕτη ἐστὶν) the witness of John,
        when the Jews sent priests and Levites from
        Jerusalem to ask him, "Who are you?" (1:19)

b1   And **this is** (αὕτη δέ ἐστιν) the judgment,
        that the light has come into the world,
        and people loved darkness rather than light,
        because their deeds were evil (3:19)

a2   For **in this** (ἐν γὰρ τούτῳ) the word is true,
        "One is sowing and another is reaping" (4:37)

b2   For **in this** (ἐν τούτῳ γὰρ) the work is marvelous!
        You do not know from where he comes,
        and yet he opened my eyes (9:30)

B' THE PATTERN OF GOD'S LOVE John 13:1-17:26

b2' **In this** (ἐν τούτῳ) everyone will know
        that you are my disciples,
        when you have love for one another (13:35)

a2' **In this** (ἐν τούτῳ) my Father is glorified, that you
        should bear much fruit and become my disciples (15:8)

b1' **This is** (αὕτη ἐστὶν) my commandment, that you
        should love one another just as I loved you (15:12)

c2   Now we know that you know all things,
        and you do not need anyone to question you;
        in this (ἐν τούτῳ) we believe you came
        from God (16:30)

a1' And **this is** (αὕτη δέ ἐστιν) eternal life,
        that they know you, the only true God,
        and him whom you have sent, Jesus Christ (17:3)

A' THE WITNESS IS TRUE John 18:1-21:25

A THE WORD OF LIFE 1 John 1:1-4

B GOD IS LIGHT 1 John 1:5-4:6

And the announcement **is this** (καὶ ἔστιν αὕτη),
  which we have heard from him, and we are announcing to you,
    "God is light and in him there is no darkness at all" (1:5)

  And **in this** (καὶ ἐν τούτῳ) we know that we have known him
    ...and the truth is not **in this** (καὶ ἐν τούτῳ) (2:3-4)
  And whoever keeps his word,
    truly **in this** (ἐν τούτῳ) the love of God is perfected;
    in this (ἐν τούτῳ) we know that we are in him (2:5)

And **this is** (καὶ αὕτη ἐστὶν) the promise
  which he himself promised us, eternal life (2:25)

  In this (ἐν τούτῳ) it is evident who are
    the children of God and the children of the devil (3:10)

For **this is** (ὅτι αὕτη ἐστὶν) the announcement
  which you heard from the beginning,
    that we should love one another (3:11)

  In this (ἐν τούτῳ) we have come to know love,
    because he laid down his life for us (3:16)

  And **in this** ([καὶ] ἐν τούτῳ) we will know
    that we are of the truth (3:19)

And **this is** (καὶ αὕτη ἐστὶν) his commandment,
  that we should believe in the name of his Son, Jesus Christ,
    and love one another, just as he gave commandment to us (3:23)

  And **in this** (καὶ ἐν τούτῳ) we know that he abides in us,
    by the Spirit which he gave us (3:24)

  In this (ἐν τούτῳ) you know the Spirit of God (4:2)

  From this (ἐκ τούτου) we know
    the Spirit of truth and the spirit of deceit (4:6)

B' GOD IS LOVE 1 John 4:7-5:5

In this (ἐν τούτῳ) the love of God was revealed to us,
  for God has sent his only Son into the world,
  that we may live through him (4:9)

In this (ἐν τούτῳ) is love,
  not that we have loved God
  but that he loved us (4:10)

In this (ἐν τούτῳ) we know
  that we abide in him and he in us,
  because he has given us of his Spirit (4:13)

In this (ἐν τούτῳ) love is perfected among us,
  that we may have confidence
  on the day of judgment (4:17)

In this (ἐν τούτῳ) we know that we love the children of God,
  when we love God and obey his commandments (5:2)

For **this is** (αὕτη γάρ ἐστιν) the love of God,
  that we keep his commandments,
    and his commandments are not burdensome,
      for all that is born of God triumphs over the world.
And **this is** (καὶ αὕτη ἐστὶν) the triumph/victory
  that triumphed over the world, our faith (5:3-4)

A' THE WITNESS OF FAITH 1 John 5:6-21

This is (οὗτός ἐστιν) the one who came by water and blood,
    Jesus Christ (5:6)

For **this is** (ὅτι αὕτη ἐστὶν) the witness of God,
  that he has borne witness to his Son (5:9)

And **this is** (καὶ αὕτη ἐστὶν) the witness, that God gave us eternal life,
  and **this** life **is** ([καὶ] αὕτη...ἐστὶν) in his Son (5:11)

And **this is** (καὶ αὕτη ἐστὶν) the confidence which we have with him,
  that if we ask anything according to his will, he hears us (5:14)

This is (οὗτός ἐστιν) the true God and eternal life (5:20)

IV. THE WITNESS TO THE WORD IS TRUE IN JOHN AND 1 JOHN

The continuity of the instructional and confessional tradition in the Gospel of John and 1 John is unique in the New Testament. The confessional and instructional purpose of 1 John (1 John 5:13) brings to completion the confessional and instructional purpose of the Gospel of John (John 20:31). Identification of the instructional themes and confessional witness and their relationship to one another expresses the way in which the community drew upon the teaching authority of Jesus as its source of instruction and the subject of its confession. Jesus remains the teacher through the ongoing work of the Holy Spirit/Spirit of truth, who leads the community into an instructional and confessional witness that is true. In these words, Jesus the "I am" (ἐγώ εἰμι) *is* present in the "we" confessions of the community.

It is instructive to see that the Gospel of John and 1 John express a continuity and authority with the instructional words in the Septuagint version of the Torah. God's instructive word to Moses is the authority to speak God's words and enact God's signs.[21] The form of the prepositional phrase with the demonstrative pronoun, "in this" (ἐν τούτῳ), identifies God's instructional and authoritative word given to Moses to speak to Pharaoh:

> Thus says the Lord, "In this (ἐν τούτῳ) you shall know that I am the Lord: behold, I will strike the water that is in the Nile with the rod that is in my hand, and it shall be turned to blood, and the fish in the Nile shall die, and the Nile shall become foul, and the Egyptians will loathe to drink water from the Nile." (Exod 7:17-18)

The authority of God's instructional word and the enacting of God's works is also given by God to Moses to speak to the people of Israel: "In this (ἐν τούτῳ) you shall know that the Lord has sent me to do all these works, and that it has not been of my own accord" (Num 16:28).

The basis of this theology of word and works, established in God's instructive "in this" (ἐν τούτῳ) word, is not only the authoritative word in the Torah, but also the authoritative word of the instructional and confessional tradition in the Gospel of John and 1 John. The God revealed to Moses is the God made known in Jesus Christ; the God who is the source of instruction in the Torah is the God made known in the instructional words and confessional witness of the community. The "in this" (ἐν τούτῳ) confessions in 1 John complete the pattern of God's instructive words to Moses in the Torah and Jesus' works and signs (ἔργα, σημεῖα) and his instructive words to the disciples in the Gospel of John.

The instructional and confessional tradition established in the witness of the Father and the Son is continued in the witness of the community through the ongoing work of the Holy Spirit/Spirit of truth. This is the foundational theology and identity of a community faithful to the Torah tradition: "Only on the evidence

---

[21]The parallel patterns between the way Moses speaks in the name of God and Jesus speaks as God are noted in Marie-Emile Boismard, *Moses or Jesus: An Essay in Johannine Christology* (Minneapolis: Fortress, 1993).

of two or three witnesses shall a charge be sustained" (Deut 19:15b; see also Deut 17:6; Num 35:30). Based on this principle, Jesus' identifying and authoritative word proclaims a witness to the Father and himself that is true: "In your law it is written that the witness of two persons is true. I am the one who bears witness to myself, and the Father who sent me bears witness to me" (John 8:17-18; see also John 5:17, 30-32; 7:18; 12:48-50). The "I am" (ἐγώ εἰμι) witness of Jesus is true because "God is true" (John 3:33). "The word became flesh" (John 1:1-18) is "the word of life" (1 John 1:1-4). Jesus' revelation of "the presence of God's light" (John 1:19-12:50) and "the pattern of God's love" (John 13:1-17:26) makes known the true confession that "God is light" (1 John 1:5-4:6) and "God is love" (1 John 4:7-5:5). "The witness is true" (John 18:1-21:25) because it is "the witness of faith" (1 John 5:6-21). The Gospel of John and 1 John reveal a true witness.

These writings create a living response that can be likened to that of experiencing a visual masterpiece. For example, one can read in secondary resources *about* Rembrandt's *The Night Watch*, but to stand in the presence of this work is to be drawn *into* its life-inviting scale. As a viewer, one ceases to remain a spectator as one is drawn into this scene and becomes a participant in the commencing procession. The Gospel of John and 1 John also draw one into the life of these works of art. Their innovative style and technique capture the subject—the living Christ—the foundation and source of faith. One can read in secondary literature *about* the Gospel of John and 1 John, but to be drawn *into* the word and its witness in the Gospel of John and 1 John is to experience the living reality of these writings.

The portrait of Jesus that emerges in the Gospel of John and 1 John captures the truth of "the Word became flesh" (John 1:14a), which is "the word of life" (1 John 1:2). As is true for every artist, the portrait created in the Gospel of John conveys Jesus in a way that is indeed different from the synoptic portraits; however, the Johannine portrait is still recognizably the same figure.

If the Gospel of John were discovered for the first time today, as the *Gospel of Thomas* was in 1945, there would be no doubt that the figure of Jesus in the Gospel of John was the same figure present in the synoptic gospels. Jesus' relationship to John the Baptist, his call of disciples, itinerant ministry, healings, controversies, teachings, entry into Jerusalem, passion events, crucifixion, death, and resurrection are attested to in all four canonical gospels. Some would see in the events recorded in the Gospel of John similarities with the synoptic portraits, and others would note how differently Jesus is portrayed. Both responses would be understandable. The Jesus who is the prophet and teacher is also the crucified and resurrected one. In this sense the Gospel of John is an indispensable source for our understanding of Jesus of Nazareth.

The earthly Jesus is the source of a coherent portrait that emerges in the Gospel of John. The historical, literary, and theological portrait of the earthly Jesus and Christ of faith are inseparably bound together. The emerging portrait is a masterpiece that invites the reader into an encounter with the living Christ and opens the door to an aesthetic appreciation of the depth, beauty, and genius of the Johannine tradition.

A primary intention of this study has been to identify the literary constructions and rhetorical forms of the Gospel of John and 1 John. In the discovery of the details of grammar and syntax, words and sentences, content and form, poetry and structure—the brush strokes and textures, colors and hues, composition and form of a visual masterpiece—we begin the interpretive task that lies before us. The literary and rhetorical artistry of these writings draws the reader and hearer into the foundation of faith, centered in Jesus Christ, the crucified and resurrected one.

In these writings the quest for Jesus comes to rest. The Jesus met in these writings is the source of a tradition in which he is the subject of the community's witness, a witness that is true. Herein lies the continuity and authority of the Gospel of John and 1 John. "In this" (ἐν τούτῳ) the people of God of every time have the word of God and the words of Jesus that instruct and sustain the life of the Christian community and its Spirit-led confession of faith and witness to the word in the world. ⊕

Word & World
Supplement Series 3
1997

Christ's Many Friends:
The Presence of Jesus in
2 Corinthians 1-7

DAVID E. FREDRICKSON

Luther Seminary
St. Paul, Minnesota

I. INTRODUCTION

2 CORINTHIANS 1-7 IS A REMARKABLE TEXT FOR MANY REASONS, NOT LEAST OF WHICH is the centrality of the earthly Jesus in the letter's argumentation. The presence of Jesus, however, must not mislead us. Paul is not presenting his answer to the vexing question of whether he invented Christianity or whether he simply follows Jesus. This question is a largely a construction of nineteenth-century New Testament scholarship and reflects its own interests and presuppositions about the relation between the church's dogma and the faith life of the individual believer. In its present sharp either/or it would have been unintelligible to Paul himself. Nevertheless, in 2 Corinthians 1-7 Paul deals with a problem that does bear a resemblance to the modern Jesus of history/Christ of faith debate. Briefly stated, the problem Paul addresses in 2 Corinthians 1-7 is this: How can that which is particular and bound by time and space and individual existence be of universal and timeless significance for all others? How can the human Jesus be related to those outside of his immediate sphere of contacts? How can one be of consequence for all?

In order to understand the way Paul answers these questions in 2 Corinthians 1-7, we must first agree that the earthly Jesus is in fact a central figure in the letter's argumentation. There are several references to the earthly Jesus in these chapters:

1:5   the passions of Christ (τὰ παθήματα τοῦ Χριστοῦ)
1:19   the "yes" happened in him (ναὶ ἐν αὐτῷ γέγονεν)

163

2:10; 4:6	on the face of Christ (ἐν προσώπῳ Χριστοῦ)
4:10	the death of Jesus (τὴν νέκρωσιν τοῦ 'Ιησοῦ)
4:10-11	the life of Jesus (ἡ ζωὴ τοῦ 'Ιησοῦ)
5:14	the love of Christ (ἡ ἀγάπη τοῦ Χριστοῦ)
5:16	Christ according to the flesh (κατὰ σάρκα Χριστόν)

These phrases will form the backbone of the present study. In the passages in which they are found we will discover Paul's conceptual framework for relating the earthly Jesus to himself and the epistle's audience.

We are not interested in an enumeration of references to the earthly Jesus for its own sake, although the collection of these phrases is an impressive witness to Jesus as the subject of action in Paul's theology. The main goal of taking this inventory is to discover the underlying pattern of thought that explains the rhetorical function and theological significance of the earthly Jesus in Paul's argumentation. We will see that Paul does not seek to mediate between the particular and the universal through a conception of Jesus as teacher of universal truths. Neither does he pursue the agenda for historical research provided by Schleiermacher's notion of Jesus as the highest example of God-consciousness. What we will find is that Paul casts the problem of the universal significance of the earthly Jesus in terms of ancient philosophical understandings of friendship (φιλία). The method of the present study will be to explain Paul's statements about the earthly Jesus by noting their relationship with and radical reformulation of relevant aspects of friendship.[1]

A preliminary comment about the topic of friendship is in order, since it may not be obvious how it had for Paul and his audience the capacity of holding together the particularity of Jesus with his universal significance. Some of the common sayings about friendship reveal its ability to overcome physical and temporal separation. Furthermore, normal boundaries between self and others are dissolved in friendship:

> friends have all things in common[2]
> a friend is another self[3]
> friends are one soul in two bodies[4]
> a friend will die for a friend[5]
> friends may be absent in body but never in spirit[6]

---

[1]Reasons for thinking that friendship is the unifying theme of 2 Corinthians 1-7 will emerge in the course of the argument. It might be noted at this point, however, that the ἐλπίζω statements in 1:13-14 and 5:11, which many scholars believe express the purpose of the letter, reflect the friendship cliché that friends have the deepest possible knowledge of one another. See Aristotle, *Nichomachean Ethics* 7.4.9-10; Cicero, *De Amicitia* 103-104; Julian, *Oration* 8.247CD.

[2]Xenophon, *Memorabilia* 2.6.23; Dio Chrysostom, *Oration* 3.110; Plutarch, *How to Tell a Flatterer from a Friend* 65A; Julian, *Oration* 8.245B; Seneca, *Epistle* 48.2-3.

[3]Cicero, *De Amicitia* 23,80; Lucian, *Toxaris* 53; *Gnomologium Vaticanum* 296.

[4]Cicero, *De Amicitia* 81, 92-93; *Gnomologium Vaticanum* 137.

[5]Cicero, *De Finibus* 2.79; *De Amicitia* 24; Seneca, *Epistle* 6.2; 9.9; Lucian, *Toxaris* 37; *Gnomologium Vaticanum* 103.

[6]The most convenient collection of this and other commonplace sayings about friendship is G. Bohnenblust, *Beiträge zum Topos* περὶ φιλίας (Berlin: Gustav Schade [Otto Francke], 1905).

Paul employs these and related notions about friendship in his presentation of the earthly Jesus in 2 Corinthians 1-7. Jesus is a friend, and Paul describes his own relationship with Jesus in terms of friendship. Similarly, Jesus' relationship to the Corinthians and to the cosmos is put in terms of friendship. By framing Jesus' identity in terms of friendship's ability to transcend the categories of time/space and self/other, Paul provides an answer to the problem of the universal significance of the particular person Jesus. As we will see, Paul must radically transform the notion of friendship, which was thought to be limited to a few persons, in order to encompass the truly startling idea that the one earthly Jesus died for all. Nevertheless, in spite of this transformation, the outlines of the ancient teaching on friendship are present in the text and shed much light on the way Paul connects the earthly Jesus to himself and his audience.

II. THE PASSIONS OF CHRIST (2 COR 1:3-7)

We find the first reference to the earthly Jesus in 2 Cor 1:5: "For just as the passions of Christ abound in us, so also through Christ our consolation abounds (ὅτι καθὼς περισσεύει τὰ παθήματα τοῦ Χριστοῦ εἰς ἡμᾶς, οὕτως διὰ τοῦ Χριστοῦ περισσεύει καὶ ἡ παράκλησις ἡμῶν.)" This verse and its context (1:3-11) characterize Paul's relationship with Jesus and the church in Corinth in terms of friendship. How does τὰ παθήματα call forth the idea of friendship?

The usual translation of τὰ παθήματα as "sufferings" does not fully communicate to readers of the English text the affective dimension of the term. Modern readers who possess the four gospel narratives and in particular the passion stories within a few pages of the Pauline epistles will inevitably think of the suffering of Jesus from an external point of view: betrayal, flogging, and crucifixion. Yet to confine the meaning of the term to actions taken against or befalling an individual is misleading. The term often denoted passion in a technical, philosophical sense.[7]

Other terms in 1:3-11 support the reading of τὰ παθήματα as passions and delineate the range of emotions experienced, although they too have suffered from the tendency to externalize what would most likely have been understood by first-century readers to be a depiction of an inner state. οἰκτιρμός (compassion) in 1:3 is related to the term οἶκτος, which was defined as grief over the evil befalling others.[8] Θλίψις (pressure or affliction) along with its verbal form θλίβομαι is mentioned in 1:4, 6 and then in 1:8-9 Paul enlarges upon the term by narrating his emotional state while in Asia.

Having ascertained the affective dimension of Christ's παθήματα we are now in a better position to see the theme of friendship running through 1:3-11. Here Paul emphasizes the identity of emotion in Christ, in himself, and in his audience:

---

[7]Well illustrated by the close connection to ἐπιθυμία ("desire") in Gal 5:24.

[8]See A. Glibert-Thirry, *Pseudo-Andronicus de Rhodes: ΠΕΡΙ ΠΑΘΩΝ*, Corpus Latinum Commentariorum in Aristotelem Graecorum, Suppl. 2 (Leiden: E. J. Brill, 1977) 227.

1:5: the passions of Christ abound in us (περισσεύει τὰ παθήματα τοῦ Χριστοῦ εἰσ ἡμᾶς)

1:6: the same passions which we ourselves have (τῶν αὐτῶν παθημάτων ὦν καὶ ἡμεῖς πάσχομεν)

1:7: partners in the passions (κοινωνοί ἐστε τῶν παθημάτων)

The notion reflected here that identity of emotion is the necessary condition for true friendship goes to the heart of traditional teaching on φιλία. In spite of separation in time and space, Christ, Paul, and the church are one because they share emotions. It is no surprise, then, that in 1:7 Paul uses the key term for this sharing of emotion in friendship: κοινωνία.[9]

Aristotle's decision to analyze the nature of friendship in terms of character and emotions sets the course for subsequent thinking about the topic and provides the deep background to Paul's emphasis on emotions in this passage.[10] Friends are homoiopathic; they have like emotions.[11] Friendship comes into being through likeness, and this includes the identity of emotions.[12] When Plutarch reflects on the reason why it is impossible to have many friends (a topic which we shall take up below in conjunction with 2 Cor 5:14-15), he cites and amplifies the widely held view that "friendship comes into being through likeness (δι᾽ ὁμοιότητος)." Since even the beasts consort willingly only with those like themselves, how would it be possible among humans

> for friendship to be engendered in different characters, unlike feelings (πάθεσιν ἀνομοίοις), and lives which hold to other principles? It is true that the harmony produced on harp and lyre gets its consonance through tones of dissonant pitch...but in our friendship's consonance and harmony there must be no element unlike, uneven, or unequal, but all must be alike to engender agreement in words (ὁμολογεῖν), counsels (ὁμοβουλεῖν), opinions (ὁμοδοξειν), and feelings (συνομοπαθεῖν), and it must be as if one soul were apportioned among two or more bodies.[13]

Not only did this identity of emotions constitute the origin of friendship, it also defined its task. Friends were eagerly to share in the emotional condition of one another, to share both joy and sorrow, or in the Pauline idiom in 2 Cor 1:3-11, affliction (θλίψις).[14] Sharing both joy and sorrow distinguished the highest form of friendship from its degraded forms, friendship based either on pleasure or utility.[15]

---

[9]Aristotle, *Nichomachean Ethics* 8.9.1; 8.12.1; 9.12.1; *Eudemian Ethics* 7.9.1; Plutarch, *On Having Many Friends* 96D; Lucian, *Toxaris* 6-7; Julian, *Oration* 8.241C.

[10]Aristotle, *Nichomachean Ethics* 8.1.7.

[11]Plutarch, *How to Tell a Flatterer From a Friend* 51E; *On Having Many Friends* 97A.

[12]Aristotle, *Nichomachean Ethics* 8.3.6-7; Cicero, *De Amicitia* 50.

[13]Plutarch, *On Having Many Friends* 96E-F.

[14]Plutarch, *How to Tell a Flatterer from a Friend* 49F; *On Having Many Friends* 95F-96D; Dio Chrysostom, *Oration* 3.100-103; *Gnomologium Vaticanum* 273; Cicero, *De Amicitia* 22, 48, 64; Seneca, *Epistle* 6.3.

[15]Aristotle, *Eudemian Ethics* 7.2.50; 7.6.7-11; 7.11.5; 7.12.18.

Great consolation could be derived from this sharing, particularly in moments of pain.[16]

Our investigation of the earthly Jesus in Paul's argumentation has shown so far that friendship supplies the connection between Christ, Paul, and the church. Through the κοινωνία that is true friendship, the passions of Christ belong also to Paul and to the church. The earthly Jesus remains quite earthy in Paul's rhetoric; he is known in the text in terms of his emotions. Through φιλία Paul and the church are both contemporaneous with Jesus, sharing deeply in his emotions.

How φιλία is able to make Jesus, Paul, and the persons in the church contemporaneous and the occupants of the same space is a matter that will be explained below. Especially problematic in Paul's use of the friendship motif is the sheer number of persons connected in friendship. The very concept that allowed for the unity through time and space of friends, that is, the likeness of character and emotions, works against extending friendship beyond one or at most two people. Paul will have to reason out how it is possible for Christ to have so many friends.

III. FRIEND OR FLATTERER? (1:15-22)

Before the investigation of that problem, however, we must turn with Paul to the topic of flattery which, as the false show of friendship, makes visible from another perspective the theoretical framework in which Paul presents the universal significance of the human Jesus. As I have pointed out above, persons were united in friendship by virtue of likeness in emotions and character. The flatterer sought to change his character and emotions artificially to conform to his professed friends. The flatterer's transformation of character was aimed at praising the victim and ingratiating himself. The forced transformation proved that the flatterer had no fixed and stable self, and thus no integrity. Flattery and friendship were enough alike to make it disastrous if they were confused. For this reason, ways of distinguishing them become a popular topic in the Roman period.[17]

2 Cor 1:15-22 abounds in allusions to the pernicious imitation of friendship. It appears that Paul had been accused of being a flatterer to the congregation at Corinth. If we can discover the tension in this text and in the philosophic discussions between the concepts of friendship and flattery, and correlate them with Paul's references to the earthly Jesus, we will establish a fruitful perspective for the

---

[16]For the consoling (παραμυθητικός) power of friendship, see Aristotle, *Nichomachean Ethics* 9.11.2 The opening of Julian's letter to Sallust (*Oration* 8.240A-B) derives consolation from shared grief and bears a strong resemblance to 1 Cor 3-7: "Ah, my beloved comrade, unless I tell you all that I said to myself when I learned that you were compelled to journey far from my side, I shall think I am deprived of some comfort; or rather, I shall consider that I have not even begun to procure some assuagement for my grief unless I have first shared (μεταδέδωκα) it with you. For we two have shared (κοινωνήσαντας) in many sorrows and also in many pleasant deeds and words, in affairs private and public, at home and in the field, and therefore for the present troubles, be they what they may, we must needs discover some cure, some remedy that both can share."

[17]See D. Konstan, "Friendship, Frankness and Flattery," in *Friendship, Flattery, and Frankness of Speech: Studies on Friendship in the New Testament World*, ed. J. Fitzgerald (Leiden: E. J. Brill, 1996) 7-19. Especially significant is Plutarch, *How to Tell a Flatterer from a Friend* 51C-E; 52A-B; 53D.

investigation of how Paul formulates the universal significance of Jesus in the remainder of 2 Corinthians 1-7.

In 1:15-22 Paul seeks to distinguish his friendship for the congregation at Corinth from mere flattery. In 1:17 the theme of flattery emerges in Paul's quotation of a popular reference to the always obliging responses of the flatterer: τὸ ναὶ ναὶ καὶ τὸ οὒ οὔ ("'Yes, yes,' and 'No, no'"). From Cicero we learn that this line originated from the Roman playwright Terence and became the standard description of the flatterer.[18] Also part of the ancient discourse about flattery is the phrase "to use the light touch" found in 1:17: ἐλαφρίᾳ χρῆσθαι.[19]

In response to these accusations of flattery, Paul lets go with a barrage of clichés about friendship, all of which point to the loyalty to the congregation displayed by God, Christ, and Paul himself. Loyalty, it should be noted, was the trait most importantly lacking in the flatterer and was constitutive of friendship. In 1:18 Paul tells the reader that God is faithful (πιστός).[20] In 1:21 God is described as "the one who makes us steadfast with you in Christ (ὁ δὲ βεβαιῶν ἡμᾶς σὺν ὑμῖν εἰς Χριστόν)." This reflects the friendship doctrine in two ways. First, since friendships were so difficult and rare, it was sometimes said that only God could establish them.[21] Secondly, the true friend is constant (βέβαιος).[22] The theme of loyalty and constancy is related to the earthly Jesus in particular in 1:19: "the 'yes' happened in him (ναὶ ἐν αὐτῷ γέγονεν)." In 1:20 we read that it is through Christ that God keeps God's promises and that agreement with God is brought about. Promise keeping and agreement are both marks of true friendship. Finally, the location of the heart for the place of sharing the down payment of the Spirit in 1:22 most likely was chosen for its friendship association.[23]

How does tracing the theme of flattery in 1:15-22 help us see the theological framework for the way Paul relates the earthly Jesus to himself and the Corinthian congregation? Clearly, Paul is pushing beyond the natural capacity of the ancient doctrine of friendship. As it was construed by Paul's contemporaries, friendship had the ability to unite two or perhaps three persons. The dissolution of the boundary between self and other was possible in rare instances only when by good fortune two persons of the same emotions and character met. When this rarity was ignored, the suspicion of flattery quickly arose. The person who through the course of a lifetime made many friends was assumed artificially to transfigure himself to fit the situation.

In 1:15-22 we have discovered the theological problem to be worked out in the remainder of chapters 1-7: if Christ does have many friends, then he is either a

[18]Cicero, *De Amicitia* 93.

[19]Plutarch, *How to Tell a Flatterer from a Friend* 65B; 71F.

[20]For πίστις as the mark of the true friend, see Aristotle, *Eudemian Ethics* 7.2.39; Xenophon, *Memorabilia* 2.6.20; Dio Chrysostom, *Oration* 3.86; Julian, *Oration* 8.243A-B; Seneca, *Epistle* 3.3.

[21]Aristotle, *Eudemian Ethics* 7.1.7.

[22]Aristotle, *Nichomachean Ethics* 8.8.5; *Eudemian Ethics* 7.2.21, 49; 7.5.2; Dio Chrysostom, *Oration* 3.86-89; Plutarch, *How to Tell a Flatterer from a Friend* 49D; 51C; 53A; *On Having Many Friends* 93E; 93D; 97B; *Gnomologium Vaticanum* 471; Lucian, *Toxaris* 6-7, 9, 20, 35, 63; Cicero, *De Amicitia* 32; 62, 64-65.

[23]Cicero, *De Amicitia* 97; Seneca, *Epistle* 3.2.

flatterer or there is a new creation through the power of God that overcomes the exclusivity inherent in friendship. In order to push beyond the capacity of friendship to unite two persons only, in this passage Paul turns to God as the one who establishes and confirms friendship and the Spirit of God as the common possession placed in hearts that makes friendship between so many diverse persons possible. God's creation of many friends with Christ is Paul's solution to our modern problem of relating the historical Jesus to the Christ of faith and simultaneously the answer he gives to his critics who charge that his ministry smells of falsely assumed identity between persons. The one solution to these two related problems is so new and involves such radical rethinking about the identity and action of God that the link between friendship and new creation will occupy Paul from this point to the end of chapter seven.

IV. The Face of Christ (2:5-4:6)

The number of times Paul refers to the human face in 2 Corinthians 1-7 is remarkable.[24] Among these many faces passing by the reader is the face of Christ. Here we discover the earthly Jesus in Paul's argumentation. In 2:10 Paul tells the congregation that he forgives anyone whom it has forgiven "on account of you on the face of Christ (δι' ὑμᾶς ἐν προσώπῳ Χριστοῦ)." At the end of this section of argumentation (4:6), Christ's face reappears as the reason that Paul preaches himself as the community's slave. What does the idea of the face of Christ, which is so earthly in its connotation, have to do with the theme of friendship?

In order to answer this question, we must first understand the connection made in the ancient world between face and personality. According to ancient physiognomists, there was no better part of the human body for detecting character traits and temperament than the face.[25] Visible on the face are character and emotions, the constitutive factors of personality.[26] There is evidence in the immediate Pauline argument that supports this understanding of face as the public presentation of the self. Moses hides his face so that the sons of Israel cannot see the result of the old covenant, shame.[27] Also significant is the ease with which Paul moves between face and heart in 3:15.

The connection of the face with the theme of friendship can now be stated. It will be recalled that friendship was defined as an identity of two persons in terms of character and emotions. The face is the place where emotion and character become visible, and therefore it may be said that the face stands for the person. If this is the case, then the phrase "you on the face of Christ" is a vivid way of

[24]2 Cor 1:11; 2:10; 3:7, 13, 18; 4:6; 5:12.

[25]Ps.-Aristotle, *Physiognomics* 814B.

[26]Epictetus (*Discourse* 1.2) devotes an entire chapter to the question of preserving one's proper character (πρόσωπον), although he is less interested in the face as revelation of personality and more concerned with the face as designation of social role. See also *Discourse* 2.10.7-8; Plutarch, *Romulus* 7.5; *Cato the Elder* 7.3; *Cimon* 2.2.6; *Phocion* 5.1.1; *How the Young Man should Study Poetry* 18B-F; 28F; *On Compliancy* 528E.

[27]For this understanding of the veil, see D. Fredrickson, "ΠΑΡΡΗΣΙΑ in the Pauline Epistles," in *Friendship, Flattery, and Frankness of Speech*, 177-178.

speaking about the friendship which exists between the Corinthian congregation and Christ. Where we would expect to see Christ's emotions and character we also see the church. Yet this should not be surprising, since it will be remembered that 1:3-7 has directed us to the sharing of emotions among the church, Paul, and Christ. There is thus implied an identity of the church and Christ. Jesus has many friends; and the many have Jesus as friend.

Yet how is it possible for Christ to have so many friends? How it possible for the exclusivity that necessarily attends true friendship to give way to a multitude of friends without compromising friendship's essential nature? In other words, how can Paul fend off the suspicion of flattery, a theme very much present in this section of the letter? These questions lead us to examine the way Paul pictures the work of God in the argument of 2:5-4:6. Somehow God makes creation anew so that the exclusivity based upon the identity of emotions and character is no longer an obstacle to universal friendship. Two passages in particular stand out in Paul's attempt to argue for Christ's multitude of friends: 3:18 and 4:5-6. The first speaks of transformation, while the second refers to new creation. We will look at each in some detail.

In 3:18 three faces become one through the work of the Spirit: "And we all with an uncovered face are being transformed into the same image as we are gazing at the glory of the Lord as if in a mirror...." The face of the self, the face of the other, and the face of Christ are all present in this verse. There are three distinct faces, and yet through the subtle mediation of the mirror they become one face and thus share the same emotion and character. Paul's metaphorical use of the mirror is no doubt influenced by the widespread fascination people in the ancient world had with mirrors. Specifically, the mirror played an important role in the theory of example in Greco-Roman moral exhortation. The person progressing in virtue was to hold up and look at a worthy person from the past as if looking in a mirror; the image seen was simultaneously the goal to be striven toward and the face of the one looking. Such gazing, it was said, worked transformation.[28] Obviously, Paul replaces individual moral striving with the work of the Spirit. Nevertheless, the connection between gazing into a mirror and transformation into the mirror's image is particularly helpful for Paul's attempt to show how the Spirit's work in the church is the creation of identity with Christ and simultaneously with one another. The Spirit's work is the creation of a multitude of Christ's friends.

In 4:5 Paul utters proudly as proclamation his critics' charge that he adopts a servile relationship to the church in Corinth through his flattery: "We do not preach ourselves but Jesus Christ as Lord, ourselves as your slaves on account of Jesus." What Paul calls friendship his critics think is slavery, a readiness to change himself in light of the needs and circumstances of the church. Paul provocatively owns the accusation, but to distinguish his voluntary slavery to the church from flattery and mark it instead as friendship, Paul turns in 4:6 to God and God's new creation: "Because it is God who said 'light shall shine from darkness' who shone

---

[28]See W. McCarty, "The Shape of the Mirror: Metaphorical Catoptrics," *Arethusa* 22 (1989) 161-190.

in our hearts for the illumination of the knowledge of the glory of God on the face of Jesus Christ." The friendship that Paul has with the church, and thus their identity of character and emotion experienced in the heart, is the new creation, every bit as reflective of God's glory as the separation of light from darkness in the old creation.

The chief characteristic of the new creation, however, is no longer separation and the exclusivity of friendship that it entails. Rather, the new creation is a matter of communion, the capacity for one person, even a multitude of persons, to appear on the face of another. Φιλία extends even to God and creation. God's separateness from creation is put to an end. God's glory appears on Jesus' face and this means that they too are friends having all things in common. So also does the church appear on Christ's face, as we learned from 1:10. The mutual presence of the friends, God, Jesus, and the church, is the new creation.[29] Paul is no flatterer, but he and the church with God on Jesus' face are a new creation.

V. THE MANY-FRIENDED SELF (4:7-6:2)

We have been exploring the relation between Paul's references to the earthly Jesus and the motif of friendship. We have seen that for Paul the particularity of Jesus, his location in time and space, is opened to the church and the church opened to him through friendship, which was theorized to have the ability to unite two persons of identical character and emotion. Yet the Greco-Roman notion of friendship, with its emphasis on the exclusivity of friendships, could not bear the weight of making Jesus and the entire church mutually available to one another. Paul asserts, therefore, that God has created anew, and now φιλία is the substance of all things and of God in God's relation with the world. In this new creation the particularity of Jesus is no obstacle to his universal presence.

In this final portion, I will demonstrate how Paul orchestrates in chapters 4-6 the three themes: the earthly Jesus, friendship, and new creation. The argument builds to a crescendo in 5:21, which is the most powerful statement imaginable of the φιλία of God and humanity created by God in Jesus: "The one who had not known sin God made to be sin in order that we become the righteousness of God in him." Along the way to the high point of the letter, we will see that Paul is engaged in a major reconstruction of the understanding of the self, both the human self and the divine self, in light of the new creation. This reconstruction is necessary in order for 5:21 to be true. Expunged in the new creation is the solitary self whose limits of time, space, particular character, and emotion are the ontological basis for the exclusivity of friendship. In its place is the many-friended self.

In order to see the many-friended self emerging in Paul's argument, I first call attention to the references to the earthly Jesus in 4:10-12:

> always carrying in the body the *death of Jesus,* so that the *life of Jesus* may also be
> manifested in our bodies. For while we live we are always being given up to

---

[29]For πρόσωπον as a motif of presence, see K. Thraede, *Grundzüge griechischer-römischer Brieftopik,* Zetemata 48 (Munich: C. H. Beck, 1970). See also Seneca, *Epistle* 35.3; 40.1; 55.8-11.

death for Jesus' sake, so that the *life of Jesus* may be manifested in our mortal flesh. So death is at work in us, but life in you [emphasis added].

It is significant that Paul uses just the name Jesus without any attending titles in 4:7-15 except for the Lord Jesus in 4:14. This latter reference is to the resurrected one, so that the unadorned name "Jesus" in these verses does bring out his earthly quality. This is reinforced by the following two phrases, both of which present Jesus as an historical person: the "dying process (νέκρωσις) of Jesus" and the "life (ζωή) of Jesus." The theme of friendship winds its way through 4:10-12 in the form of two clichés: "friends have all things in common" and "a friend will die for a friend." Notice, in that regard, the "communication of properties" between the self described in verses 10-12 and Jesus, and the self's willing to die for the one who died for it. Furthermore, Paul brings the church into the φιλία relationship between himself and Jesus in verse 12 with the notion of friends sharing all things: "So death is at work in us, but life in you." Finally, the theme of new creation enters the argument in verse 14: "knowing that he who raised the Lord Jesus will raise us also with Jesus and bring us with you into his presence." The ultimate cause of separation—death—is overcome, and God brings together Jesus, Paul, and the church.[30] Through the power of the resurrection, Paul with Jesus and the church become many-friended selves.

Paul returns to the theme of the many-friended self in 5:14-15 when he states twice that "one on behalf of all died." Not only is this an obvious reference to the earthly Jesus, but here also we have an explicit reference to the motif of a friend dying for a friend. Yet Paul has Christ violate the canons of friendship by having him die for all. From the perspective of the Greco-Roman understanding of friendship, this universality of Jesus' affections is an unthinkable perversion of friendship, since it assumes that Christ shares in the character and emotions of all and that all are made to share in the same character and emotions of Jesus. Christ would appear to be guilty of what the philosophic theorists of φιλία condemned as πολυφιλία (having many friends), a vice so harmful that Plutarch dedicated an essay to define, expose, and condemn it.[31] Only the polytrope, the person who could transform his character like a chameleon changes its coloring, was capable of having many friends.[32] So we are left with the typical Pauline adoption and adaptation of his intellectual and social world. Christ's death for all must be understood within the framework of friendship in the sense that Jesus here is for his friends, and yet at the same time he destroys the exclusivity which was emphasized to flow from friendship's very nature. Pressing further, we see that the concept of the "self" as a bounded and centered accumulation of unique character traits and emotions is exploded in Jesus' death for all. If he did die for all, then he is no longer a solitary self. He is the many-friended self, a new creation.

[30]Cf. 2 Cor 7:3, where the common notion that friends live out their lives together is mentioned.

[31]Plutarch (*On Having Many Friends* 93B-97B) follows the outlines of Aristotle's argument (*Nichomachean Ethics* 9.10.1-6).

[32]Aristotle, *Nichomachean Ethics* 8.3.8; 8.5.3; 9.9.10; 9.10.3; 9.12.1-6; Plutarch, *How to Tell a Flatterer from a Friend* 65A; Lucian, *Toxaris* 37; Cicero, *Amicitia* 20, 44-45.

Neither are those for whom he died any longer solitary selves. Paul reasons in verse 14 that, since it is the case that one died for all, "therefore all have died." He goes on: "and on behalf of all he died, in order that those who are living might no longer live to themselves but to the one who died for them and was raised." The language of "living to" is borrowed directly from the ancient discourse of friendship and describes the mutuality and exclusive dedication of friends to one another.[33]

Paul weaves in the new creation theme at the beginning of verse 14 by alluding to another dimension of friendship, although, by rendering the term used there "compel," "constrain," or "urge," modern translations make the allusion impossible for readers in English to detect. Paul says, "The love of Christ *holds us together*" (emphasis added). The operative term here is συνέχω, which occurs in discussions of friendship when the union of friends results in a new being greater than the total of its individual parts.[34] Thus, what we have in 5:14-15 is the narration of Christ's act of friendship, his death for all, which is not isolated but actually a sample of the new creation so that all those who live now because of Christ's death live to him in complete mutuality.

The concept of the many-friended self has provided us with a running start at the proper interpretation of one of the most debated passages in the New Testament, 2 Cor 5:16: "So that we from now on know no one according to the flesh; even if we had known Christ according to the flesh, nevertheless now no longer do we know him." I am suggesting that we read "according to the flesh" as Paul's way of speaking of the solitary self, bound by time and space, and distinct in character and emotions. It is the self presupposed in all the quests for the historical Jesus. Paul has no interest in *this* self, even if this self is the historical Jesus. His interest is the Jesus whose self is so permeable that it is possible for others to exist in him, as we read in verse 17: "so that if any one is in Christ...." This new self exists because of God's new creation, of which it is a part: the old world that would make φιλία possible between two or perhaps a few has been replaced by the new in which φιλία is its deepest principle.

Just how deep φιλία runs in the new creation is revealed in 5:18-19. These verses broaden the scope of new creation to include not only anthropological but theological dimensions as well. God, it is said in 5:18, reconciled us to God's self. Reconciliation does not simply mean the cessation of animosity; the term is used regularly to refer to the establishment of the friendly relations and the sharing of possessions that this relationship implies.[35] This means that in Christ God with us has become the many-friended self. All the clichés of friendship identified at the

---

[33]Cicero, *De Finibus* 2.79; *De Amicitia* 29-31; Seneca, *Epistle* 48.2-5; 55.5.

[34]Aristotle, *Nichomachean Ethics* 8.1.4; *Gnomologium Vaticanum* 82. See especially Plutarch, *On Having Many Friends* 95A: "For friendship draws persons together and unites them and keeps them united (συνέχει) in a close fellowship by means of continual association and mutual acts of kindness—'Just as the fig-juice fastens the white milk firmly and binds it,' as Empedocles puts it (for such is the unity and consolidation that true friendship desires to effect)."

[35]Aristotle, *Nichomachean Ethics* 8.6.7; and Dio Chrysostom, *Oration* 38.11, 41, 47-48.

beginning of this paper can in Christ be applied to our relationship with God: friends have all things in common; a friend is another self; friends are one soul in two bodies; a friend will die for a friend; friends may be absent in body but never in spirit. And what is true for us is true also for the entire cosmos according to 5:19: "God was in Christ reconciling the world to God's self."

VI. CONCLUSION

We have traveled in this paper what might appear to be a huge distance, from the emotions of the earthly Jesus to the friendship of God with creation in Christ. At times it may have been difficult to understand what all of this has to do with the core questions arising from the quest for the historical Jesus. I hope that this paper has made it clear that, from a Pauline point of view, the notion of questing after the solitary self of the historical Jesus, the attempt to get to know him across the great divide of history, is in the end not very interesting. This is so because the quest presumes the opposite of what Paul proclaims. From the quest's perspective, Jesus' identity is separable from the question of who he is for us. Paul makes the opposite move. Christ's identity is nothing other than who he is for us, because he is our friend with whom we have all things in common.

I wish to close with a paragraph from Luther's essay, *The Freedom of a Christian*. Note how Luther, in a very Pauline fashion, has no interest in Christ according to the flesh, although he recognizes a fascination with the subject among his contemporaries. Although Luther does not mention friendship explicitly, he nevertheless follows in the Pauline direction by stressing that the identity of Christ and what he shares with us are issues that cannot be separated. Christ's identity resides in what he shares with us, his very own self:

> I believe that it has now become clear that it is not enough or in any sense Christian to preach the works, life, and words of Christ as historical facts, as if the knowledge of these would suffice for the conduct of life; yet this is the fashion among those who must today be regarded as our best preachers....Now there are not a few who preach Christ and read about him that they may move men's affections to sympathy with Christ, to anger against the Jews, and such childish and effeminate nonsense. Rather ought Christ to be preached to the end that faith in him be established that he may not only be Christ, but be Christ for you and me, and that what is said of him and is denoted in his name may be effectual in us. This is done when that Christian liberty which he bestows is rightly taught and we are told in what way we Christians are all kings and priests and therefore lords of all and may firmly believe that whatever we have done is pleasing and acceptable in the sight of God.[36] ⊕

---

[36]Martin Luther, *The Freedom of a Christian* (1520), LW 31:357.

Word & World
Supplement Series 3
1997

Jesus' Resurrection as Presupposition for the New Testament

CRAIG R. KOESTER

Luther Seminary
St. Paul, Minnesota

"**W**HY DO YOU SEEK THE LIVING AMONG THE DEAD?" THIS WAS THE QUESTION that the angels asked on the first Easter morning. Several women had come to the tomb looking for the corpse of Jesus, but their quest was interrupted by the announcement that "he is not here, but has risen" (Luke 24:5). The Easter question is a good one to ask of our quests for the historical Jesus, since an underlying assumption of many who seek to reconstruct Jesus through a critical analysis of the sources is that we are studying the story of a dead man. Yet when we turn to the New Testament in order to find out who Jesus *was*, we encounter voices who persistently tell us who Jesus *is*, in the present tense. When summarizing the story of Jesus, Peter declares that Jesus "*is* Lord of all" (Acts 10:36), and the Fourth Evangelist concludes his gospel by telling readers that he wrote in order that they might believe that "Jesus *is* the Christ, the Son of God" (John 20:31; emphasis added).

Early Christians did not consider the resurrection to be merely one incident among others in the story of Jesus but the reality that undergirded their telling of the whole story. A gospel writer might choose to omit the stilling of the storm, a parable about the kingdom, or the feeding of the five thousand from his account without significantly altering the picture of Jesus; but omitting the resurrection would decisively change the character of the entire narrative, since the evangelists take the crucifixion and resurrection to be the culmination of the story and the key to knowing who Jesus is. Moreover, apart from the four gospels, the remaining twenty-three books of the New Testament recount very little about Jesus' ministry;

but they regularly do speak about Jesus' identity and the character of Christian faith and life out of the conviction that the Jesus who was crucified has been raised from the dead.

I. RESURRECTION AND GOSPEL TRADITION

Belief that God had raised Jesus from the dead has long been recognized as one of the presuppositions undergirding the gospel narratives, even by the sharpest biblical critics. First, belief in Jesus' resurrection made the accounts of his life worth preserving. This was noted over a century ago by David Friedrich Strauss, who has gained notoriety for his thorough deconstruction of biblical narratives. Strauss himself was convinced that Jesus' resurrection was an absolutely groundless idea that could only be described as "a humbug of world history." Yet Strauss recognized that all the teachings of Jesus, however true and good they may have been, "would have been tossed and scattered like individual leaves by the wind were these leaves not held together" and preserved by what Strauss called "the deluded belief" in Jesus' resurrection, which served as a "tough and firm bond."[1]

Second, belief that Jesus was alive and active shaped the present form of these accounts. Thirty years ago Norman Perrin wrote that early Christians "made no attempt to distinguish between the words the earthly Jesus had spoken and those spoken by the risen Lord through a prophet in the community, nor between the original teaching of Jesus and the new understanding and reformulation of that teaching reached in...the Church under the guidance of the Lord of the Church." Rather, the early church "absolutely and completely identified the risen Lord of her experience with the earthly Jesus of Nazareth."[2] Perrin did not offer these remarks as a preface to a devotional tract but as an introduction to his own scholarly attempt to get behind the gospel presentations of Jesus by stripping away the early church's accretions to Jesus' words in order to recover earlier forms of Jesus' teachings.

The comments of these scholars invite us to ask why belief in Jesus' resurrection would move Christians both to preserve and to recast accounts of Jesus' life and teachings. The first point noted above was that resurrection made traditions about Jesus' life worth preserving. Early Christians understood that Jesus had lived as an embodied human being who had traveled and taught, suffered and died. Yet God raised Jesus to life again, and by raising him in bodily form, God showed the value of what Jesus had said and done in the body. The New Testament accounts of the resurrection appearances do not suggest that people experienced a generic sense of spiritual power on and after Easter, but that they encountered as a living being the Jesus who had been crucified. Paul insists that resurrection means bodily resurrection (1 Cor 15:44, 49), and the gospels speak of the bodily character of the risen Jesus who met the disciples (Matt 28:9, 17; Luke 24:36-43; John 20:20, 27). God did not abandon the body of Jesus but raised it to

---

[1]David Friedrich Strauss, *Der alte und der neue Glaube. Ein Bekenntnis* (Leipzig: S. Hirzel, 1872) 72-73; noted by Gerd Luedemann, *The Resurrection of Jesus* (Minneapolis: Fortress, 1994) 9.

[2]Norman Perrin, *Rediscovering the Teaching of Jesus* (London: SCM, 1967) 15.

new life, and Christians did not abandon the traditions about what Jesus had done in the body but allowed the stories of the embodied Jesus to have a life within their communities.

The second point was that resurrection faith led to the recasting of traditions about Jesus. According to the New Testament, God did not simply reanimate Jesus' body but transformed it. Resurrection of Jesus' body involved transformation of Jesus' body.[3] Paul contrasted the body that was perishable with one that is imperishable (1 Cor 15:42-44; 2 Cor 5:1-5), and the gospel accounts of encounters with the risen Jesus tell of someone who is no longer confined by ordinary structures of time and space, but who suddenly appears in closed rooms or along roadways and then disappears (Matt 28:9; Luke 24:31, 51; John 20:19, 26; cf. Acts 9:3). Just as Jesus himself was transformed through his resurrection, the traditions about Jesus were transformed in light of his resurrection. Early Christians were not content to resuscitate the stories about the preacher from Nazareth but recast these stories in a manner that could more effectively bear witness to the reality of the one who was now risen.[4]

Those who wrote the four gospels understood that the story of Jesus' life and ministry had to be understood in light of its ending. In itself, the story of Jesus' life and death was filled with a profound ambiguity. We might compare it to a mystery story in which the chief character utters cryptic sayings that elicit conflicting responses from bystanders; next, an unexplained healing creates a local sensation; there are encounters with demonic powers, prophecies of doom, and a sudden outburst among the crowds in a sanctuary that confuses some and alienates others. Ordinary readers find it impossible to construct a coherent picture from the available pieces of information until the end, when a detective like Sherlock Holmes, speaking from his omniscient perspective, discloses the meaning of the mystery and enables others to see the identity of the central character and the plan behind the action.

The four gospels make clear that the significance of incidents in Jesus' life was far from transparent. Modern scholars often preoccupy themselves with questions as to whether Jesus actually uttered a particular saying or performed a certain action; but the gospels show how often people who agreed *that* Jesus said or did something still disagreed about what it *meant*. For example, Jesus' followers and his adversaries agreed that he performed exorcisms, but they differed sharply on the significance of these actions. Jesus' foes argued that his exorcisms showed that he was in league with the devil, while his friends understood that he was in league with God (Mark 3:22-27; cf. John 10:20-21). Jesus was also known for other types of healings, but his opponents thought that he violated the will of God by healing on

---

[3]On resurrection, Pheme Perkins, *Resurrection: New Testament Witness and Contemporary Reflection* (Garden City: Doubleday, 1985); Reginald Fuller, *The Formation of the Resurrection Narratives* (New York: Macmillan, 1971) 57; Raymond E. Brown, *An Introduction to New Testament Christology* (New York: Paulist, 1994) 162-170.

[4]A valuable study of the interplay between preservation and change of traditions about Jesus is J. Louis Martyn, "Attitudes Ancient and Modern Toward Tradition about Jesus," *USQR* 23 (1968) 129-145.

the sabbath, while his followers believed that he carried out the will of God by healing, even on the sabbath (Mark 3:1-6; John 5:16-21).

The Gospel of John offers valuable insights into the way that the resurrection shaped the perspective from which the ambiguity of Jesus' life was understood. John relates that Jesus once came to the temple, drove out the merchants, and turned over the tables of the money changers who did business there. When bystanders challenged him, he replied, "Destroy this temple and in three days I will raise it up" (John 2:19).[5] This saying only confused matters, however, since the crowd could not comprehend how a temple that had been under construction for forty-six years could be rebuilt in three days by one man. Significantly, the by-standers were not the only ones baffled by Jesus; even his own followers failed to understand the incident at the time that it occurred and were able to discern its meaning only after his death and resurrection. The evangelist comments that Jesus "was speaking about the temple of his body. After he was raised from the dead, his disciples remembered that he had said this; and they believed the scripture and the word that Jesus had spoken" (John 2:22). Something similar occurred when Jesus rode into Jerusalem on a donkey to the acclaim of the crowds. All four gospels record the incident in different forms, suggesting that it rests on early Christian tradition; yet the meaning of the action was far from clear. In his account of the episode, John quotes the words of Zech 9:9 about the king coming to Zion upon a donkey's colt; but he acknowledges that Jesus' "disciples did not understand this at first; but when Jesus was glorified, then they remembered that these things had been written of him and had been done to him" (John 12:16).

The Fourth Evangelist related this kind of post-resurrection preserving and interpreting of traditions about Jesus to the work of the Holy Spirit. In the farewell discourses, Jesus prepared his disciples for life after his return to the Father by saying, "I have said these things to you while I am still with you. But the Advocate, the Holy Spirit, whom the Father will send in my name, will teach you everything and remind you of all that I have said to you" (John 14:25-26). "Teaching" and "reminding" are two aspects of the process reflected in the gospel narrative itself. The Spirit's work is bound to the life and teachings of Jesus in that the Spirit *reminds* Jesus' followers of his teachings in the period after his resurrection. Yet the Spirit not only brings to mind the things that Jesus said and did in the past, but *teaches* or discloses to subsequent generations a depth of meaning that may not have been apparent before Jesus' death and resurrection. Such a post-resurrection perspective means that even in passages that recall incidents from Jesus' life, it is the risen Christ who seems to do the teaching. For example, John's Gospel says that Jesus met with Nicodemus near the beginning of his ministry. Yet when Jesus tells Nicodemus that "no one has ascended into heaven except the one who descended from heaven, the Son of Man" (John 3:13), he uses the perfect tense, implying that

---

[5]In a recent study Gregory J. Riley accents the importance of the bodily resurrection of Jesus in Johannine theology, although his contention that the Fourth Evangelist was arguing against a spiritual-ized view like that of the *Gospel of Thomas* seems unlikely. See his *Resurrection Reconsidered: Thomas and John in Controversy* (Minneapolis: Fortress, 1995).

he already "has ascended," even though his return to the Father would not occur until the end of his ministry some two years later.

The way that John presents the story of Jesus through the lens of the resurrection has often meant that John's Gospel is discounted in studies of the historical Jesus, a practice that I consider to be a problem. On the one hand John does not dismiss the importance of Jesus' life, ministry, and death; indeed, he preserves as well as develops traditions about the pre-Easter Jesus like the cleansing of the temple, the entry into Jerusalem, and the crucifixion.[6] On the other hand, the synoptic writers as well as John tell the story of Jesus from a post-resurrection perspective. One of the contributions made by form-critical and redaction-critical studies of the gospels has been to show the extent to which early Christians shaped traditions about Jesus as they passed on the tradition within their communities of faith. The comments by Norman Perrin, which I quoted earlier, were occasioned primarily by his study of the synoptic gospels.

The Gospel of Mark, which is probably the earliest of the synoptics, concludes by bringing readers to the empty tomb and announcing that Jesus, who was crucified, has been raised (Mark 16:6). Although Mark does not describe any appearances of the risen Jesus, a post-resurrection perspective is evident throughout the gospel. Various outlines for Mark's Gospel have been proposed, but most interpreters recognize that a pivotal moment occurs when Jesus announces his coming death and resurrection (Mark 8:31; 9:30-32; 10:33-34), and when he appears in glory at his transfiguration (Mark 9:2-8). Scholars have sometimes wondered whether the transfiguration is actually a misplaced resurrection account—which seems unlikely—but whatever the history of the tradition behind the text, Eugene Boring has observed that the transfiguration is "a post-Easter reality which is expressed in a pre-Easter time frame. And this is not only typical, but paradigmatic, for Mark's christology as a whole."[7] In Mark's Gospel, the post-Easter Christ speaks and acts within the story of the pre-Easter career of Jesus. The best-known literary feature of Mark is the secrecy motif, in which a display of divine power or a disclosure of Jesus' messianic identity is quickly followed by a command not to make this known. The presupposition for this motif is that Jesus' identity cannot be rightly understood prior to his death and resurrection; therefore his identity must not be proclaimed openly during his public ministry. Mark does not work with a simple temporal sequence in which he first tells of the earthly Jesus and later of the risen Christ. Rather, the earthly Jesus and the risen Christ are present at the same time, with the resurrection providing the perspective from which the whole story is understood.

The Gospel of Matthew appropriates and builds upon the post-resurrection

---

[6]On the portrayal of Jesus in John, see my *Symbolism in the Fourth Gospel* (Minneapolis: Fortress, 1995) 32-45. See also Marianne Meye Thompson, "The Historical Jesus and the Johannine Christ," in *Exploring the Gospel of John: In Honor of D. Moody Smith*, ed. R. Alan Culpepper and C. Clifton Black (Louisville: Westminster John Knox, 1996) 21-42.

[7]M. Eugene Boring, "The Christology of Mark: Hermeneutical Issues for Systematic Theology," *Semeia* 30 (1984) 125-153. The quotation is from pp. 141-142.

perspective of Mark. The gospel concludes when Jesus stands upon a mountain in Galilee before a group of disciples who worship him. He says, "All authority in heaven and on earth has been given to me. Go therefore and make disciples of all nations, baptizing them in the name of the Father and of the Son and of the Holy Spirit, and teaching them to obey everything that I have commanded you. And remember, I am with you always, to the end of the age" (Matt 28:18-20). This message of the risen Christ offers a valuable perspective on the shape of the gospel as a whole. In Matthew's account of Jesus' birth, the magi come looking for Jesus even though they are not Israelites but members of other nations, like those to which the disciples will later be sent to preach; and the magi "worship" the infant Jesus just as the disciples will later "worship" the risen Jesus (2:11; 28:17). Matthew's account of Jesus' feeding of the five thousand and walking on the water resembles the account found in Mark, but where Mark says that the disciples failed to comprehend what these events meant (Mark 6:51-52), Matthew says that they worshiped Jesus as Son of God (Matt 14:33); the latter would be the proper response from a post-resurrection perspective. Matthew's account of the crucifixion also mirrors that of Mark in its references to mockery, darkness, and Jesus' own cry of abandonment; but Matthew brings Easter into the middle of this account by saying that when Jesus died the tombs were opened and many saints were raised, who, after Jesus' resurrection "appeared to many" (Matt 27:52-53).[8]

Luke's Gospel offers additional insights into the post-resurrection perspectives of the evangelists. Perhaps the most succinct presentation of the centrality of the resurrection in the evangelist's perspective is in the story of Jesus' appearance on the road to Emmaus. Two disciples were walking away from Jerusalem after the crucifixion when the risen Jesus appeared to them, although they did not recognize him. When asked why they were so sad, Cleopas gave a brief account of the story of Jesus of Nazareth, "who was a prophet mighty in deed and word before God and all the people, and how our chief priests and leaders handed him over to be condemned to death and crucified him" (Luke 24:19-20). Without the resurrection, that information only produced disappointment and confusion in Cleopas, since he had hoped that Jesus would redeem Israel. Therefore, the risen Jesus supplied the perspective needed to comprehend the story of his life and work by showing them from the scriptures that it was necessary for the Christ to suffer and then enter into his glory (24:26-27).

II. RESURRECTION AND OTHER NEW TESTAMENT WRITINGS

The pivotal role of the resurrection is also evident in the other New Testament writings, sometimes in surprising ways. Many of the modern quests for Jesus seek to establish his identity on the basis of his teachings. From this perspective the natural first step in answering the question, "Who is Jesus?" would be to cite Jesus' own words about himself. For example, it is common to call Jesus "the Christ" or

---

[8]On the post-resurrection perspective of Matthew, see Robert H. Smith, *Matthew*, ACNT (Minneapolis: Augsburg, 1989) 15-16.

"Messiah," a term that means "anointed one" and identifies him as the fulfillment of the promise God made to David (2 Sam 7:12; Ps 2:2, 6-7). Before applying this title to Jesus, those who base their understanding of his identity on his teachings would presumably like to have a statement from Jesus saying, "Yes, I am the Messiah." The problem is that if Jesus said that he was the Messiah, his words would not settle anything, since we would still need some evidence that his words were true. A saying in the gospels warns that if anyone simply says, "'Here is the Messiah!' or 'Look! There he is!'—do not believe it. False messiahs and false prophets will appear and produce signs and omens to lead astray, if possible, the elect" (Mark 13:21-22). A rough analogy might be the question of how we determine whether someone can be considered a hero. The person might claim to be a hero, but that would not settle the issue, since someone who claims to be a hero might be deluding himself and others, while a true hero might not make any public claims to heroism. The question would have to be decided on other grounds.

In the case of Jesus, early Christians commonly called him the Christ or Messiah, but they did not do so by appealing to Jesus' own words; in fact they probably could not do so on the basis of Jesus' words since there is little evidence that he openly declared himself to be the Messiah. In Luke's Gospel, for example, we find that Jesus is identified as the Messiah by the angels at his birth (Luke 2:11) and by Peter during his ministry (9:20), but when John the Baptist sent messengers to ask, "Are you the one who is to come, or are we to wait for another?" Jesus responded indirectly by summarizing the miracles that he had performed (7:18-23). Yet this might actually confuse the issue since there is little evidence from earlier Jewish traditions that the Messiah was expected to be a worker of miracles.[9] Later, when his adversaries asked if he was the Messiah, Jesus replied, "If I tell you, you will not believe" (22:67). Several verses later, Jesus' opponents declare that he has been forbidding people to pay taxes to Caesar (23:2b), which readers know is not true (20:25), then they add that Jesus has been calling himself the Messiah, a king (23:2c); this also seems misleading, since Luke has not given evidence that Jesus explicitly used the title for himself during his public ministry. Jesus uses the title more directly only after the resurrection, when he explains that it was necessary for the Messiah to suffer before entering into his glory (24:26, 46).

Given these traditions about Jesus, it is not surprising that early Christians did not appeal to Jesus' teachings but to his resurrection when identifying him as the Messiah. The book of Acts, the second volume written by the author of Luke's Gospel, contains a number of speeches ascribed to the early followers of Jesus. These speeches are almost certainly not transcriptions of what was said, but were probably set down in their present form by the author of Luke-Acts.[10] Significantly,

[9]See J. Louis Martyn, *History and Theology in the Fourth Gospel*, 2nd ed. (Nashville: Abingdon, 1979) 95-99.

[10]The classic work is Martin Dibelius, "The Speeches of Acts and Ancient Historiography," in *Studies in the Acts of the Apostles*, ed. Heinrich Green (London: SCM, 1956) 138-185. On the theology of the speeches in Acts, see James D. G. Dunn, *Unity and Diversity in the New Testament*, 2nd ed. (Philadelphia: Trinity International, 1990) 16-21.

the speeches proclaim Jesus' identity on the basis of his resurrection, not his teachings. When Peter proclaims the messiahship of Jesus on Pentecost, he does not say that Jesus claimed to be the Messiah, but that "God has made him both Lord and Messiah" by raising him from the dead in fulfillment of the scriptures (Acts 2:36; cf. 2:31-35). Paul's preaching in Acts follows a similar pattern, as Paul proclaims that God fulfills the promises that he made to David by raising Jesus from the dead (13:30-39; cf. 17:3; 26:23). Both Peter and Paul also declare that Jesus is the one who will judge the world in righteousness, and the basis for this claim is not that Jesus claimed to be the judge but that God appointed him to this position by raising him from the dead (10:40-43; 17:31).

The centrality of Jesus' death and resurrection in Paul's own letters is well-known. Paul had not been a follower of the earthly Jesus, but for a time persecuted the early church. Paul's perspective shifted when, by his own account, the risen Christ appeared to him as to "one untimely born" (1 Cor 15:8; cf. Gal 1:16). The conviction that Jesus, who was crucified, had been raised from the dead under-girded Paul's proclamation and shaped the perspective from which he viewed the earthly life of Jesus. Paul's letters provide no narrative of Jesus' life and ministry, yet it would be an overstatement to say that for Paul it was enough simply to know *that* Jesus had lived and died, and nothing more.[11] For example, Paul understood that it was important that Jesus was Jewish, for Jesus was descended from David according to the flesh (Rom 1:3) and he was "born under the law" in order to redeem those who are under the law (Gal 4:4). Paul knew and occasionally quoted some of Jesus' sayings, such as his teaching about divorce (1 Cor 7:10-11), his provision that those who proclaim the gospel should be supported in this work (1 Cor 9:14), and his words over the bread and cup at the last supper (1 Cor 11:23-25).[12] Paul also knew that Jesus died at the time of Passover (1 Cor 5:7) and that he died by crucifixion, which was offensive to both Jews and Greeks (1 Cor 1:18, 23) and meant that Jesus was accursed under a statute in the Jewish law (Gal 3:13; Deut 21:22-23).

The resurrection is the perspective from which Paul discerns the meaning of Jesus' earthly life. Jesus may have been descended from David, but of course so were many other people. What is unique about Jesus is that "he was declared to be the Son of God with power according to the Spirit of holiness by resurrection from the dead" (Rom 1:4). Many were born under the law and many were crucified, but Jesus alone has been raised from the dead. It is from this perspective that Paul discerns that Jesus did not simply die but that he "was handed over to death for

[11]Rudolf Bultmann is remembered for arguing that "Paul proclaims the incarnate, crucified, and risen Lord; that is, his kerygma requires only the 'that' of the life of Jesus and the fact of his crucifix-ion....The eschatological and ethical preaching of the historical Jesus plays no role in Paul....The decisive thing is simply the 'that'" ("The Primitive Christian Kerygma and the Historical Jesus," in *The Historical Jesus and the Kerygmatic Christ*, ed. Roy A. Harrisville and Carl E. Braaten [New York: Abingdon, 1964] 20).

[12]The "word of the Lord" in 1 Thess 4:15-17 is probably a saying of the earthly Jesus (cf. Matt 24:30-31; Mark 13:26-27), although it could be a word of the risen Jesus delivered through an early Christian prophet.

our trespasses and raised for our justification" (Rom 4:25). Without the resurrection, the foolishness of the cross remains mere foolishness; but in light of the resurrection it can be seen that it is the power of God. Therefore, Paul's understanding of the faith by which people are justified or set into a right relationship with God is a faith that trusts in the God who raised Jesus from the dead (Rom 4:24); "because if you confess with your lips that Jesus is Lord and believe in your heart that God raised him from the dead, you will be saved" (Rom 10:9).

Jesus' resurrection is also basic to Paul's view of human life and the future of the world. Since this aspect of the topic is so large, let me simply make several brief points: (1) Paul understood that Jesus lived a human life and died a human death; by raising Jesus from the dead, God provides assurance that when people of faith die they too have hope of being raised to new life. Therefore, when the Thessalonian congregation mourned the death of a loved one, Paul assured them that, just as Jesus died and rose, we can be confident that Christians who die will also rise (1 Thess 4:13-14; cf. 2 Cor 4:14). (2) Paul understood that Jesus' resurrection was a bodily resurrection, not simply a release of his spirit from its material prison. The same will be true for others. God does not confine his interest to the soul but lays claim to the entire person, the embodied person. Christians do not hope for escape from their bodies but for the redemption and transformation of their bodies—from bodies that are subject to dishonor, decay, and death into bodies that are glorious and immortal (1 Cor 15:42-43; 2 Cor 5:1-5). Hope for bodily resurrection is one of the reasons that Paul warns the Corinthians against immoral behavior (1 Cor 6:13-14). What they do with their bodies matters, because God claims their bodies and has a future for their bodies. (3) By raising Jesus from the dead, bodily, God shows his purposes for the whole creation. The creation groans in its present bondage to decay just as human beings groan in their mortal bodies; the creation awaits liberation just as those who have the first fruits of the Spirit await the redemption of their bodies. The resurrection hope is not finally hope for escape from the created order but for the redemption and the transformation of the created order (Rom 8:18-23).[13]

Like the gospels and Pauline letters, the writings that appear at the end of the New Testament are written from a perspective that presupposes Jesus' resurrection. Hebrews begins with an elevated portrayal of the risen Christ in glory, seated at God's right hand, adored by the hosts of heaven (Heb 1:1-14). From this vantage point, the author turns to the problem confronting his readers, which involved the apparent contradiction between the promises of God and the reality of life in the world. When the readers came to faith, they embraced the hope that they would inherit a share in God's glorious kingdom (1:14; 2:1-4); yet at the hands of others in their society they were abused, dispossessed, and imprisoned (10:32-34). The author has them consider their situation in light of the story of Jesus, who, before being raised to heavenly glory, had been tested as severely as the readers were

---

[13]See J. Christiaan Beker, *Paul the Apostle* (Philadelphia: Fortress, 1980) 152-81; Hermann Ridderbos, *Paul: An Outline of His Theology* (Grand Rapids: Eerdmans, 1975) 537-551.

being tested (2:8-9, 18; 4:15). During his lifetime Jesus offered anguished prayer to God for deliverance (5:7); he endured the hostility of others (12:3) and was crucified outside the city gate (12:2; 13:12).[14] God did not respond to Jesus' prayers by exempting him from suffering but by bringing him through suffering to everlasting life and glory. Therefore, the faithful who suffer can be confident that God will not abandon them but bring them to glory in his presence. Moreover, the author interprets Jesus' death and resurrection in light of Old Testament sacrificial practices to show that after shedding his blood as a sacrifice for sins, Jesus entered into the heavenly sanctuary where he makes intercession for others (7:23-25; 9:11-12, 24). Therefore, Christians can turn to the risen Jesus for help while they continue their pilgrimage of faith on earth (4:14-16).

Several other books show similar patterns. According to 1 Peter, the salient feature of Jesus' earthly life was the steadfast and innocent suffering through which he offers redemption and an example to others, who are called to follow in his steps (1 Pet 2:21-24). Since God raised Jesus from the dead (1:21), those who trust and follow him may be confident of inheriting a share in the glorious life to come (1:3, 9; 4:13; 5:10). According to 1 John, Christians can confess their sins because the Jesus who made atonement for sin by his death continues to live and act as the advocate before God on their behalf (1 John 2:1-2). Finally, the book of Revelation has as a central image the Lamb who was slain and raised to new life (Rev 5:6). The author of Revelation takes the reality of Jesus' suffering and death as a given; from the perspective of resurrection faith, he seeks to show that by faithfully withstanding the forces of evil, Jesus' death was truly a victory that brought him into the presence of God. From the vantage point of the resurrection one can declare that the Lamb who was slain has "conquered" (νικάω) by faithful obedience (5:5-6) and that the risen Christ can call upon Christians to "conquer" (νικάω) by remaining faithful in the face of sin and evil, trusting that the God who raised Jesus from the dead will raise them up by his power (2:7, 11, 17, 28; 3:5, 12, 21; 12:11).

III. RESURRECTION AND CONTEMPORARY QUESTS FOR JESUS

This survey of texts has been designed to show how faith in Jesus' resurrection functions as a presupposition for various writings in the New Testament. Early Christians preserved sayings of Jesus and stories about Jesus, but they understood and recast this material in light of the culmination of Jesus' ministry in crucifixion and resurrection. Luke Johnson has recently observed that "Christianity in its classic form has not based itself on the ministry of Jesus but on the resurrection of Jesus, the claim that after his crucifixion and burial Jesus entered into the powerful life of God, and shares that life" with others.[15] I would add that

[14]On the historical Jesus in Hebrews, see Erich Grässer, "Der historische Jesus im Hebräerbrief," in *Aufbruch und Verheissung: Gesammelte Aufsätze zum Hebräerbrief*, BZNW 65 (Berlin and New York: Walter de Gruyter, 1992) 100-128; Graham Hughes, *Hebrews and Hermeneutics* (Cambridge: Cambridge University, 1979) 75-78.

[15]Luke Timothy Johnson, *The Real Jesus* (San Francisco: HarperSanFrancisco, 1996) 134. Compare his *The Writings of the New Testament: An Interpretation* (Philadelphia: Fortress, 1986) 1-20, 87-140.

those who believe that God raised Jesus of Nazareth from the dead understand that accounts of his life and teachings have an ongoing place in the life of the church because the risen Jesus has an ongoing place in the life of the church. At the same time, the church's existence is not centered on the teachings of the pre-Easter Jesus in and of themselves, but on the proclamation of his death and resurrection.

A number of current studies seek to move the crucifixion and resurrection to the periphery of our understanding of Jesus and to make central a reconstruction of Jesus as a sage or purveyor of wisdom sayings. Robert Funk, for example, argues that the focus on Jesus' death and resurrection derives largely from Paul, who interpreted Jesus along the lines of hellenistic mystery religions with their interest in divine figures who died and rose. Therefore, once "the discrepancy between the Jesus of history and the Christ of faith emerged from the smothering cloud of the historic creeds, it was only a matter of time before scholars sought to disengage the Jesus of history from the Christ of the church's faith," a faith that Funk himself identifies with "the dark ages of theological tyranny."[16]

It is important to recognize at the outset that the historical Jesus is not so much rediscovered as he is recreated by modern scholars. The expression "the historical Jesus" is usually applied not to Jesus as presented by the New Testament but to Jesus as imaginatively reconstructed by academicians of the nineteenth and twentieth centuries. Briefly, the process involves two steps. In the first, bits of information about Jesus are extracted from the New Testament and other sources. Sayings of Jesus are detached from their present narrative contexts and are stripped of elements that appear to show signs of post-resurrection reflection in order to provide a small collection of sayings that are considered to represent the true teachings of Jesus. The sayings that are admitted into this collection of Jesus material vary depending on the criteria that are used for selection: the previous generation of scholars found Jesus' apocalyptic sayings to be integral to his message; the current generation brackets those out, so now we have a wisdom teacher rather than an apocalyptic prophet.[17]

In the second step, the material that has been removed from the gospel narratives is placed in some other interpretive framework. The importance of this step cannot be underestimated. For material that has been extracted from the gospels to be meaningful, it must be placed in some interpretive context. This point, again, is nothing new. For over a century scholars have recognized that

---

[16]Robert W. Funk, Roy W. Hoover, and the Jesus Seminar, *The Five Gospels* (New York: Macmillan, 1993) 7-8. This is nothing new. A century ago Martin Kähler perceived that it was "antipathy to the Christ of dogma which constituted the real interest of the Life-of-Jesus movement," and that "for many historians the recovery of the historical Jesus provided the dynamite to explode once for all the christological dogma of the ancient creeds" (in Carl Braaten's introduction to Kähler's *The So-Called Historical Jesus and the Historic Biblical Christ* [Philadelphia: Fortress, 1964] 19). Kähler's own work was published in German in 1896. Similarly, Albert Schweitzer noted that the "historical investigation of the life of Jesus did not take its rise from a purely historical interest; it turned to the Jesus of history as an ally in the struggle against the tyranny of dogma" (*The Quest of the Historical Jesus* [New York: Macmillan, 1968] 4; German original, 1906).

[17]For a survey, see Ben Witherington III, *The Jesus Quest: The Third Search for the Jew of Nazareth* (Downers Grove, IL: InterVarsity, 1995).

some "outside force must rework the fragments of the tradition," and that this force is the scholar's imagination, "an imagination that has been shaped and nourished by the analogy of his own life and of human life in general."[18] Today, those who remove fragments of tradition from the narrative framework provided by the gospels most often try to make sense of these fragments from a perspective shaped by the social sciences.

When a reconstruction of Jesus' pre-Easter sayings is made the basis of an interpretation of Jesus, the phenomenon of faith in his resurrection is moved from the center to the periphery, but it must still be explained, since its influence is too powerful to be ignored. Interestingly, the process of explanation often tells us more about ourselves than it does about Jesus. Lesslie Newbigen has observed that we "accept something as an explanation when it shows how an unexplained fact fits into the world as we already understand it. Explanation is related to the framework of understanding we inhabit, the firm structure of beliefs we never question, our picture of how things really are. Explanation puts a strange thing into a place where it fits and is no longer strange."[19]

Politics is one way to explain what the New Testament has to say about Jesus' resurrection. Elaine Pagels has argued that "the doctrine of bodily resurrection serves an essentially *political* function: it legitimizes the authority of certain men who claim to exercise exclusive leadership over the churches as the successors of the apostle Peter."[20] Her comments are based primarily on second-century sources, but others insist that the same thing is evident in the New Testament itself. Scenes recounting an appearance of Jesus to early Christians are said to serve mainly as ways of legitimating the authority of Peter and the other apostles. For Funk, "the resurrection is entirely self-serving for the leaders of the Jesus' movement," since it has to do primarily with "empire building and office politics."[21] Crossan argues similarly, concluding that the resurrection appearances "are not about Jesus' physical power over the world but about the apostles' spiritual power over the community."[22]

Identifying political motives behind the resurrection accounts helps to make them less strange and more plausible, since political maneuvering is a common part of day-to-day life. Yet such explanations are finally unpersuasive. Luke, for example, only briefly mentions an early appearance to Simon Peter (Luke 24:12, 34); he gives most attention to Cleopas and another unnamed figure on the Emmaus road (24:13-35), men who apparently never assumed positions of leadership.

[18]Martin Kähler, *The So-Called Historical Jesus*, 55; Schweitzer, *The Quest of the Historical Jesus*, 8. For a critique of the methods used by the Jesus Seminar to extract words of Jesus, see Richard B. Hays, "The Corrected Jesus," *First Things* 43 (May 1994) 43-48. On the problem of reconstructing Jesus on the basis of models from the social sciences, see Johnson, *The Real Jesus*, 81-133.

[19]Lesslie Newbigen, *Foolishness to the Greeks: The Gospel and Western Culture* (Grand Rapids: Eerdmans, 1986) 22.

[20]Elaine Pagels, *The Gnostic Gospels* (New York: Random House, 1979) 6.

[21]Robert Funk, *Honest to Jesus* (San Francisco: HarperSanFrancisco, 1996) 272-273.

[22]John Dominic Crossan, *Jesus: A Revolutionary Biography* (San Francisco: HarperSanFrancisco, 1994) 170.

Moreover, if Luke recounted the appearances of the risen Christ primarily to bolster the authority of Peter and his circle, Luke's continuation of the story in the book of Acts actually subverts his own purpose. Peter is the central figure in the opening chapters of Acts, but control of the church's mission quickly slips from the grasp of the twelve as Stephen and Philip—who were not commissioned to preach but to serve tables—become the focus of attention and carry the story forward (Acts 6-8). Peter occasionally reappears in Acts, but the last half of the book focuses on Paul, whose ministry stems from an encounter with the risen Christ, but who never occupied a position of governance in the church. Moreover, when Paul began his missionary career, he did not embark on his own authority or on the authority of Peter, but through the commissioning of several members of the congregation in Antioch (Acts 13:1-3).

Matthew's Gospel evinces high regard for Peter (Matt 16:18), but does not single him out as a witness to the resurrection. The first to meet the risen Jesus and to be commissioned to "go and tell" are Mary Magdalene and another Mary (28:9-10), neither of whom are known to have been authority figures in the church. When Jesus appears to the eleven, he says that "all authority in heaven and on earth has been given to *me*" (28:18); instead of commanding his followers to assume control of the community, he sends them out to make disciples of all nations. If this climactic scene was designed to establish the eleven in ecclesiastical office in the post-resurrection church, we might have expected to find some traces of this earlier in the gospel. Instead, we find that discipline is not delegated to a select group of apostles but is a matter for the whole community (18:15-17).[23]

The resurrection appearances in John's Gospel do pertain to the role of Jesus' disciples, but not in the political sense suggested by some. The first person to see the risen Jesus and the first to be commissioned to "go and tell" is not Peter but Mary Madgalene (John 20:11-18), who did not hold ecclesiastical office as far as we know. The risen Jesus later appears to the disciples as a group, giving them the Holy Spirit and commissioning them to forgive and retain sins (20:22-23). None of the disciples is singled out for special mention. Moreover, elsewhere in the gospel "the disciples" represent the whole Christian community and not merely one group of authorities within it (e.g., John 13:5, 14). The commissioning can best be understood as a charge given to the whole community.[24] The conclusion of John 21 does underscore the roles of Peter and the beloved disciple, but not with the "political" connotations suggested above. When entrusting Peter with responsibility for tending Jesus' flock, Jesus warned that Peter would become subject to others and suffer martyrdom (21:15-19). The testimony of the beloved disciple also re-

---

[23]John Meier, a leading Roman Catholic New Testament scholar, noted that the warnings against preoccupation with titles and honors (Matt 23:1-12) indicated that the evangelist was "obviously concerned about a type of nascent 'clericalism' in his church" (Raymond E. Brown and John P. Meier, *Antioch and Rome* [New York: Paulist, 1983] 70-71).

[24]Raymond E. Brown, a leading Roman Catholic biblical scholar, commented that exegetically there does not seem to be "sufficient evidence to confine the power of forgiving and holding of sin, granted in John xx 23, to a specific exercise of power in the Christian community" (*The Gospel According to John*, 2 vols. [Garden City: Doubleday, 1966-70] 2:1044).

ceives special attention (21:20-24), but the resurrection appearance does not ascribe to him a role in church governance. The Johannine epistles show that even in later times a leader in Johannine Christian circles had to exercise influence that came from "prophetic witness rather than that flowing from jurisdiction or structure."[25]

Psychology is an even more popular way to explain resurrection faith. To speak of resurrection in terms of the inner workings of the human mind helps to make it more palatable and less strange, so that it does not so profoundly challenge our accepted ways of understanding the world. John Dominic Crossan, for example, has written, "I do not think that anyone, anywhere, at any time brings dead people back to life."[26] In Crossan's view there probably was not much of a corpse to bring back to life anyway, since he argues that Jesus was not placed in a tomb but in a shallow grave where his corpse would have been eaten by dogs or other scavenging animals. For Crossan, resurrection faith was not occasioned by an encounter with a person who had come back from the grave; it was the sense that his followers could live their lives after Jesus' death much as they had before. Crossan has said that he imagines what happened was that the peasants in lower Galilee who followed Jesus before his death had adopted a caring lifestyle characterized by open table fellowship. After Jesus' death they found themselves as empowered as before to carry on in this way; thus, Easter faith is not something new but a continuation of this pre-Easter experience.[27] Arguing somewhat differently, Burton Mack points out that Jesus' death created a theological problem for his followers, since God should not have allowed him to die. Some Jewish sources promised that if God did not protect the righteous from martyrdom he would surely reward them after death, and Mack proposes that Jesus' followers found in this "martyr myth" a way to "rationalize" the death of their community's leader.[28]

Other psychological interpretations offer variations on these ideas. In a recent study of the resurrection, Gerd Luedemann concludes that the New Testament reports of encounters with the risen Jesus in bodily form are largely unhistorical, but from the perspective of depth psychology Luedemann does find it plausible that Peter and other early Christians had visionary experiences in which they experienced forgiveness, received a sense of new life in the present, and found their hearts able to look into eternity.[29] In a more popular vein, Shelby Spong composed a scenario in which he imagines that, after Easter, Simon Peter "felt himself to be embraced even with his doubts, his fears, his denials in a way that he had never before been embraced." That feeling of acceptance was "the dawn of Easter in human history."[30]

Psychological explanations help to make the strange idea that God brought

[25]Raymond E. Brown, *The Epistles of John* (Garden City: Doubleday, 1982) 651.

[26]John Dominic Crossan, *Jesus*, 95.

[27]Ibid., 161-163; Crossan, *Who Killed Jesus?* (San Francisco: HarperSanFrancisco, 1996) 209.

[28]Burton Mack, *A Myth of Innocence: Mark and Christian Origins* (Philadelphia: Fortress, 1988) 109-110.

[29]Luedemann, *The Resurrection of Jesus*, 176-177.

[30]Shelby Spong, *Resurrection: Myth or Reality?* (San Francisco: HarperSanFrancisco, 1994) 255.

Jesus of Nazareth back to life seem less strange, because they make resurrection essentially a resurrection of hope within the human heart. This fits with reality as we already understand it. There are, of course, psychological aspects to human faith; the issue is whether Jesus' resurrection can be explained in terms of psychology. For example, if faith in Jesus' resurrection emerged as a way to rationalize his death through a conventional martyr myth, why was Jesus not treated simply as yet another martyr? Why did the risen Jesus become the object of faith in a way that other martyrs did not? Or if Easter faith was essentially Peter's feeling of forgiveness and hope, how did his feeling spread to so many groups of people, and why did they identify it with the presence of the risen Christ?

Psychological explanations of the resurrection take us to the heart of contemporary debates about the nature of theological discourse itself. Where we want to limit ourselves to speaking about human experience, the New Testament speaks about God and God's action in Christ. Where we want to focus on Easter faith as a human experience, the New Testament insists that Easter faith is produced by an encounter with a divine reality that comes to us from outside ourselves. When we turn to the New Testament, we find texts that not only refuse to surrender easily to contemporary modes of explanation, they also persist in challenging our own views of reality. Where we would say, "Hope is alive," the New Testament says that "Jesus is alive"; and where we would say, "Faith is risen," the New Testament says that "Jesus is risen." Put sharply, many modern interpreters consider faith or hope to be the fundamental realities, with Jesus' resurrection as a secondary symbol for faith or hope, whereas the New Testament considers Jesus' resurrection to be the fundamental reality that evokes human faith and hope. Given what the scriptures say, how can we be sure of our own presuppositions?

The New Testament's proclamation that God raised Jesus from the dead resists conforming to our usual ways of understanding reality. Rather, as Erich Auerbach put it, the Bible "seeks to overcome our reality: we are to fit our own life into its world, feel ourselves to be elements in its universal history."[31] The New Testament presents the story of Jesus' life through the lens of his resurrection, and it insists that our own human stories must be viewed in light of the hope of our own future resurrections and the resurrection of the creation itself. God intruded into the vision of reality of Mary Magdalene and the other women who came to Jesus' tomb. They had embarked on a quest for a dead man, but were told that "he is not here, but has risen" (Luke 24:5). God intruded into Paul's vision of reality. Paul once sought to suppress the Christian faith by persecuting the human beings who proclaimed it, but he later testified that it was God who revealed the risen Jesus to him and who commissioned him to proclaim the faith to the nations (Gal 1:13-17).

Through the New Testament presentations of Jesus, God also intrudes into the way that people in the late twentieth century understand reality, by placing us

[31]Erich Auerbach, *Mimesis: The Representation of Reality in Western Literature* (Princeton: Princeton University, 1953) 15.

189

within a story that is defined not by current trends in psychological or political theory but by Jesus' resurrection and God's new creation. The biblical portrayals of Jesus as the crucified, risen, and living Christ constitute a problem for many modern readers because their presuppositions do not correspond to our presuppositions. Yet we do well to let the New Testament press its claims about reality even as the modern world presses its claims, for in doing so we come to know more deeply the one to whom the New Testament bears witness. ⊕

Word & World
Supplement Series 3
1997

The Quest for Jesus and the Church's Proclamation

JAMES L. BOYCE

Luther Seminary
St. Paul Minnesota

I. WHAT CAN WE KNOW?

"**H**OW DO WE KNOW?" "WHAT CAN WE KNOW?" "OF WHAT SIGNIFICANCE IS that knowledge for faith?" The quest for Jesus, or, as it is more often put, the quest for the "historical" Jesus carries with it implications for these underlying and more basic questions. Questions about our knowledge of Jesus remain of interest in part at least because they belong to the more basic question of our understanding of the activity of God in the world. To ask the question of Jesus is to ask the question of what God is doing. It is the question of revelation. When we ask about the "historical" Jesus, we press the question of what is authoritative for us in life, what serves as the basis for our Christian faith, on what does faith ultimately rest.

The answer to this question of what is the basis for knowledge and faith (or as the Evangelical Lutheran Church in America constitution puts it, what is authoritative for faith and life) commonly has been: the word of God. But however readily given, that answer requires further specificity: Of what does the word of God consist? How is the word of God to be interpreted?

Any audience schooled in issues of theology and the church will recognize that questions about authority for the church as a whole and for individual Christians have through the centuries balanced on the two poles of scripture and doctrine. The church has deemed certain writings to be authoritative and, at the same time, has developed traditions and teachings regarding the proper transmission and interpretation of that scriptural witness. In establishing a canon for the preservation of that which was authoritative, the church has assumed that certain traditions could be included and trusted as authoritative only because (or insofar as) they were accurate witnesses to or about Jesus, in some way extending back to the very events to which they bore witness.

It should not surprise us then, nor should we consider it only some modern invention or corruption, that the enterprise of "questers" should find its engagement in the question of Jesus and what we can know about Jesus. Implicit from the outset in ascribing to certain writings the status of "scripture" or "New Testament," has been the assumption that what is ultimately authoritative is not doctrine or interpretations, but Jesus himself in his life, death, and resurrection, in his ministry and his teachings. Jesus is the basis of the New Testament witness. This has been clear, for example, in the overwhelming consensus to focus on the Gospel of Matthew, to the exclusion of the other gospels, in the church's lectionary (at least until the adoption of the three-year lectionary in the last generation). That Matthew's witness was primary was not a judgment about historicity, but a judgment about the fullness of the first gospel's witness to the life and teachings of Jesus—above all in the sermon on the mount and the twenty-eight chapters of narrative detail.

Nevertheless, as part of the tension between scripture and tradition, while the scriptures bear witness to the life and teachings of Jesus, the doctrine of the church—the ongoing and at times controversial and heated interpretive conversation and tradition of the community of faith—not only shaped the scriptures themselves but also determined how these scriptures were to be interpreted in light of the community's experience of Jesus. We are reminded of this within the New Testament itself when, for example, Acts 17:11 calls attention to those believers who "examined the scriptures every day to see whether these things were so." The witness and experience of faith and the gathered interpretation of the community are in constant conversation with the scriptures. We see another example in 2 Peter where, after an exhortation to remember the authoritative words spoken through the apostles (3:2), the author goes on to signal the presence within the community of alternative interpreters and to underscore the importance of orthodox interpretations: "So also our beloved brother Paul wrote to you according to the wisdom given him, speaking of this as he does in all his letters. There are some things in them hard to understand, which the ignorant and unstable twist to their own destruction, as they do the other scriptures" (3:15-16). Nils Dahl, for one, has ably developed this insight in his emphasis on the community's memory in shaping and interpreting the traditions about Jesus, particularly in regard to its use of the Old Testament.[1]

It is almost a truism by now to note how this tension became only more acute in the aftermath of the reformation and the enlightenment. One effect of the reformation was to tip the balance of this tension in favor of the scriptures rather than the authority of the church, at least to the degree that the church is understood as the repository of tradition and doctrine. For the church as the community of believers, however, there was a different effect: exposing the scriptures and their

---

[1]Nils Dahl, "The Crucified God and the Endangered Promises," WW 3/3 (1983) 251-262.

interpretation—and ultimately their authority—to the "whims" of individual interpreters, to the moods of the times, and thus to a multiplicity of competing traditions of which we are at one time or another the thankful or frustrated heirs.

Our frustration has been amplified by the addition of a third partner to the polarity of tensions we have just been discussing. Modern discussions of the character of knowing and the limitations of historical knowledge have compounded the issue of what we can know about Jesus. Modern consciousness is convinced that our individual perspectives shape and determine our understanding of history. Thus, given the fact that the primary witness to Jesus is contained in writings produced not by dispassionate or neutral observers, but precisely by those who were convinced of having experienced in his life, teaching, death, and resurrection the very revelation of God, it is no wonder that questions about what we can know and how we can know it should continue to occupy the modern mind. Such interest is not limited to the historian bent on remaining objective, but also affects the person of faith who seeks to understand the relationship of the tradition to the continuing proclamation of Jesus as the gospel and revelation of God.

II. A Matter of Perspective

In relation to our questions (What can we know? What is God doing?) each of the so-called quests for Jesus has made its own particular contribution: the first quest with its rationalist despair at capturing the historical Jesus, paralleled by a romantic turn to a Jesus in the heart and Jesus as a moral teacher; the second with its reassertion of the importance for theology and the church's witness of a Jesus who is "historical" and "in" history; and the third with its careful delineation of the necessary distinctions between the actual Jesus, his "historical" reconstruction, and the resurrected Jesus present to the eye of faith. Yet when all is said and done, Albert Schweitzer's evaluation of the first quest a century ago remains in many ways essentially applicable today. In the introduction to his investigation of the various nineteenth-century lives of Jesus, Schweitzer writes:

> The historical investigation of the life of Jesus did not take its rise from a purely historical interest; it turned to the Jesus of history as an ally in the struggle against the tyranny of dogma. Afterwards when it was freed from this πάθος it sought to present the historic Jesus in a form intelligible to its own time....Thus each successive epoch of theology found its own thoughts in Jesus; that was, indeed, the only way in which it could make Him live....But it was not only each epoch that found its reflection in Jesus; each individual created Him in accordance with his own character. There is no historical task which so reveals a man's true self as the writing of a Life of Jesus.[2]

As he concludes:

> Those who are fond of talking about negative theology can find their account here. There is nothing more negative than the result of the critical study of the Life of Jesus. The Jesus of Nazareth who came forward publicly as the Messiah,

[2]Albert Schweitzer, *The Quest of the Historical Jesus* (New York: Macmillan, 1964) 4.

who preached the ethic of the Kingdom of God, who founded the Kingdom of Heaven upon earth, and died to give his work its final consecration, never had any existence. He is a figure designed by rationalism, endowed with life by liberalism, and clothed by modern theology in an historical garb....But the truth is, it is not Jesus as historically known, but Jesus as spiritually arisen with men, who is significant for our time and can help it. Not the historical Jesus, but the spirit which goes forth from Him and in the spirits of men strives for new influence and rule, is that which overcomes the world....Jesus as concrete historical personality remains a stranger to our time, but his spirit, which lies hidden in His words, is known in simplicity, and its influence is direct. Every saying contains in its own way the whole Jesus.[3]

Schweitzer's comments are presented here at some length, not to suggest agreement or sympathy in all respects, but to note how little has really changed since he wrote. No matter how much effort has been expended in the various quests, no matter how much soil has been turned over in efforts to recover the real historical Jesus through objective research, the fact remains that the textual "data" available to such research remains much as it has throughout the history of the church. There is no new data with which to work. As the many works on Jesus summarize, the New Testament itself offers the narratives of the four gospels and the non-narrative writings of Paul. Outside the New Testament are the sketchy references or allusions in the writings of Josephus, Tacitus, Suetonius, and the *Babylonian Talmud*, and, perhaps most important, the collection of sayings in the *Gospel of Thomas*.[4] The evidence has not changed. What has changed and what calls attention to the essential correctness of Schweitzer's remarks is the way in which that evidence is presented, managed, and evaluated. The perspective of individual interpreters is crucial to the evaluation and handling of the evidence. It clearly makes a difference in talk about Jesus whether one is generally optimistic or pessimistic about the historical reliability of the gospel narratives. That stance is further influenced by philosophical or methodological presuppositions about the nature of historical evidence, standards of evidence, and issues of the nature of truth and meaning.

When it comes to authoritative evidence concerning Jesus we often take a much different stance from that of the early Christian community. Early Christians typically moved from their conviction and belief that Jesus was the Messiah (Acts 2:36) to the collection and telling of stories about him. It was through the eyes of this faith that the stories about Jesus had authority and meaning. Luke 24, for example, makes clear how the encounter of the disciples with the risen Lord empowers and shapes their understanding of the traditions. As Luke tells the story, before the risen Lord met them and "opened their minds to comprehend the scriptures" (24:45), they remained unconvinced and unbelieving. The experience of the risen Christ occasioned their conviction of the continuity between Jesus the

---

[3]Ibid., 398-401.

[4]For a convenient summary of this data or evidence, see Luke Timothy Johnson, *The Real Jesus: The Misguided Quest for the Historical Jesus and the Truth of the Traditional Gospels* (San Francisco: HarperSanFrancisco, 1996) 112-125.

Christ whom they worshiped and the Jesus from Nazareth who had been crucified in Jerusalem (John 20:31; 1 Corinthians 2). The earliest Christian witness seems far more interested in Jesus as the living and present Lord whose imminent return was expected (1 Thess 1:10) than in the "historical" Jesus.[5] On the other hand, our modern perspectives regarding authority often lead us to move in the reverse direction from that of the early church. We often seek to establish or define the historicity of Jesus and the stories about him and from that imagine we have secured a basis or authority for faith or proclamation.

III. THE PERSON OF JESUS

Norman Perrin has provided a helpful way to delineate the different perspectives on Jesus found in the New Testament. When we seek to describe the Jesus reflected in the New Testament, we find a complex figure consisting at least of three facets: first, there is the person[6] of Jesus, the "historical Jesus," the one who actually lived and proclaimed his message in Galilee and Judea; second, there is the Jesus who as risen Lord was present in the lives of the Christian community; and third, there is the Jesus who, as living Lord, is expected to return "on the clouds of heaven" as redeemer and judge of the living and the dead. The sayings and stories of Jesus were shaped and traditioned by this three-fold personage, based on the interaction of reminiscence, experience, and expectation or hope—actual reminiscences of Jesus' ministry and teaching, the present experience of him within the life of the community, and expectation that this Jesus would come again in the near future.[7]

These three facets—reminiscence, experience, and expectation—are inseparably bound together in the Christian community's imagination of the person of Jesus. Yet, of these three facets, the reminiscence of Jesus as historical figure is always profoundly shaped by the other two, namely, the experience of Jesus as present and living Lord and the expectation and hope that this same Jesus will come again. The witness that calls forth faith in Jesus as the risen Lord shapes both the character and the depth of conviction with which the Christian community holds to those matters that can be described as historical reminiscences about Jesus. At every point, then, the church's proclamation shapes the figure of Jesus in the church's reminiscence.

---

[5]Norman Perrin and Dennis C. Duling, *The New Testament: An Introduction*, 2nd ed.(New York: Harcourt Brace Jovanovich, 1982) 397. See also Dahl, "Crucified God."

[6]Perrin (see note 5) uses the term "figure" of Jesus. In this section, I have used the term "person" of Jesus as essentially interchangeable, albeit not intending to fill it with modern implications of personhood or personality. The use of "person" alongside that of "figure" is intended to underscore the "historical" or "in the flesh" character of the one to whom the church bears witness. Jesus is not just a "figure" of the imagination, though he is that; nor can he be reduced to a "historical" person, unconnected to the "figure" of Jesus who belongs to the tradition of the church's imagination.

[7]Perrin and Duling, *The New Testament*, 397-98.

IV. THE PERSON OF JESUS AND THE CHURCH'S PROCLAMATION

We now turn to look briefly at several New Testament texts to illustrate and expand on this point. In Matt 11:2-6 we read:

> When John heard in prison what the Messiah was doing, he sent word by his disciples and said to him, "Are you the one who is to come, or are we to wait for another?" Jesus answered them, "Go and tell John what you hear and see: the blind receive their sight, the lame walk, the lepers are cleansed, the deaf hear, the dead are raised, and the poor have good news brought to them. And blessed is anyone who takes no offense at me."

Although located in the context of the Matthean narrative of Jesus' ministry and specifically in the interaction of Jesus with John the Baptist, the reader quickly recognizes that John's question is not his alone; it is one spoken on behalf of the potential believer of any age who is confronted with the proclamation of Jesus as Messiah. In fact John's question might well serve as the theme for the Gospel of Matthew as a whole. It anticipates the same question put by Jesus, albeit in rephrased form, to the disciples at Caesarea Philippi: "Who do you say that I am?" As the gospel narrative unfolds, it becomes increasingly clear that any answer to this question can only be forthcoming within the context of a resurrection encounter with the risen Lord Jesus whose claims of authority accompany his promise to be with the disciple community to the end of the age (Matt 28:18-20). Furthermore, the particular form of the question here—"Are you the one who is to come?"—places the hearer in a double stance in relation to the person of Jesus, referring to him as a present historical figure and also alluding to the hope of his coming again.[8] Finally, Jesus' answer to John's question seems an evasion or almost no answer at all. It is instead a call to faith in this Jesus as the risen Lord who indeed will come again, a faith that will give shape to every understanding of the figure of Jesus. "Blessed is the one who takes no offense on my account." This faith, in turn, calls to further proclamation in the specific shape of a narrative about the ministry and teaching of Jesus: "Go and tell John what you hear and see." Proclamation, faith, and continuing witness to Jesus in the form of narrative are bound together in this text and in the gospel as a whole.

This interrelationship is true not only within the gospel narratives, but also in the non-narrative proclamation of Paul. Though Paul's letters are notable for their apparent lack of so-called "historical" detail of the life of Jesus, still for him the hearing that leads to faith is always integrally tied to proclamation that assumes and is grounded in the person of Jesus as the one who came in the flesh. This becomes clearest in Paul's witness to the crucifixion: "I decided to know nothing among you except Jesus Christ and him crucified" (1 Cor 2:2). In Gal 3:1-4, Paul begins his crucial argument that righteousness consists not in works of the law but in the faithfulness that has become ours in Christ Jesus:

---

[8]Note the reference to expectation ("waiting") in the verb προσδοκάω. The only other use of this verb in Matthew's Gospel is in 24:50, where it explicitly refers to the coming or return of the "Lord" at a day and hour that the servant does not know.

> You foolish Galatians! Who has bewitched you? It was before your eyes that
> Jesus Christ was publicly exhibited as the crucified one! The only thing I want
> to learn from you is this: Did you receive the Spirit by doing the works of the
> law or by the hearing that led to faith? Are you so foolish? Having started with
> the Spirit, are you now ending with the flesh? Did you experience so much for
> nothing?—if it really was for nothing.

Here the perfect tense of the verb "crucify" signals that the Jesus present for the
community of faith is constantly the crucified Jesus. Then, this Jesus, constantly
enmeshed in history, is linked precisely to the faith that comes in response to the
proclamation of the gospel—the hearing that led to faith. Finally, through the
explicit characterization of the Galatian response as "your experience,"[9] experience,
proclamation, and the figure of Jesus crucified have all been bound together. The
figure of Jesus as the crucified one is explicitly linked to and available only to the
experience of faith that comes in response to the proclamation. For Paul, this linkage
of the figure of Jesus to proclamation and response is not limited to Jesus' death and
resurrection. Later in this same argument, proclamation implies a reminiscence of
particular narrative details: "But when the fullness of time had come, God sent his
Son, born of a woman, born under the law, in order to redeem those who were under
the law, so that we might receive adoption as children" (Gal 4:4-5).

V. Treasure in Earthen Vessels

In another context Paul speaks in yet another way about the incorporation of
the figure of Jesus in proclamation. When in 2 Corinthians 4 he is describing his
ministry of apostleship in terms of the proclamation of the word of God, he asserts:
"But we have this treasure in earthen vessels, to show that the transcendent power
belongs to God and not to us" (2 Cor 4:7). In this passage, where Paul's ministry,
the particular manner of his life, and the character of his preaching are on the line,
the proper perception of the word of God is also at stake, along with what it means
to believe in this Jesus whom Paul proclaims as Christ and Lord. Central to Paul's
understanding is that the truth of God's word and the validity of faith are intimately bound up with life experiences; in the particular argumentation of Paul's
speaking and preaching the hearer experiences the glory of God, precisely in the
human face (πρόσωπον) of Jesus the Christ (4:6). Here in this world, in the ambiguity of language, in opinion and argument, in the interplay of doubt and faith and
of grace and decision, here it is that the Christian experiences the complexity of the
New Testament's witness to Jesus. The life of Jesus, the proclamation of Jesus, and
human language all belong together. As much as we might sometimes wish it were
not so, proclamation and religious discourse rescue neither us nor even the story of
Jesus from the implications of historical existence in this world. Language about
Jesus can never, therefore, simply declare objective truths. Being human and
fallible means that all human language and the reality described and shaped by

---

[9]The word translated "experience" here is actually the verb ἐπάθετε (cf. *pathos*). The reader is
invited to reflect on associations with the remarks on Paul's use of the related word παθήματα in 1
Corinthians in the essay by David Fredrickson included in this volume (pp. 163-174).

language is always true and functional only within specific contexts, in the midst of specific historical relationships.

A specific witness to Jesus as well as a specific response to that witness always takes shape and is lived out in this world. In the interplay of authors, discourses, and audiences, of God, sacred texts, and believers, a specific word of God is created, understood, and appropriated as new words are woven into new and relevant meanings for new occasions. Christian faith and existence are at heart rhetorical in that the particular shaping of the word of God and the faithful response and adherence to that word of God are mediated through specific stories and arguments that call the hearer to a particular response of faith and life to the address of God's love and mercy.

Paul speaks of this reality as a "treasure" that shows the "transcendent power" that belongs to God, but the treasure and power come "in earthen vessels." The word "in" should be construed both in the sense of "contained in" and in the sense of "composed of or consisting of." I take this to be similar to Martin Luther's "in, with, and under," as analogous to the sacraments, in which we understand that transcendent power is present in and through earthly signs. The power and the sign can never be separated or distinguished. Without both there is no sacrament.

In similar fashion, in the message of the New Testament, in the narratives of Jesus, common human language becomes the medium of revelation. To speak of treasure in earthen vessels implies that the revelation of God, even in the life of Jesus, is enmeshed in the human experience of this world, words and all—with all their imperfections and ambiguities, with all language's rhetorical perspectives, problems, and promises. If the consistent emphasis in the New Testament is on testimony, on bearing witness to this Jesus who is the Christ, then Paul asserts that this testimony rests on the persuasive power of the one who ultimately bears witness, namely, God. God is the ultimate authority and it is to the transcendent power of God that Paul's language bears witness. Yet it is still Paul and his words that are the bearer of that witness. It is the disciples and apostles, the letter writers and gospel storytellers, who are called to bear witness, both then and now. The call to witness and the word of witness which they bear "to Judea, to Samaria and to the uttermost parts of the world" (Acts 1:8) is, as always, couched in the persuasive rhetoric of human language addressed to each specific audience of potential believers. Through the same human language, the call continues to be extended to those who hear and read today and who are persuaded to respond to that call.

That God's revelation to us and ultimately, then, our own religious stories should be so at risk, so bound up with the ambiguities and perversities of human language, is unnerving to some. A particular library copy of Amos Wilder's book, *Early Christian Rhetoric: The Language of the Gospel*, which I happened once to be reading, contained an especially fitting illustration of this unnerving connection. In a section in which Wilder emphasizes how the narratives of the New Testament remind us that Christian existence is bound up with the historicity of particular language, with particular tellings of the story of Jesus, he makes the comment:

> Perhaps the special character of the stories of the New Testament lies in the fact that they are not told for themselves, that they are not told only about other people, but that they are always about us. They locate us in the very midst of the great story and plot of all time and space, and therefore relate us to the great dramatist and storyteller, God himself.[10]

In the margin alongside this paragraph an earlier reader had written, "Rot!" Perhaps the affront was that such transcendent power should be limited by such a fragile and unassuming "earthen vessel," a vessel that might just as well be relegated to the "rot" of a garbage heap as become the bearer of the refreshing water of life. The rhetorical character of the New Testament makes clear that Christian existence and experience are always bound up with language and so with history; still, this is so "irreligious" and so unthinkable that students of the New Testament and those who proclaim its message must be reminded of it again and again.

VI. WORD OF GOD AND HUMAN WORDS

The word of God in earthen vessels constantly calls attention to what might be described as the rhetorical mode of Christian faith and existence. The Christian witness to Jesus and the life of faith depend on persuasive argumentation that pursues adherence or commitment of the hearer in the face of other choices in issues that are, for human experience, matters only of probability. Thus, the risk of language always accompanies the witness to Jesus' life, death, and resurrection. God is ever new and each day presents new possibilities for understanding what God is doing in the world. There is truth, yes; but it is not unambiguous. Truth, even the truth that we call revelation, dare we say even the "truth" about the historical Jesus, is always truth for and belonging to a particular historical context, for a particular people of God. It is constantly moving. Like the language which contains it, it needs to be hammered out in constant dialogue with the scriptures, the tradition, and the world—the language of the present—in order that it may be constantly fresh with images for tomorrow. We see this "movement" in the fact that there are four gospels, not one, and so four narratives of the life of Jesus belonging to four differing contexts. As in human life in general, seeking the word of God for today is never the search for an absolute "truth," hidden for all eternity, but for clues to the transcendent power of God, which we are convinced is active in the reasonable, the probable, and the contingent elements of life in this world.

One of the most important components of this contingent character of life—which might be called historicity—is the necessarily argumentative and persuasive function of language, the gift so often identified as that which separates humans from other forms of life. Human beings live among probabilities and uncertainties that even for the life of faith imply a plurality of options. Christian witnesses today need to recognize that the word of God, entrusted as it is to human words, is never self-evident or unambiguously verifiable. It takes its chances in the arena along

---

[10]Amos N. Wilder, *Early Christian Rhetoric: The Language of the Gospel* (Cambridge: Harvard University, 1978) 57.

with all other competing claimants to allegiance and adherence which argue in the human marketplace.

This is another way of stating the notion of revelation that is captured so aptly in Paul's phrase "treasure in earthen vessels." This is not revelation as history or revelation equated with a particular history, but it is revelation in history and not separate from it. Christian witness to Jesus is never free of the complex enterprise of rhetoric. Just as there is in the original narrative of John's question to Jesus in Matthew 11 an intricate interdependence of speaker, audience, and message, each interpreting and shaping the other, so there is in today's hearing of that story a new speaker-interpreter and a new audience, along with the same discourse that is still in need of reshaping, rethinking, and rewording. Again, all interpret and shape each other in a new historical context, creating a new event of revelation. The linking of the two rhetorical events is never simply that of formal or logical demonstration. Neither revelation nor proclamation is ever simply unpacking the kernel of truth about the historical Jesus or the logic of the text and making them available. Instead, the treasure is always hidden within the unassuming common language of human speech, whether oral or written, or in the actions of human beings towards one another as those actions are understood and interpreted within the framework of language available to the recipient. It involves a persuasive argument, an invitation to a point of view, a new image of reality.

The word of God in human language, just as in the human life of Jesus of Nazareth, comes as radical address, as persuasive word of life, as miracle to which there is no automatic assent. What is spirit and life to me today is mere letter tomorrow, when new events call for a new language and a new word for which yesterday's language is unsuited. Rhetoric and language are always for a particular moment, a particular hearing, and call for a particular response. This call for response implicit in the New Testament literature is signaled in Paul's words to the Romans: "So faith comes from what is heard, and what is heard comes by the preaching of Christ" (Rom 10:17).

Whether in oral or written form, the narratives of Jesus are purposive; they are about persuasion, about bringing or promoting adherence to a particular way of being, thinking, and living in this world—all of which is captured under the New Testament's multifaceted word "faith." As Paul says, faith comes ultimately through hearing, and so these stories and documents are always about proclamation, about preaching.

So when Paul speaks of the transcendent power of God that we have "in earthen vessels," he speaks of the message of the gospel and the nature of its transmission, that is, of his own preaching. In preaching—in the preaching of the New Testament writers, the preaching of those writers through the written text of scriptures, and the faithful preaching of the Christian church today—the treasure in earthen vessels continues to have power. The Word of God remains alive in, with, and under the common discourse of human language as it takes shape in specific human situations.

To say this another way, the New Testament stories of Jesus are part of a literature of persuasion that seeks to bring about conviction and response to what it represents as the very word of God, first become flesh in Jesus of Nazareth and now present again in its own proclamation and hearing. According to that New Testament witness, hearing the word of God always implies an openness to the persuasive movement of the transcendent power of God that takes form in the earthen vessels of human language and communication. By its involvement in human form, the word of God is always also focused in a world of action, of past, present, and future. It takes shape in the contingent realm, where decisions and responses shape the present and the future as well as our understanding and interpretation of the past. It belongs to the realm of argumentation that seeks to persuade amid a plurality of options and visions of reality within which the word of God is always at risk.

VII. THE WORD OF GOD AND THE RISK OF PREACHING

So, too, the word of proclamation participates in the realm of risk. Risk is implied in each new context of persuasion; each new hearing brings the potential for the altering of attitudes, convictions, and actions. Risk is present in the hearers who live within an ever changing understanding of the data of history. It is present in the goal of argumentation, in its call for commitment, to which there always exists the potential response of hearing and obedience, on the one hand, or of rejection and unbelief, on the other.

Since preaching always takes place amid a plurality of alternatives among which there are no absolute or self-evident formulations, proclaiming the word of God in human form runs the risk of finding more or less successful forms of argumentation. Like it or not, preaching is never free of the argumentative and rhetorical nature of language. The argumentation of proclamation is never "proof" as logically conceived. There is no rhetorical technique that will always do the trick or be absolutely faithful to the demands of the task. Yet in such preaching that persistently has as its goal the persuasion or conversion of the hearer, the gospel fulfills its essential character. Argumentation persuades through its effective linking of ideas, as images and experience become intimates and are woven together. As we tell the story, we always do so with an eschatological sense that the word of God is still present in our world. We tell the story in a way that does not gloss over the painful realities of our present world but rather glimpses with imaginative vision and the hope of faith God's promise that death is swallowed up in victory.

This was certainly true for Paul. As he writes about his own ministry and preaching in the verses surrounding his talk of "treasure in earthen vessels," one notes how quickly and easily his discussion takes on a variety of forms of personal argumentative technique. Our own preaching, too, cannot be comprehended or communicated without our becoming personally involved in the complex realities of tradition, experience, emotions, attitudes, and reason by which we seek to understand and extend the faithful witness to the word of God as we have come to know it.

One thing seems clear. Effective preaching always ends where it begins, with that transcendent power that has come close to us in the earthen vessels of our own human experience, with the conviction that there is indeed a power in the word, and that the word of preaching is grounded in the historical word made flesh. As students and proclaimers of that word, we read the Bible ultimately not as a collection of propositions or rules about life, nor the New Testament only as the official story of the life of Jesus, but as proclamation, as a message, a story that wants to involve us in God's activity in the world, as a story which we are convinced becomes, in its very telling, a means of the Spirit and the power of God—reaching out to claim us and involve us as God's people in the story of God's faithfulness.

As Luke T. Johnson has put it:

> Christian faith has never—either at the start or now—been *based on historical reconstructions of Jesus*, even though Christian faith has always involved some historical claims concerning Jesus. Rather Christian faith (then and now) is based on religious claims concerning the present power of Jesus....At the very heart of Christianity, therefore, is an experience and a claim. The experience is one of the transforming, transcendent, personal power within communities that can be expressed in shorthand as "the gift of the Holy Spirit." The claim is that this power comes from Jesus, who was crucified but who now lives by the life of God.[11]

Experience and conviction belong together. In this thickening[12] together of experience and conviction, through the witness to this word, the scriptures have a central place. They are not an afterthought or an embarrassment. The preaching of the word will be persuasive as long as it speaks with clarity and drinks deeply of the conviction that through persuasive human language, by the mystery and power of God, we are brought again and again to believe that all of the promises of God have found their Yes in the word made flesh; through persuasive human language God continues to give life to the dead and to call into existence things that do not exist. ⊕

[11]L. Johnson, *The Real Jesus*, 133, 135.

[12]For the use of this word, see C. Perelman, *The Realm of Rhetoric* (Notre Dame, IN: University of Notre Dame, 1982) xiv-xv.

Word & World
Supplement Series 3
1997

What Difference Does the Quest for Jesus Make for the Christian Faith?
A Panel Discussion

HULTGREN

Two positive points, two negative ones. My first positive comment is this: there is a general public function that biblical scholars play, and that has some implications for the Christian faith.

Back in April of this year I received a message on the internet that said that a researcher in Virginia has done a survey of books around the world with Jesus as their primary subject. As of that date—April 18, 1997—the researcher had found that there were 65,571 books on Jesus (apparently since the invention of the printing press), and that four new ones come out daily.

My point should be obvious. There is an interest in Jesus, and biblical scholars have a responsibility to enter into the broader public arena. Many people in the public, and certainly many in the churches, wonder what we are getting paid for if we do not enter into the discussion.

But now the question is, "What difference does this rather secular task make for the Christian faith?" I think it has importance. The Christian faith is worldly, secular, down to earth, public, mired in the stuff of human existence—even though there are some people who would want to rob us of that understanding. And if we cannot see a connection between Jesus and the world, we have no right to assert a connection between Jesus and God. And if there is a connection between Jesus and the world, we have to use worldly ways of knowing in order to know him.

As Christians seeking to know the earthly Jesus, we cannot say that our ways are inspired or revealed, as if we have some inside track on this kind of investigation.

We know Jesus as the Christ only by faith, and that is a gift of God. One of the most wonderful insights in Christian literature is in Martin Luther's *Small Cate-chism*: "I believe that I cannot by my own reason or strength believe in Jesus Christ my Lord, or come to him, but the Holy Spirit has called me through the Gospel, enlightened me with his gifts, and sanctified and preserved me in true faith." We can paraphrase that: "I believe that I cannot by my own historical research believe in Jesus Christ my Lord..." I think that is important. Historical study is not a way of getting to belief. We cannot remove the miraculous nature of faith.

With all this interest in the historical figure of Jesus, scholars in the field of New Testament studies have a responsibility to enter into the broader public arena and give an accounting of what can be said about one of the major figures of human history. This rather secular task should not be underestimated in its impor-tance for Christian faith. If the Christian faith is to be intelligible, let alone credible, it must be sponsored in part by persons who have thought deeply—and done the hard work of historical probing—about Jesus as a public figure in history.

A second positive point is that faith seeks understanding. Faith cannot rest on the shifting sands of historical research, but the person of faith cannot help but ask questions about Jesus. If a person grows up in the church and hears all those children's sermons about how wonderful Jesus was, it seems that that person, if thoughtful at all, will someday wonder, "Well, why was Jesus executed if he was so great?" and "What about all this talk about the kingdom of God? What does that mean?"

A couple negative points:

One of the things that I have concluded lately is that the so-called "third quest" is more like the first quest of the nineteenth century than the second. Let me try to explain.

The second quest was initiated in 1953 by Ernst Käsemann within a circle of scholars that shared many theological views and held much in common about what is possible. They affirmed that the historical element in the gospels has significance, namely, to secure the identity of the exalted, post-Easter Christ, the Lord of the church, with the earthly Jesus. As a matter of principle, the proclama-tion of the church should have continuity with the proclamation of Jesus. These questers were intrigued by the continuity they discovered, such as Jesus' accep-tance of sinners and the gospel of justification. That quest was carried on by persons who were passionately committed to a larger theological context and to scholarship for the church. That larger framework is missing today, just as it was with the nineteenth-century quests.

But of course other frameworks are in place—all kinds of them. Some of them are institutional, as David Tiede said in his presentation. Religion departments in state universities cannot be departments of theology. Yet they should give atten-tion to Jesus.

Other frameworks are more conceptual. Since people are saying these days that there is no such thing as historical objectivity, everyone can have his or her own Jesus. Your Jesus is simply your own interests projected and incarnated in someone long gone, but still able to command authority.

My last point: I think we should also be asking the related question, What difference does the current culture make for the current quests for Jesus? There is no one quest in our time. There really are several. But the more popular presentations of Jesus, I think, serve spirituality more than they do the Christian faith. What I mean by that is that the interest in Jesus is driven in large measure today by individualistic spirituality. That interest is by its very nature anti-institutional.

At one time it was said, *extra ecclesiam non salus est* ("There is no salvation outside the church"). That slogan had its excesses and abuses, and the reformation sought to correct them. But even the churches of the reformation have perpetuated the sense—the good sense—that salvation is not a solitary or purely private matter; it is a corporate reality. But now it seems that the slogan is, "There is no salvation *inside* the church; it is only in my own spirituality." The church is no good, but Jesus is my favorite spiritual guide. So I shall use what I can from the library or my favorite bookstore on Jesus, as long as I like it.

TIEDE

What do I think, what do I know, what do I believe? Within the Christian community we make credal statements about Jesus' crucifixion under Pontius Pilate and about the resurrection. People are now trying to sort these pieces out, and they are trying to understand "how then shall I live?" Clearly one reason people are interested in this discussion is some sense that it influences how they are going to live and what their values are about. One of the things for you to think about as leaders of Christian communities is the connection between this discussion and the things we have hoped, believed, confessed, and lived by in our deep confessional statements. We have engaged this question within the Christian community. It has been and should be a consistent part of what we are about here at Luther Seminary. There is a wonderful opportunity now to extend that conversation.

Perhaps you can gain a greater sense of security out of this conversation. Your confession can become clearer and more forthright. You will know that your faith is not based in your own reason or strength, but that it is not alienated from that either.

My hope is that we help you find some ways to think about this, about how to relate what we can from history, from the texts of our tradition, and from elsewhere, and the question of how to speak of all that in terms of what we believe.

JACOBSON

I agree with the quotation from Paula Fredriksen that Sarah Henrich used in her paper, that not caring about the historical Jesus is a form of theological docetism. We have to care! I care about the character, word, and actions of the one in whom God is incarnate. How can we not care about such things?

One analogy that came to mind is the end of the book of Job. When I teach that book and read articles about it, people often say, "The most important thing about the end of Job is that God cares enough to show up!" And my response to that is always, "But then he talks for three chapters. Don't you want to know what he has to say?" Doesn't the content matter as much as the showing up? This is how I feel about knowing about Jesus.

The irony is that I also agree with what Jim Boyce said in his presentation, that finally you can't get to the actual content of Jesus' words through historical research. We are trapped. Yet I share Jim's tone about this trap as well. We find constant engagement and joy in this task. Just as the end of Job is continually engaging and difficult, so are the gospels and Paul, and that is what keeps us in this enterprise. It would be a great disaster if we only had one gospel instead of four, because then we might think we own Jesus instead of being owned by him.

JUEL

Two comments:

1. We participate in this conversation about the historical Jesus because we have been asked to do so by people for whom Christ died and who have questions. And whether you are personally interested in it or not doesn't make one bit of difference. The fact that other people are interested means that you are obliged to play the game. What I object to most about the kind of Jesus scholarship that has appeared in the last 20 years is that it is so poor, and that people who ought to know better are so impressed by it. We can do better than that, and the fact that the church has not done better, that it hasn't trained pastors and lay people to detect shoddy work, is an indictment of those of us who teach. We can do better than we have done. We can out-think the culture. The Christian church has done best when it has been able to do that.

2. One of the things that the whole enterprise discloses is the yearning of exegetes to be something more than we can be. I was talking to a colleague once about the story of Jesus' death in Mark and Matthew. The question arose: Did Jesus really experience abandonment by God or didn't he? "My God, my God, why have you abandoned me?" The scholarly question was, did Mark just find that quotation in the Bible and use it, or did Jesus really experience abandonment? My fellow scholar's life has been absolute chaos. He has known every moment of his life that it is suspended by a very slender thread. "If Jesus didn't experience that sense of abandonment, I'm not interested in him," he said. "So what have you got to say about that?" I told him that as an historian, I could not give him what he needed. I can't tell you what Jesus experienced. What I can say is, there is warrant in the story for me to promise that God is there in the darkness and will bring life out of death. But that is all I can say. I have no direct access to the experience of Jesus. I have no direct access to the experience of God, and neither do you. If you imagine that you need such access in order to survive, then you will be disappointed. You want to know as God knows, and you won't. In some ways, this discussion provides a wonderful opportunity to try to figure out what it means to be justified by a promise. Because we don't live by anything but promises. If anyone imagines that doing historical research will provide the kind of stable foundation that will make risk and faith unnecessary, they are simply succumbing to the temptation. This is a great chance for us to discover that we don't need that kind of stability. It

is not available to us, and what the study of history does is to expose us, to place us at the mercy of God. Which is not a bad thing!

KOESTER

There are three questions that emerge for me when reflecting on the quest for Jesus. The first two questions yield negative answers. The third question yields a more positive answer.

First, have the various quests for Jesus allowed us to lay hold of Jesus? The answer to this question is persistently negative, I think. What we find again and again is that in attempting to find the Jesus who lies behind the biblical texts we actually encounter ourselves. In his book *The Quest of the Historical Jesus*, Albert Schweitzer wrote that "each successive epoch of theology found its own thoughts in Jesus; that was, indeed, the only way in which it could make Him live. But it was not only each epoch that found its reflection in Jesus; each individual created Him in accordance with his own character. There is no historical task which so reveals a man's true self as the writing of a Life of Jesus."[1]

Contemporary quests for Jesus often tell us more about ourselves than they do about Jesus. They provide occasions to ask about the norms to which we want God to conform and about the plausibility structures within which we want God to work. In the nineteenth century the historical Jesus often emerged as a moral teacher, and morality was precisely what was valued by so many of the questers. When a rereading of the texts yielded a Jesus who was an apocalyptic prophet, the interest in the historical Jesus dropped dramatically, since that Jesus was too strange to be appealing to the generation living before the first world war. After the second world war, interest in Jesus the apocalyptic prophet became much more pronounced, in part because our renewed capacities for self-destruction made the end of the world seem much more real. Similarly, Jesus the sage, who utters witty aphorisms and practices inclusive table fellowship, who is vigorously anti-hierarchical yet spiritually in tune, is precisely the kind of Jesus one might expect to appeal to the aging children of the sixties.

Second, does that mean that the historical Jesus is unimportant? No, the Jesus who lived and died, who taught and healed, is immeasurably important for us, because faith clings to a particular person, not to a generic spiritual presence. Christian faith is centered on the crucified and risen Jesus. That does not mean that the life and teachings of Jesus are unimportant; rather, Jesus' life and teachings are important precisely because Jesus is the one whom God raised and the one whom we confess to be Lord and Savior.

One and two generations ago some scholars almost reveled in the fact that so little could be said with certainty about the historical Jesus. They pressed this lack of certainty in order that people might recognize that faith is precisely faith and not security. Yet the scriptures themselves do preserve the traditions of what Jesus said and did. They bear witness to the living Lord not by theological abstraction but by

---

[1] Albert Schweitzer, *The Quest of the Historical Jesus* (German, 1906; New York: Macmillan, 1968) 4.

recounting his miraculous signs and his teachings (John 20:30-31). The resurrection of Jesus does not make his life unimportant, but the reverse. God raised Jesus in bodily form, which means that what Jesus did in the body upon earth is of abiding significance for Christians.

Third: My first two points seem to place us in something of a bind. On the one hand we cannot lay hold of Jesus by means of historical investigation, and on the other hand we cannot simply dismiss the importance of Jesus' life and teachings. So what does it mean to embark on a quest for Jesus? To pursue a quest for Jesus means to search the scriptures that present Jesus to us, trusting that through our encounter with the scriptures Jesus can and will reveal himself to us.

The quest for Jesus is, at its most fundamental level, a quest for God. Augustine was correct when he confessed to God, "You have made us for yourself, and our hearts are restless until they rest in you" (*Confessions* 1.1). We cannot prevent ourselves from seeking a God of some sort. Our own time provides eloquent testimony to the inborn human drive to know God. Some seek God in the recesses of their own spirits, others seek to enter Heaven's Gate on the tail of a comet. The Fourth Gospel testifies that no one has ever seen God, yet the only Son—who became flesh in Jesus of Nazareth—can and does make God known (John 1:18). We embark on the quest for Jesus not in the hope that we can find the real Jesus through all the contrivances of the human mind, but in the hope that as we search the scriptures, the living Lord will meet us there—and that as he meets us, he will reveal the God whose hidden presence we seek to know.

BOYCE

Three brief comments about why the quest is important to me:

First, it is important because of the "tapes" that still play in me from my younger days. As I grew up, I tended to read the scriptures flat, to expect and to say that they simply mean what they say on the surface. The story of Jesus is as the gospels portray it. If the gospels say that Jesus did thus and so, that is the way it was. I was rather naïve about issues of history and biblical narrative. Those tapes continue to play within me. I can't get away from them. It is because of those tapes that I still shudder when I read the quote Craig Koester just read from Schweitzer's evaluation of the quest almost a century ago. What do you do with the stuff that is in you that cares a lot about what you can really know about Jesus?

Secondly, the quest interests me because it has implications for our understanding of what God is doing in this world and the way in which scholarship addresses and shapes that understanding. There is a sense in which education and research in western culture represent attempts to control the world we know. They can lead us to assume that we have the world under control, to assume that the more we can know, the more we can control God and what God is doing. The historical research that belongs to the quest for Jesus does not escape these implications.

Thirdly, the quest is important because it presses the issue of what we mean when we say, especially in our Lutheran tradition, that the word of God comes to us in our experience in this world. The word of God is not out there somewhere;

when God meets us, God meets us precisely in that strange offense of a babe born in a manger. It is sometimes easy to assume that everything about God's word is fully human except the story of Jesus. Something in us works to put that story off in a compartment by itself. One can't tamper with it because at least *that* story is real. I continue to ask what it means that the word of God is at risk, even in the story of Jesus. A preacher has to deal with this reality. God truly meets us in the story of Jesus; yet even that story is at risk in our experience in this world.

DISCUSSION

A participant observed that he was struck by the difference in tone between these remarks and the earlier presentations. He found much more passion in the present statements.

GAISER

All of us here would probably agree that theological conversation is richer and more fun than "mere" historical investigation. Theological discourse is what we do every day in class—on top of history.

Like my own beloved teacher, Gerhard von Rad, I am much more interested in the "theological maximum" than in the "historical minimum." But, also like him, I care about history. We care about the historical minimum for its own sake, of course, but also for the sake of apologetics. We must be able to enter into conversation with the world, including the historians.

TIEDE

One might say that we must do the compulsory figures before we can skate free-style. Those compulsory figures are largely dictated to us by the world of scholarship, by a tradition of thought, and we must be responsible about what we think in that arena. Every one of you has the same problem. There are places where, if you are going to give an account of what you know and what you think, you have to work differently, using a different and perhaps more careful vocabulary. But when we say what we believe, we can sing!

JUEL

It is more fun, in some ways, to get together with your own folks, to sing and listen to testimonies, than it is to make arguments to people who don't agree. The problem with the church is that it has enjoyed the experience of getting together and listening to the singing, but has not always welcomed the strangers by taking their questions seriously. There is a big difference between persuasion and pronouncement. I get tired of hearing preachers talk only about their own experience, imagining that that somehow does it for me and for other people. We have to get into the imagination of people who are different, of strangers, and we have to make persuasive arguments to them. That is just plain hard work. It need not be boring, and it may be that we can be much more artful in what we do. But persuasion is a different business than making pronouncements.

A participant asked for comments on the popularity of the historical Jesus literature. Should we not be asking some of the questions raised by that literature in our churches and in the world? Does the church stand in the way of Jesus?

JACOBSON

I think you are right. There are many times that the church undermines its own message by its actions and attitudes. I think the historical Jesus question is trying to get at something here. Many of the people in the Jesus Seminar were raised in the church and hate it. Well, we should take some responsibility for that. Why do they hate the church?

If we disallow feminist questions, or questions about the authority of the church, or historical questions, we aren't doing our job as evangelists. We aren't listening.

HULTGREN

To be sure, the church is often its own worst enemy; but the church has also been a means of life for me and the others here, or we would not be here. Were it not for the church, I don't know that I would be a Christian. It is primarily by the encouragement of Christians around me, the communion of saints, that I am sustained.

I see in our culture a move away from that way of thinking, and I think it is unfortunate.

TIEDE

Things are awkward now. People read the quest for Jesus books and they recognize values and communities that they share in many ways, but that they are not hearing in the church. All of a sudden Jesus is over in a different community of meaning and reference. I hear in your question an appeal to the church to understand the force of Jesus in our cultural setting. There are new and different ways to appropriate the Jesus tradition, ways that are interested in other things than simply cross and resurrection. The church needs to take seriously that concern.

A participant observed that Jürgen Moltmann and Robert Funk agree about "a hole" in the middle of the Apostles' Creed. The creed leaps from Jesus' birth to his suffering and death, saying nothing of parables or miracles, of Jesus' fellowship with outcasts, of Jesus' life and teaching. Is this not a problem?

TIEDE

Particularly at the center of our preaching, we do focus on the cross and resurrection. Still, I am intrigued by the statement in Luke/Acts, it is *this* Jesus that God raised up. The "this" is important. It wasn't just anybody. The resurrection is the vindication of *that* life. Jesus' life includes his death, of course, but it is not just the death of Jesus that is vindicated, but this Jesus who did signs and mighty works among the people. That is part of the New Testament proclamation.

JUEL

The trouble is, I hardly ever hear any cross and resurrection preaching. What

I hear mostly is a king of ordinary wisdom, that really is ordinary and often not very interesting. I don't hear much solid cross and resurrection gospel. By the way, emphasis on that message didn't prevent Paul from saying all kinds of things about ordinary aspects of daily life. Where are people being engaged? What kind of preaching and teaching is going on? What are people hearing? Much of what people say that they learn in church has little to do with the Pauline tradition.

A participant suggested that we need to pay closer attention to the body, to the bodily aspects of Jesus' ministry, including, for example, his washing of feet. The questioner quoted Luther to the effect that in order to understand the divinity of Christ "we must begin from the bottom" with Jesus' humanity.[2]

BOYCE

An aspect to be noted in this conversation about the adequacy of the creeds is that the creeds are not for proclamation. To pretend they are is to miss the point. The creeds may, in some sense, sharpen our proclamation, but they don't *do* our proclamation. If there is a hole, it is not in the creeds but in our preaching.

I have often been impressed by Ignatius' comments, precisely when he was struggling with the question of Jesus in the flesh in response to the docetists. Ignatius makes the crucial observation that the docetists, who professed that Jesus did not come in the flesh, also didn't care much about the widows and orphans in the congregation. There are strong implications in the question of the Jesus of history for the Jesus that the Christian knows Monday through Saturday. If we aren't concerned about the historical Jesus, it may be that we can stay "religious," but we won't have to deal with the nitty-gritty realities of how God meets us daily in this world—not merely on Sunday, but precisely in the middle of the week.

GAISER

It may be that both the traditional or theological Jesus and the more human or bodily Jesus have been neglected. Maybe our trouble is in trying to lay too much on the historical Jesus. It will be hard for Christians to make the case that Jesus is special because he is a better teacher and a better foot washer than anyone else. But we don't have to! We don't have to get everything into the second article. We have two other ones. The first and third articles, God's work in creation and in the Spirit, move us profoundly into the world. As long as theology is trinitarian, and if it is true that we see the Father through the Son, then what we see of Jesus will greatly influence what we think about creation and everyday life and what kind of God we proclaim. The point of our confession is not merely that Jesus was a wonderful guy who did wonderful things; the point is that *God* was in Christ, in the flesh, doing wonderful and worldly things. Concentration on all three articles together will get us into the world without either truncating the Jesus of tradition or inventing a Jesus who has to be better in every way than everyone else.

[2] See a fuller citation of this quotation in the introduction to this volume (pp. 10-11).

BOYCE

Christian tradition points to the death of Jesus as somehow special or unusual; still one needs to take account of the apparent incongruity that nobody really took notice of it in the larger world. It wasn't really all that strange a death, and not as bad a death as many people die. The gospels tell us that two others were crucified alongside Jesus, and that even on the cross Jesus' suffering was cut short. Other people tended to suffer longer during crucifixion. In other words, the tradition suggests that the death of Jesus was not all that extraordinary. We will need more than historical reconstruction to get at what we think is going on here.

A participant noted that some of the things we see in the Jesus Seminar we have sown ourselves in the reformation tradition, saying, in effect, not that "I believe in the Holy Spirit, the Holy Catholic Church," but "I believe in the authority of the autonomous self." We are still struggling with what it is to be the church and how the scriptures must be understood in the context of the community of faith. They cannot be understood apart from that context.

HULTGREN

The problem is not just ecclesiology, but church and culture. We have in the culture not only the autonomous self, but now also the autonomous Jesus, ripped out of history. I agree with Fred Gaiser that to claim that our guru is better than any other guru will not work. We can't convince the world that this is so. We have all these things converging in the culture—the autonomous self, the sayings of Jesus apart from a social context, and a form of spirituality that too often seeks salvation within the self rather than from the external word.

A participant asked about the relation between the apocalyptic Jesus and the historical Jesus. What is the role of Mark 13?

TIEDE

I think that a legitimate question about the historical Jesus is whether he predicted the destruction of Jerusalem. I think he did. In the prophetic tradition, Jeremiah spoke about the destruction of Jerusalem the first time. The gospel writers all see Jesus entering that discussion. Somehow what happened to Jesus was fundamental to what happened to Israel. So as those two get wed, the rich tradition of Jewish apocalyptic, which sees God intervening dramatically in judgment or in vindication, is tied up with Jesus. Where is the historical Jesus in that? This is a very important historical and theological question—not the least because, as Christianity became gentile, the way in which that intense Jewish debate was picked up became, of course, virulently anti-Semitic.

HULTGREN

Whether or not Jesus had an apocalyptic message is one of the big debates going on today. My sense is that those who want to deny it are not only wrong in their historical assessment, but they then go on to construe a Jesus who is more familiar to us, more comfortable, and less a stranger. But I think reading the Bible is a cross-cultural experience. It is a book out of distant times and places, and we have to learn the accents, the language and metaphors, and let it do its work with our own imagination. We should not try to make the Bible "perfect" for our times by removing those things we find offensive.

KOESTER

Historically, why is this issue important? Because it connects us with the Jesus who is presented in the scriptures. It is historically responsible to preserve Jesus' connection with apocalyptic, not to try to shy away from it. I think it is also theologically important to give due weight to the apocalyptic side of Jesus' preaching. This keeps Jesus' work within the scope of the whole work of God. Apocalyptic eschatology has to do with what God is doing and with the future of the whole world. It is not simply about the redemption of individual souls, but it has to do with the way in which the Creator relates to the creation and about the future of the creation. It is important to see the work of Christ within that broad scope of God's work within the creation. We don't collapse everything about God into Jesus of Nazareth; instead we recognize that Jesus of Nazareth reveals something about what God is doing with the creation.

JUEL

What is important about apocalyptic then, theologically, is that it indicates that for Jesus, for the gospel writers, for the church, and for us, we don't know yet how it is going to come out. We live by a promise. It all remains to be seen.

KNUTSEN

For a lot of churches, Hal Lindsey has become the lens through which apocalyptic texts like Mark 13 are read—which seems to imply that this is a scenario of the end of this world and the inauguration of doom. Dr. Tiede is suggesting that Jesus may be using the vivid apocalyptic imagery of Mark 13 to talk about an utterly cataclysmic event that actually happened in the first century. What was coming to an end was the very thing Israel had been focused on—the temple of God.

JACOBSON

N. T. Wright's new book, *Jesus and the Victory of God*, does a good job of talking about apocalyptic, especially apocalyptic in Israel. I would commend that book to you as a way of getting into the question. Also, people who are interested in the connection between apocalyptic and wisdom—they aren't to be pitted against each other—might read the helpful essays in *In Search of Wisdom*, edited by Perdue, Scott, and Wiseman.

TIEDE

Mary Knutsen's mention of Hal Lindsey reminds me that many of you here have teaching responsibilities at a very popular level. The series *Understanding Jesus Today* is where my little book on *Jesus and the Future* appeared. That book was specifically addressed to this question. It is an effort to describe fairly simply what

213

was happening in the period of the writing of the book of Daniel, the period of the birth of Jesus, during the life of Jesus, and then during the writing of the gospels and the book of Revelation. Of course, the book of Revelation refers to a very different historical arena than the synoptic apocalypse does. In Revelation we are now talking about the Roman order. It helps to get these apocalyptic witnesses projected against their real historical environments. How might this stuff have sounded in the time of Pontius Pilate? How would it have sounded in the time of Vespasian? How would it have sounded to believers in the time of Domitian?

A participant suggested that the Jesus Seminar troubles us because it attacks some of the things upon which we have placed our hope. That is scary. Sometimes, he said, people only want the eternal heavenly insurance policy that they think the church offers. They are not prepared to think about the issues raised by the quest for the historical Jesus.

KOESTER

Early in the conversation, Schweitzer came up. One of the things that I value most about Schweitzer is his constant press for self-criticism. Scholars who relentlessly critique the scriptures must be just as relentless in critiquing their own constructions. When we have deconstructed certain ways of looking at Jesus, we inevitably put something else in their place. The only question is what that "something else" will be. The words of Schweitzer continue to haunt me, because they get at the question of what we now put in the place of the Jesus proclaimed by the New Testament. Self-criticism is an absolutely essential part of the ongoing life of faith, and we must ask how the new visions of Jesus stand up in light of what the scriptures say. Many now read Borg's *Jesus, A New Vision*, but that does not mean we can forget about reading Matthew, Mark, Luke, and John. In fact the quest becomes most productive when writers are able to engage in their own self-criticism on the basis of scripture itself.

JUEL

The Bible will not answer all our questions. There is no atonement theory in the New Testament. That is something we have to come up with ourselves. It is a way of imaginatively answering the question, "What does it mean that Jesus died for you?" The church has invented some terrible ways to answer that question that hardly have anything to do with the Bible at all! While the preaching of the church may be cross and resurrection preaching, it is often not very good. What people get from it is that God needs blood. And fortunately, Jesus paid. Or God has debts to pay and will stop at no lengths to pay them. My heavens! That is hardly an apt portrait of the God one finds in the scriptures. But one of the tasks, then, is for us as theologians, as thinkers, as preachers, to figure out how we want to say those things. What does it mean to say that Jesus died for us? He did die. The violence is right there at the center of the story, but what one understands by that can be constructed in very different ways. ⊕